Collections of the
New Jersey Historical Society,
volume 19

SILK CITY

Published by the Society as a
Thomas Alva Edison Study in
New Jersey Economic History,
with a Grant from the
Charles Edison Fund

Dedicated to the Memory of
Herbert G. Gutman (1928–85),
scholar, educator, and
historian of industrial Paterson

PELGRAM AND MEYER SILK RIBBONS. No. 3076, 3/1917 (*upper left*) was woven in 1917 and described as a "moire velour warp print." It is a particularly fine moire-finished fabric with a soft all-over effect, imitating the velvety lines of a true velour. The choice of a cotton weft or filling resulted in a pronounced rib, which was mechanically crushed to produce the "watered" effect. **No. 3731, 10/1922** (*upper right*) is a "Jacquard Persian" ribbon, inspired by the contemporary fascination with the Middle East. Its silk threads were dyed before weaving, and the pattern is formed by the complex weave alone, requiring 2,880 Jacquard cards per repeat. **No. 3267, 2/1919** (*lower left*) is a warp-printed Jacquard ribbon, referred to in French as a "taffeta façonné." A standard number 800, or 110 *lignes* (9.8 inches) wide, this silk ribbon is woven with over 375 threads per inch. **No. 3348, 2/1919** (*lower right*) is a "Satin Jacquard" ribbon woven in a distinctly Art Decco pattern. The design and card punching—1,696 Jacquard cards were needed to weave one repeat—were probably done on the outside, costing $36.75 and $40.80 respectively. [*Reproduced courtesy of the Passaic County Historical Society*]

SILK CITY

Studies on the Paterson Silk Industry, 1860-1940

Edited by
PHILIP B. SCRANTON

NEWARK 1985
New Jersey Historical Society

© Copyright 1985 by the
New Jersey Historical Society

Printed in the U.S.A. by BookCrafters,
Chelsea, Michigan

Library of Congress Card Number 85–42869
ISBN 0–911020–12–8

Library of Congress Cataloging in Publication Data
Main entry under title:

Silk city.

(Collections of the New Jersey Historical Society;
v. 19)
  Bibliography: p.
  Includes index.
    1. Silk industry—New Jersey—Paterson—History—
Addresses, essays, lectures. 2. Strikes and lockouts—
Silk industry—New Jersey—Paterson—History—
Addresses, essays, lectures. I. Scranton, Philip.
II. Series.
F131.N62 vol. 19   974.9 s   85–42869
[HD9918.P38]   [338.4′767739′0974924]
ISBN 0–911020–12–8

Contents

List of Illustrations

Introduction

IN MOST CHRONICLES OF American economic history, Paterson, New Jersey, can be expected to appear only twice. First, the city grew around the site where Alexander Hamilton and his associates in the Society for Establishing Useful Manufactures (SUM) began to harness the water power of the Great Falls of the Passaic River in the 1790s. Second, one hundred and twenty years later, Paterson was the location of the mammoth, disorderly, and protracted 1913 strike, a struggle that involved the dreaded Industrial Workers of the World (IWW). Otherwise, the economic history of one of the nation's most specialized manufacturing cities has long been ignored.[1] In the 1960s Herbert G. Gutman, the distinguished social historian, rekindled interest in Paterson through the publication of two essays (on metalworking proprietors and on community power relationships), which by now are required reading at many American universities. The present volume, offering the fruits of recent research on the Paterson silk industry, is in a sense a response to Professor Gutman's call for historians to treat the "factory town . . . the industrial city as a legitimate subject for detailed and careful inquiry."[2]

The six studies offered here do not by any means constitute a full history of Paterson or of its most significant industry, but together with the accompanying illustrations, they will invite readers to view its development through a number of lenses and from a variety of angles. Taken as a whole, they should stimulate renewed concern for the economic and cultural dynamics of second-tier industrial cities like Newark, Bridgeport, and Providence, as well as thoughtful comparison with the urban experience of major manufacturing centers like Pittsburgh or Detroit. As a center for specialty manufacturing in both the silk industry and metal trades, Paterson also offers a fully realized example of the historical alternative to mass production, a skill-intensive productive flexibility that has recently been introduced into public-policy debates through the work of Charles Sabel, Jonathan Zeitlin, and Michael Piore.[3] Most concretely, these six essays are a contribution to the local history of a city becoming increasingly aware of its rich industrial heritage.

Paterson was founded on the speculations of a cluster of eighteenth-century gentlemen and named for Gov. William Paterson of New Jersey, who signed their charter of incorporation in 1791. The site for establishing the useful manufactures that SUM envisioned was chosen in 1792, after two agents sent out scouting by Hamilton enthusiastically recommended the Great Falls of the Passaic River. Once seven hundred acres surrounding its spectacular cataract were purchased (for a little more than $8,000.00), Pierre Charles L'Enfant received a commission to design the new town and supervise its erection. Within a year, the planner of the nation's capital was dismissed and replaced by Connecticut's Peter Colt as superintendent general. Under his direction, the first factory to draw the Passaic's water power was completed and set in motion in June 1794. The factory was devoted to cotton spinning; no weaving was attempted, but cotton printing was tried on materials "purchased in New York." Despite bright hopes, the SUM ended its manufacturing efforts in 1796–97, a victim of skilled-labor shortages, the personal bankruptcies of its directors, and insufficient technical knowledge. Over the next fifteen years, Colt family members gained control of the corporation through the purchase of most of its 2,620 shares and began promoting leases of the falls' power.[4]

The stimulus to domestic manufacturing provided by Jefferson's 1807 embargo and the War of 1812 was felt in Paterson. Samuel Colt opened a rolling mill in 1811. John Clark, a refugee from Samuel Slater's mill at Pawtucket, Rhode Island, expanded the textile machine works he had begun in 1801, helping outfit several of the new local spinning mills, which soon supplied cotton yarn to Philadelphia's hand-loom weavers. Many of the new textile enterprises collapsed during the postwar depression, but the mills remained and were reoccupied by new hopefuls who built Paterson's spindlage to forty thousand by 1832. Power looms were, however, not adopted with anything like the verve shown by the cotton corporations of Massachusetts; Paterson partnership mills long remained yarn specialists. By 1860 eleven local textile firms employed just under nine hundred workers, but they had slipped to second place among Paterson manufacturers (after locomotive builders) in terms of employment.[5]

Railroad equipment construction had commenced about 1830, when Paterson textile-machinery craftsman John Rogers turned his talents to the casting of wheels and axles for the South Carolina Railroad. From this he progressed to building entire steam locomotives; in 1837 he completed the *Sandusky*, an engine modeled after an English-made George Stephenson locomotive used on the Paterson and Hudson Railroad. Its initial reliability brought other orders, and as Rogers was willing to experiment with improvements, the Rogers Locomotive Works soon gained a reputation for flexibility which added to its clientele. By the time of Rogers' death in 1856, his works rivaled Philadelphia's Baldwin and Norris companies, becoming one of the nation's "big three" locomotive manufacturers. The firm and its local competitors, all formed by veteran Rogers' workers, employed 1,230 mechanics in 1860; the Paterson firms had built as many as 183 engines in their best year of the preceding decade. Although cotton textile manufacturing had stagnated, machinery building had come to stay.[6]

Christopher Colt, a member of the Connecticut family, was responsible for the first silk production in Paterson. At the close of the 1830s, he installed machinery from his failed Hartford silk mill in Paterson's Old Gun Mill. Though the operation failed within a few months, its crude equipment drew the attention of John Ryle, an immigrant silk worker from Macclesfield, an industrial town in northwestern England, situated seventeen miles south of Manchester. Purchasing the machines on behalf of paint manufacturer George Murray, Ryle made a successful restart by 1840, superintending production of "sewing silk." In three years, he joined Murray as a partner; in six, Ryle had bought full control of the firm, in part through financial assistance provided by his brothers in Macclesfield. By mid-century, demand for "machine twist" (spooled silk for the new sewing machines) and weaving and embroidery yarns kept five hundred employees at work in vastly expanded facilities. The mill's profits enabled Ryle to travel to Europe, where he visited silk mills on working vacations. During the last decade before the Civil War, Benjamin Tilt arrived from Boston to revitalize the Phoenix Manufacturing Company, once a cotton firm; two of Ryle's workers, Robert Hamil and James Booth, left his shops to start their own spinning mill. Though little weaving had yet been attempted, by 1860 Paterson was home to a half-dozen silk companies, including its first silk dye works, employing six hundred workers, four-fifths of whom were women and girls.[7]

From the Civil War era through the Great Depression, aided by protective tariffs and the immigration of both skilled workers and eager entrepreneurs, Paterson built and sustained an international reputation as "The Lyons of America." Its population soared from under 20,000 in 1860 to 138,000 in 1930. No other North American city rivaled its prowess in silk manufacturing, the most fashion sensitive division of the textile industry, with the highest-priced products. From the handful of firms present in the mid-nineteenth century, the Paterson silk industry grew by 1900 to include 175 companies and over 20,000 workers. Every imaginable variety of silk was fabricated in the mills—yard goods for dresses, ribbons for decoration, drapery and upholstery silks, veiling, linings, and braids. [8] Raw silk bales from Europe and Asia were transformed into yarns; specialist dyers added colors in every degree of intensity and hue. Under the motto *spe et labore* (or "with hope and hard work"), Paterson entered the twentieth century as the focal point of American silk manufacturing.

Yet by 1900 a pervasive sense of foreboding had settled in over the city. Just as the Latin root "spero, sperare" in its motto can be read either as "to hope (for good things)" or "to fear (ominous developments)," depending on the context, Paterson's industrial trends were filled with ambiguity. Within the city, both competition and labor conflict had intensified by the turn of the century. Also, rival firms were sprouting rapidly, especially in northeastern Pennsylvania; as Paterson's silk output rose, its share of total national production ebbed. Federal industrial statistics document this shift. In 1890, New Jersey held nearly 12,000 silk looms, 359,000 spindles, and about 17,500 silk workers, chiefly located in Paterson. Pennsylvania reported appreciably smaller totals (3,500; 320,000; and 9,000 respectively). Ten years later, though New Jersey's capacity had grown to over 20,000 looms and 500,000 spindles, its western neighbor had quadrupled its loom count to 13,000 and had passed the Garden State in spindlage, soaring to 942,000. [9] By the end of World War I, Pennsylvania had surged far ahead. In 1919 its silk output was valued at $231 million, as 373 companies were employing 53,000 workers, dwarfing Paterson's $140 million production and 22,000 workers. [10] Over the 1890–1920 period, while New Jersey's silk employment had doubled, Pennsylvania's had increased nearly sixfold. Meanwhile, Philadelphia, never a rival in woven goods, was adapting its prodigious knitting capacity to silk hosiery, whose boom would sustain the Quaker City's textile complex for the next generation. Paterson firms had no experience with knitting. The founding generation of immigrant proprietors was dying out; many of their substantial enterprises were already liquidated, being replaced by dozens of struggling, undercapitalized concerns. If there was much to fear, however, there remained cause for hope because two "natural" advantages remained undiminished. First, Paterson's proximity to the city of New York and its vast market, the national center for textile sales, enabled its companies to detect fashion shifts and continue the rapid responses that had helped foster Paterson's rise to prominence. Second, the soft water drawn from the Passaic River was so well suited to silk dyeing that carloads of fabrics woven elsewhere were shipped to Paterson for coloring. Moreover, the city's pool of skilled workers was being replenished with the immigration of a sizable Italian population, a fraction of which had experience gained in the textile factories of northern Italy.[11]

Looking back from their late-1930s' vantage point, the compilers of the New Jersey volume in the American Guide Series documented the city's gains and losses. Through a "curb exchange" on Washington Street, the Paterson silk shopmen continued to meet New York commission merchants and to negotiate contracts, often verbal, to suit their needs. More importantly, however, Paterson's dye works had emerged as the dominant sector of the silk industry. In 1901 two dozen city dyeing firms had engaged about twenty-five hundred largely male "hands," 11 percent of Paterson's textile workers. By the late 1930s, five thousand dyers and helpers operated vats and tubs that processed three-quarters of the nation's silks and represented over half of the city's textile work force.[12] Yet the dyers' success was offset by the decay of the old weaving sector, the prevalence of explosive strikes both before and after the famous 1913 confrontation, and the hand-to-mouth existence of hundreds of "cockroach shops," whose operators tried to earn a few dollars' profit from their curb-side commissions. Running a few looms in partitioned sections of aging mills, these "family shops" were testimony to a local industrial evolution that ran counter to national developments. Whereas in steel, ceramics, or glass, major consolidations increased the scale and decreased the numbers of producers, in silks, the large integrated concerns of the 1880s were gradually succeeded by hundreds of workshops.[13]

Though these firms had multiplied dramatically during World War I, doubling the number of Paterson silk-weaving companies from 291 to 574 in five years,[14] they faded away within the next two decades. Their tiny scale made them obviously vulnerable to every shift in market and materials prices; but worse, they entered the silk industry just at the moment when the first synthetic fiber, rayon or artificial silk, was gaining wide acceptance. By the late 1920s, the pioneering Vicose plant at Chester, Pennsylvania, alone reported employing over four thousand workers engaged in spinning rayon yarn, as silk production commenced its rapid decay.[15] In the last years of the Great Depression, 63,000 American men and women were turning out acres of rayon goods, but silk-weaving employment had shrunk to 17,000, only 12 percent of which remained in New Jersey.[16] The coming of World War II eliminated the supply of raw silk from Japan, where mulberry acreage was converted to food production and rayon quickly replaced silk.[17] Even after 1945, when peace ended the wartime interruption in silk supply, the industry continued to languish, as 1947 census figures indicate that production had recovered to only one-quarter of the modest 1939 levels.[18] Though a few firms survived by converting to the manufacture of rayon, and skilled dyers continued their labors, Paterson's reign as Silk City and silk's days as the "queen of fibers" had ended.

Given this brief overview, the articles that follow address a broad range of issues germane to the silk industry's development and recurrent crises. Richard D. Margrave begins with an evaluation of the role English immigrants played in the transfer of European technology and skills to Paterson (carrying forward into the later-nineteenth-century questions raised by David J. Jeremy).[19] This writer then assesses the continuities and changes in the system of silk production during the quarter century after 1885, focusing on business practice, technology, and labor-capital relations. Steve Golin reviews the manufacturers' strategy in the 1913 general strike, exploring the roots of the unity maintained despite a fiercely competitive market environment. Patricia C. O'Donnell's study of the ribbon silks produced at Pelgram and Meyer represents one of the first efforts to examine Paterson fabrics as historical artifacts. Rivalries among trade unions and their ethnic and ideological bases are the central concern of David J. Goldberg's analysis of the labor situation during and after World War I. Philip J. McLewin scrutinizes the "family shop" of the 1920s and 1930s, setting its emergence in the context of technological change, market power, and labor conflicts. The illustrations, selected and described by Delight W. Dodyk and John A. Herbst, provide a visual introduction to Paterson's mills, masters, and workers from the era of John Ryle, the first prominent proprietor, to the 1930s. A bibliographical note supplements the source notes, which are appended to each article.

The editor wishes to express his appreciation to the Charles Edison Fund, whose generous grant supported the preparation and publication of this volume. In addition, thanks are due the Rutgers Research Council, which undertook the expenses of manuscript typing; Monica DeCarlo, who handled drafts and revisions with her customary skill; Don C. Skemer, editor of publications at the New

Jersey Historical Society, who conceived this project and offered valued advice throughout the past two years; Joanne R. Walroth, copy editor at the Society; and the contributors, who responded graciously to pages of badly typed comments on earlier versions of the work presented here.

NOTES

[1]Economic historians occasionally recall that in the nineteenth century, Paterson was known nationally as the birthplace of the Rogers Locomotive Works (1832) and the Colt Patent Arms Manufacturing Company (1842).

[2]Herbert G. Gutman, "Class, Status, and Community Power in Nineteenth-Century American Industrial Cities: Paterson, New Jersey: A Case Study," reprinted in *Work, Culture and Society in Industrializing America* (New York, 1976), 235.

[3]See Michael Piore and Charles Sabel, *The Second Industrial Divide* (New York, 1984); Charles Sabel and Jonathan Zeitlin, "Historical Alternatives to Mass-Production," *Past and Present*, forthcoming, 1985; Charles Sabel, *Work and Politics: The Division of Labor in Industry* (New York, 1982).

[4]Morris W. Garber, "The Silk Industry of Paterson, New Jersey" (Ph.D. diss., Rutgers University, 1968), 6–18 (quotation from 11). For an old but reliable study of SUM, see Joseph S. Davis, *Essays in the Earlier History of American Corporations*, 1 (New York, 1968), 349–518.

[5]Ibid., 30–45.

[6]Ibid., 63–77; John H. White, Jr., "Introduction," in *The Rogers Locomotive Catalog, 1876* (Newark, N.J., 1983), v–vii. Locomotive construction continued through World War I in the city, and other machinery builders flourished, particularly those serving the needs of silk manufacturers.

[7]L. R. Trumbull, *A History of Industrial Paterson* (Paterson, N.J., 1882), 165–85.

[8]Broad silks (for dresses, drapes, and linings) were defined as fabrics over twelve inches in width, and goods of unpiled surface, thus excluding plushes and velvets. All woven silks twelve inches or less in width were classed as narrow or ribbon goods, principally used for ornament and decoration in millinery, clothing, and home furnishings.

[9]U.S. Department of the Interior, Census Office, *Twelfth Census of the United States: 1900*, Volume 9: *Manufactures*, part 3, "Special Reports on Selected Industries" (Washington, D.C., 1902), 206–10.

[10]U.S. Department of Commerce, Bureau of the Census, *Fourteenth Census of the United States: 1920*, Volume 9: *Manufactures: Reports for States with Statistics for Principal Cities* (Washington, D.C., 1923), 911, 928, 1266, 1294.

[11]See Caroline Golab, "Comments," in Paul A. Stellhorn, ed., *New Jersey's Ethnic Heritage* (Trenton, N.J., 1978), 61–64.

[12]U.S. Department of Commerce, Bureau of the Census, *Biennial Census of Manufactures: 1937*, part 2 (Washington, D.C., 1939), 69–70.

[13]Federal Writers Project (WPA), *New Jersey: A Guide to Its Present and Past* (New York, 1939), 349–54.

[14]*Fourteenth Census*, 9:928.

[15]Pennsylvania Department of Internal Affairs, *Sixth Industrial Directory of the Commonwealth of Pennsylvania: 1928* (Harrisburg, Pa., 1928), 246.

[16]U.S. Department of Commerce, Bureau of the Census, *Census of Manufactures: 1937, Man-Hour Statistics for 105 Selected Industries* (Washington, D.C., 1939), 27–28, 30–31.

[17]Rachel Maines, "Wartime Allocation of Textile and Apparel Resources: Emergency Policy in the Twentieth Century," *The Public Historian* 7 (Winter 1985): 44.

[18]U.S. Department of Commerce, Bureau of the Census, *Census of Manufactures: 1947, Product Supplement* (Washington, D.C., 1950), 26.

[19]David J. Jeremy, *Transatlantic Industrial Revolution: The Diffusion of Textile Technologies between Britain and America, 1790–1830* (Cambridge, Mass., 1981).

1

Technology Diffusion and the Transfer of Skills: Nineteenth-Century English Silk Migration to Paterson

■ RICHARD D. MARGRAVE ■

IN THE WINTER OF 1872 A Paterson newspaper published a poem entitled "The Silk Weavers," written in a northern English dialect by an immigrant domestic hand-loom weaver.[1] The poem is not a backward romantic glance toward an almost-forgotten time of English artisan activity in the Old World. Rather, amid the rapid industrialization of post–Civil War America, resided a large group of English-born silk workers actively pursuing their traditional means of earning a living. English immigrants were among the many European population groups that crossed the Atlantic Ocean to North America in the nineteenth century.[2] Numbers, timing, and motivations diverged widely throughout the century. But important among the English were those industrial workers who chose to emigrate to the United States. All varieties of skilled and semiskilled workers relocated in America as the British economy continued to develop. Their contribution to the establishment and growth of industrial processes in America has long been recognized. Yet many questions remain unanswered as to the exact extent of their roles in specific industries and particular North American communities.[3]

The English-born industrial immigrant was to be found in Paterson from the very earliest days of development and the initial schemes of the Society for Establishing Useful Manufactures (SUM). Through-

out the first half of the nineteenth century these immigrant technicians continued to be integrally involved in the expansion of the city's
industrial base, comprising workers and entrepreneurs in textile–machinery manufacture, locomotive works, factories, and
workshops.[4]

By the time of the 1850 federal census, of a total of 578 men, 60.4
percent of the English-born enumerated in employment in Paterson—English immigrants accounted for about a tenth of the city's
population—were engaged in occupations that involved a knowledge
of industrial skills. This group found work as machinists, weavers,
mule spinners, and molders, who were involved in industries forming
the very basis of nineteenth-century industrial growth. Another 23.8
percent had skills that were craft-orientated or preindustrial in
nature, skills largely unchanged by the process of industrialization to
this date. The remainder worked as industrial laborers (10.2 percent), tertiary-sector employees—clerical, commercial, profes-
sional, and gentlemen (5.1 percent), and agricultural workers (0.7
percent).[5] Paterson was mirrored elsewhere in other northeastern
industrial centers. Hundreds of similar immigrants, for instance,
worked in the cotton hand-loom weaving and framework knitting
sectors of Philadelphia, the textile factories of New England cities,
the pottery industries of Trenton, New Jersey, and of East Liverpool,
Ohio, and the coal mines of Pennsylvania.[6]

While the American silk industry enjoyed only faltering fortunes
and slow growth before the Civil War, a firm base for the infant
industry was established in centers such as Paterson, Philadelphia,
New York, and New England. The chief product at this time was
sewing silk for domestic consumption, which demanded few of the
specialized skills of the European silk immigrant. Nevertheless, previous entrepreneurial or supervisory experience in European silk
manufacture enabled immigrants to found several of the pioneer
American silk companies. This was especially true in Paterson,
where the number of English-born silk manufacturers gradually increased from the first establishment in the early 1840s.[7]

Twenty years later, the local industry was concentrated largely in
the hands of the English-born. From the available statistics, it would
appear that fully one-fourth of the entire Paterson silk work force was
English-born in 1860.[8] Of the male English-born workers, almost
one-quarter (24.2 percent) of their number was classed as manufacturers engaged in the production of sewing silks and trimmings, while
nearly three-quarters (72.7 percent) had known industrial skills, and
a small number (6.1 percent) held managerial positions in the Paterson mills. (See table 1.)

Table 1

OCCUPATIONS OF ENGLISH-BORN SILK WORKERS, PATERSON, 1860–80. PERCENTAGE DISTRIBUTION

	Entre-preneurial		Super-visory		Skilled		Semiskilled		Totals	
	no.	%	no.	%	no.	%	no.	%	no.	%
1860										
M[a]	8	24.2	2	6.1	14	42.4	9	27.3	33	100.0
F[a]	—	—	—	—	6	33.3	12	66.7	18	100.0
T[a]	8	15.7	2	3.9	20	39.2	21	41.2	51	100.0
1870										
M	11	4.0	8	2.9	152	55.7	102	37.4	273	100.0
F	—	—	—	—	6	4.5	128	95.5	134	100.0
T	11	2.7	8	2.0	158	38.8	230	56.5	407	100.0
1880										
M	42	4.3	19	1.9	456	46.2	469	47.6	986	100.0
F	—	—	—	—	74	15.7	396	84.3	470	100.0
T	42	2.9	19	1.3	530	36.4	865	59.4	1456	100.0

Source: U.S. Department of the Interior, Census Office, MSS., Population, Paterson, N.J., 1860–80. Percentages have been rounded.
[a]M = Males; F = Females; T = Totals.

Table 2

OCCUPATIONAL MOBILITY: MALE ENGLISH-BORN SILK WORKERS, PATERSON, 1870–80

Year	Entre-preneurial		Super-visory		Skilled		Semi-skilled		Totals	
	no.	%	no.	%	no.	%	no.	%	no.	%
1870	8	7.5	5	4.7	56	52.3	38	35.5	107	100.0
1880	11	10.3	1	0.9	50	46.7	45	42.1	107	100.0

Source: U.S. Department of the Interior, Census Office, MSS., Population, Paterson, N.J., 1870–80. Percentages have been rounded.

TRANSATLANTIC RELOCATION

The imposition of high tariff barriers against products of foreign manufacture during the Civil War conferred upon the infant American silk industry a degree of protection, which was to help foster immense domestic growth. In Paterson the early silk-throwing and silk-sewing establishments expanded as new ventures began first in narrow goods, or ribbon-weaving production, then later in broad-silk weaving. Paterson came to represent the most highly skilled area of silk manufacture in the United States, a reputation based in part upon its relatively long experience of the trade, plus the considerable reservoir of local skills and expertise. Further arrivals of English-born and other skilled European silk workers during the next thirty years acted to strengthen the reputation for excellence of Paterson.[9]

The arrival in Paterson of immigrant workers, entrepreneurs, and even machinery imports was greatly encouraged by the economic climate in contemporary Great Britain. The Cobden trade treaty of 1860 acted to accelerate drastically the already downward trend in British silk production. Old established centers of excellence in silk manufacture in Britain, such as Coventry and Macclesfield, entered a period of rapid decline. Preexistent links between the old Cheshire silk town of Macclesfield and Paterson in particular led to the establishment of an informal network of migration. Increasingly during the period 1860–80, workers, entrepreneurs, and their families moved directly from Macclesfield to Paterson. The post–Civil War growth in American silk was to be supplied readily with further inputs of skills and expertise as immigrants from England and other European silk centers continued to arrive.[10]

As traditional employment opportunities in the old English silk centers contracted during the post-Cobden period, several hundred workers and their families chose emigration as the means of alleviating their economic distress. Many such workers found their way to North America, drawn there by the growing network of communications between the British and American silk centers. The chief economic components of this emigration response—dynamic in the sense that traditional craft workers threatened by unemployment and economic change were able to uproot themselves and journey several thousand miles, and passive in the sense that the objective of their move was to preserve their old hand-processing skills—provided an interesting counterpoint for their subsequent adaptation to a new life in America. Both pushed and pulled by strong economic forces, the migrants fully expected to be able to use their skills in Paterson, while at the same time avoiding change at home.

The percentage distribution of English-born silk workers in Paterson in 1870 and 1880 is shown in table 1. The influx of skilled workers after the Cobden trade treaty and the Civil War tariff changes is clearly visible when compared with the figures for 1860. The total number of English-born silk workers in the industry climbed from 51 in 1860 to 407 in 1870; it rose further during the 1870s, to reach a total of 1,456 in 1880.

The relative proportion of male entrepreneurs to the toal number of English-born male silk workers fell dramatically in the 1860s, from almost one-quarter (24.2 percent) in 1860, to less than one-twentieth (4.0 percent) by 1870. This was due solely to the arrival of large numbers of new immigrant workers during the decade, thereby diluting the overall proportion; it should not be inferred that the role of the English-born silk manufacturer declined within the industry. The dominance of the early English-born "pioneers" in the industry actually increased following the relocation from New England of two other silk companies owned and operated by English-born immigrants. Together these companies continued to expand during the 1860s to take full advantage of the higher level of tariff protection. (See table 1.)

ENTREPRENEURIAL MOBILITY

In the 1870s the widespread introduction of the production of new woven goods and the consequent increase in the number of small silk companies helped to increase the number of English-born silk manufacturers and merchants from eleven in 1870 to forty-two in 1880. British immigrants generally were more likely than other immigrants to assume entrepreneurial positions in American manufacturing companies during the nineteenth century. The size of the English population in the Paterson silk industry remained surprisingly high, despite the general decrease in the overall importance of the English-born in new American industries after the Civil War. [11] The large increase in the numbers of English-born silk entrepreneurs was not enough to be reflected in the overall distribution of the English-born silk worker labor force in 1880. Despite a heavy immigration of additional workers during the 1870s, the relative proportion of those in entrepreneurial positions only rose from 2.7 percent of the total to 2.9 percent. Did this rise in overall numbers reflect the arrival of entrepreneurs who simply transferred their operations across the Atlantic, or were the new breed of Paterson woven-goods entrepreneurs recruited from the ranks of earlier immigrants?

There was a widespread belief that the Paterson silk industry offered opportunities for upward occupational mobility to the skilled worker which were far in excess of those in the English silk centers: "The Macclesfield operative must be content to remain an operative all his life, but the Paterson operative sees all around him successful manufacturers who have but recently sprung from the loom."[12] The perception was that skilled factory workers could become self-made men—"the various silk manufactories of Paterson are like bee-hives in the regularity with which they turn out the nuclei of new establishments."[13] The same perception also applied to domestic weavers who worked in their own homes: "Some of the heaviest manufacturers of to-day began with a loom or two in their own houses. Even now when the city is ringed around with great three and four storey factories, it is not impossible for a skilful, industrious workman to commence business with a single loom and in a few years become the head of a large concern. The production of some articles which meet with marked favour in the market will often bring an offer of capital sufficient to start a mill."[14] Contemporary sources stressed repeatedly the unique opportunities open to the European, and especially English, immigrant skilled in the silk business. It was widely held that considerable numbers of local manufacturers had emigrated from Macclesfield where they had been employed as weavers: "There are dozens of men who, a few years ago, were wage-earners in Macclesfield, yet who are to-day extensive employers, and prosperous mill-owners and manufacturers in Paterson."[15]

The finest example was provided by the partnership of two Macclesfield silk weavers, Henry Doherty and Joseph Wadsworth. Their partnership was described in 1882 as "one of the most remarkable instances of recent success in the silk manufacture of any in the business."[16] Born around 1850, Doherty and Wadsworth were the sons of a silk weaver and a silk man (or merchant) respectively. They lived together in the same Macclesfield neighborhood and worked for the same mill. The story was related that the pair labored long hours in the silk mill, only to return home each evening to study the intricacies of the trade to an even further extent. Both were said to have become extremely skilled workers before their decision to emigrate to America in the late 1860s. "They learned the manufacture of silk from the carrying of the bobbins to the completion of the finest fabric; there was not a branch of the silk industry in which they were not proficient when they concluded to come to this country."[17]

Doherty emigrated in the latter part of 1868, and Wadsworth followed six months later. Both traveled directly to Paterson and found well-paid positions in the mills of fellow Macclesfield immigrants—

Doherty as foreman of the Mackay mill, Wadsworth in a similar capacity at the Grimshaw mill. After a period of almost ten years spent working for fellow immigrants, during which time both began raising families, Doherty and Wadsworth decided to start a business together. "Although both commanded liberal salaries, they found that others were reaping the larger harvest of their skill and experience and once more they joined their fortunes together which had been so often linked when they were boys."[18]

The newly formed partnership of Doherty and Wadsworth immediately negotiated the lease on a small workroom situated on the third floor of the Second National Bank building and in October 1879 began to weave their own silk goods upon a single loom. Business quickly prospered and by January of the following year the company had moved to the second floor of the Arkwright mill and operated a total of eight looms. Only a few months later winding machinery was installed, a section of the first floor leased, and the company employed fifty workers and operated thirty looms. By June 1881 the remainder of the first floor was leased and over a hundred other looms were added. The company produced a wide variety of broad silks, dress goods, handkerchiefs, millinery goods, scarfs, grenadines, laces, satins, and brocades, and it provided work for 250 employees. The following year, Doherty and Wadsworth were able to purchase the Arkwright mill, and over the next three years they extended the building to include a total of four storeys. Expansion of the business continued throughout the remainder of the century; employment had reached almost a thousand workers by the early 1890s. It was Henry Doherty who, in his attempt to raise loom assignments in 1913, precipitated the Paterson silk strike of that year.[19]

The extraordinary success of Doherty and Wadsworth attained a degree of local prominence for them equal only to the "pioneers" of the Paterson silk industry, John Ryle, Catholina Lambert, and William Strange; they were by no means isolated examples of self-made immigrant men. During the course of the late nineteenth century, dozens of English and other European immigrant workers, with largely similar backgrounds, attained considerable entrepreneurial success in the Paterson silk industry. Names such as Joseph Bamford, Sr., Alfred Crew, and Thomas Henshall became synonymous with the success that could be achieved by the ordinary English immigrant in the Paterson silk industry.[20]

A variety of specific economic circumstances favored the establishment of these predominantly small-scale businesses. Little initial capital outlay was required, as both machinery and materials were easily available on credit.[21] New mill buildings were gradually added to the existing superfluity of cotton mills in the city to provide a constant supply of rented mill accommodations. The mills were subdivided into small units, and potential manufacturers were able to rent the amount of floor space they required to suit both the methods and the scale of production. In 1883, for instance, the third floor of the Dale mill housed four newly established silk manufacturers from England, each of whom specialized in a particular branch of the trade.[22] The tremendous growth and specialization of the industry presented unique opportunities for the small firm throughout the remainder of the century. A leading authority on the industry was later to comment, "it has always been comparatively easy for a skilled weaver, or designer, to start out as a manufacturer. . . . because of the highly specialized nature of the industry, the great value of the product and the opportunity for personality and individual skill."[23] The necessary degree of specialization dictated that the overall structure of the industry remain on a small scale; this allowed the basic unit of industrial activity to remain either the single proprietorship or the partnership. This resulted in easier access for the skilled worker, who simply combined with family or friends from England to establish a small company of his own.[24] Finally, the existence of a well-established and efficient wholesale market, based upon the New York silk commission houses, obviated problems with regard to the eventual sale of the final product.[25]

These opportunities were available specifically for the immigrant, rather than the native-born American, because of the specialized knowledge required to enter the business and the continually growing immigrant network. Friends, family, and even former employers from home who were already established in Paterson were more than willing to provide assistance. When Coventry-born Edward Riley formed his own business in 1882, after thirteen years of work in Paterson silk-dyeing establishments, he was able to call upon considerable help from an influential fellow immigrant. John Ryle provided space in a rented mill for the new company and supplied references and recommendations to potential customers. Riley's proposal was described by Ryle as commercially sound and sufficiently capitalized and his work as well known by the principal silk companies in Paterson. Ryle added, in a letter of recommendation, "I should not hesitate to give him whatever quantity or color I might wish to give out."[26]

It is much more difficult to describe the cases of immigrants who established small businesses after years of hard work only to fail a relatively short time afterwards. This is due to a consistent bias in the contemporary sources towards successful examples rather than to a high success rate among all ventures. A detailed examination of biographical sources and contemporary newspaper reports does shed some light on the origins of those migrants whose concerns later failed.

Philip Walmsley, superintendent of a Paterson mill for three years, established his own company in the city in the late 1860s. After only two years, the business collapsed and Walmsley moved to New York and became a silk commission dealer. John Jackson Scott, thoroughly acquainted with silk manufacturing in Leek before his emigration, continued to add to his experience in America by working almost twenty years in the Massachusetts silk industry and then for John Ryle in Paterson. In 1871 he established his own silk-thread company in Paterson, yet within ten years he had been forced out of business. In May 1886 the stock and silk machinery of the failed business owned by Macclesfield-born John Lockett was sold by the Paterson sheriff for $6,000.00. Coventry-born John Day twice failed in business in Paterson before he was able to establish his own company successfully; Ernest Barber of Macclesfield worked hard as a weaver for many years prior to becoming a manufacturer in Paterson, only to be ruined in the panic of 1893, when he was forced to return to work as an ordinary weaver. Even the "father" of the American silk industry, John Ryle, came close to bankruptcy in 1857 and only survived with the aid of a generous loan from his brothers in Macclesfield. Indeed, in 1872 even Ryle failed and was forced to organize a new silk company in Paterson.[27]

Many more European and native-born entrepreneurs must have suffered a similar fate in the early 1880s, a period of exceptional growth in the industry that attracted an increased number of "amateur" newcomers but also saw an unusually high number of bankruptcies.[28] The origins of those English-born immigrants who subsequently failed are not appreciably different from their fellow countrymen who were successful. As Herbert G. Gutman wrote of a comparable situation in the Paterson metal industries, "many had failed in comparison to the number that succeeded. Although the printed sources tell little about those who started unsuccessful manufacturing enterprises, there is no reason to think that most of them differed in social origin from their more favored contemporaries."[29]

On the basis of fairly conventional methods of historical analysis, it is already apparent that the contemporary view of rapid and easy upward mobility in nineteenth-century Paterson silk as presented in the local biographical directories and city histories was a distortion of reality. To obtain a more exact measurement of the degree of intra-occupational mobility open to the skilled immigrant, a group composed of 107 English-born workers and manufacturers in the Paterson silk industry was traced over the census period 1870–80.[30] The experience of this cohort proved beyond doubt that it was indeed possible to advance from worker to entrepreneurial status within only ten years, but the absolute numbers involved (less than 3 percent of the total) were relatively few. The classic self-made-men stories also masked other important trends already evident among skilled immigrant workers during this decade, such as a pronounced loss of supervisory positions and a relative shift away from positions requiring higher skills toward purely mill-based occupations among members of the cohort. (See table 2.)[31]

Though opportunities for upward mobility may have been considerably overstated in contemporary accounts, the fact remained that the English immigrants themselves believed that Paterson had more opportunities to offer than Macclesfield. Of course, concrete examples of such successes were to be seen all around. John Ryle, in an 1887 letter from England to his sons in Paterson, noted the following conversation between himself and the owner of a Lancashire machine-building shop: "The other day when old Mr. Smith (79 years old) was showing me a fine loom, I said that would be no good in America, he said why, I said we should have nobody competent to put it to work oh, he replied I could send you out a man that could put it to work for you, without any delay, Yes, I said and in a weeks time he'd own the place, I said we were not willing to part with our property on such easy terms, the old man laught, I think he'd been there."[32] Traditionally, such upward mobility was regarded as extremely rare in contemporary England. Catholina Lambert, for instance, was said to have believed a quotation he had read in a book as a young man in England: "In England the chances for success are one out of ten unless born of rich parents; in America, nine out of ten."[33] Interesting by comparison is a remark in the 1920 Macclesfield town guide: "Probably the Silk Industry of Macclesfield stands unique in the trades of the country in the fact that out of fifteen firms engaged in silk production almost all are either owned or managed by men who have risen either from the loom itself or from other operative positions in the industry."[34]

The predominance of the English-born among the mill owners in the Paterson silk industry during the 1850–90 period was due both to small numbers of ordinary workers achieving entrepreneurial status and to the transfer of existing businesses across the Atlantic. In 1869 the *Paterson Weekly Press* noted, "most of the manufacturers of Paterson have spent years of apprenticeship in Europe."[35] This preponderance of English and other European-born mill owners, an unusual situation in nineteenth-century America, was to influence directly the subsequent course of growth in the Paterson industry. [36]

TECHNOLOGICAL IMPROVEMENTS

In the years before the Civil War, the American silk industry produced only sewing silks and trimmings and provided few opportunities for the skilled immigrant. The imposition of high protective duties and the extension of the native industry into the more complex production of woven silk goods changed the situation radically. Introduced primarily by immigrant manufacturers, the new woven goods were extremely similar to those previously imported from Europe. Indeed, for many years the American-based entrepreneurs even went so far as to append "foreign" labels to their goods. [37] By the late 1870s, Paterson manufacturers had introduced a wide variety of narrow- and broad-silk products, using European technology: "Beginning with the simple process of twisting and dyeing sewing silk, the industry has widened until it now embraces the richest flowered and damask dress goods." [38] The Paterson industry was to develop new techniques in time, but the late 1860s, 1870s, and early 1880s offered opportunities to the skilled European silk worker almost directly comparable to those quickly disappearing at home. [39]

The clear similarity in manufacturing processes was due in part to the use of actual European silk machinery in the expanding American industry. The collapse of the British silk industry created spare capacity. As mills closed down, quantities of surplus machinery were sold and shipped to the United States. In 1865 John Stearns established silk-spinning companies in New York City and Staten Island using machinery purchased at low prices from Manchester mills ruined in the aftermath of the Cobden commercial treaty five years earlier. After a fire destroyed the entire contents of John Ryle's mill in 1869, a large new mill building covering one and a half acres was stocked throughout with machinery from England. The machinery was bought from the estate of the late William Wanklyn, a noted Ashton-under-Lyme silk throwster, and arrived in October 1869 packed in seventy-eight cases aboard the steamship *Java*. There were other such instances of English mills selling their machinery to entrepreneurs in the United States. L. P. Brockett reported in 1876, "today the spindles of some of these mills, purchased at a mere nominal price, are running in American silk mills." [40]

The purchase of European silk machinery was not confined solely to bankruptcy stock from Britain, with the selective importation of specialized technology a constant feature of the American silk industry in the late nineteenth century. In 1874 Catholina Lambert revisited England to purchase a "plant" of power looms, which he shipped back to Paterson to use for broad-silk weaving. A year later, the Phoenix Manufacturing Company imported the first damask loom to be seen in the United States and engaged a Mr. Sisserson, "a veteran weaver . . . who worked at the first Jacquard loom set up in England" to operate it. [41] An advice note concerned with the dispatch of four cases of machinery from Liverpool to New York is still in existence among the Ryle Family Papers. In 1879 W. B. Cochran imported a card-cutting machine from England, which enabled him to produce ten thousand textile cards daily. A year later French-born Claude Greppo was reported to have "recently imported some very costly machinery for dyeing and finishing velvet," and Crew and Henshall purchased a quantity of English finishing machinery. In 1882 Pfeffer and Wells, previously large spun-silk manufacturers in Germany, established a silk company in Paterson and "imported a large and costly plant of spun-silk machinery from Europe."[42] Even late in the century machinery of rather anachronistic wooden construction was imported to Paterson. The mills of local entrepreneurs such as Macclesfield-born Thomas Henshall were packed with such machinery: "His works are stocked with the most improved and costly machinery, much of it of special design and a great deal imported from Europe."[43]

The purchase of specialized European machinery usually was carried out either by the entrepreneur himself or by a European agent retained specifically by the American silk company. Coventry-born Charles Barton secured employment with Dexter, Lambert, and Company, first in Boston, then later in Paterson, and was sent on several occasions to England, "mainly on business for the firm, and to purchase machinery."[44] John Ryle visited England in 1887 and immediately dispatched a consignment of eighteen looms back to America (purchase price: £9 each) for eventual trial among the largely unskilled workers in his new mill in Pennsylvania. His comments in an accompanying letter explained with surprising simplicity the economics of the purchase: "This matter of buying looms here, gives me some serious thought and you will have to judge, will they cost, duty included more than you can buy as good a loom for in America, or are they so much better that it is an advantage to have them."[45] While American machinery manufacturers were soon to develop their own varieties of silk machines, European industries made both specialty silks and the machinery to produce them. John Ryle avidly described to his sons in Paterson the enormous variety of specialized machinery available in a Lancashire machine shop he visited in 1887: "Oh my; you should go thro. Smiths shop to see a place where they make silk looms; it beats all, they have looms that are going all over Europe, and for all kinds of silk goods, they have velvet looms making double cloth and cut in the middle and for making plush imitation of seal skin, they make looms of all kinds for silk, if you want posting, you should come to Smiths."[46] The immigrant manufacturer established in the American silk industry knew only too well the enormous scope of the traditional European machine builders.

Naturally the increasing scale of the Paterson silk industry and the considerable expense involved precluded the possibility of the majority of the silk machinery in use being of European origin, and gradually during the late 1860s and 1870s the manufacture of silk machinery began in the city. Paterson enjoyed a comparative advantage in this new industry because a central feature of the earlier, now largely defunct, cotton textile industry was the widespread manufacture of textile machinery. As the silk industry grew in stature, local machine shops began to switch production to cater to the needs of the new industry. Once more the role of the immigrant was of great value, as earlier arrivals such as Thomas Wrigley, Benjamin Buckley, James Atkinson, and John R. Daggers, from Lancashire and Yorkshire, largely controlled the manufacturing of textile machinery.[47]

To these long-established machine shops were soon added the local locomotive and metal-working companies, which themselves began to cater to the needs of local silk companies during the severe business depression of the mid-1870s. The first products were confined to the throwing, or spinning, side of the industry, which required a simpler technology and offered great potential for the refinement and "speeding up" of the machinery. During the mid-1870s local silk mills began to stock this less expensive and improved throwing machinery and by 1875 were said to use a mixture of imported and locally manufactured machinery: "The machinery of the Phoenix mill was made in England and this country."[48]

By the time of the 1876 U.S. Centennial Exposition in Philadelphia, thrown-silk machinery manufactured in Paterson had attracted widespread attention among the American manufacturers. "What immense strides young America is making towards full rivalship with old England in the most intricate processes of the silk manufacture," the newspaper editorials announced.[49] The three-tier spinning frames manufactured by the Danforth Locomotive and Machine Company, local locomotive builders, were to revolutionize the thrown-silk business; "a fact recognized . . . by veteran English silk manufacturers in this country" by 1876.[50]

Construction of the more complicated machinery for weaving developed more slowly in Paterson; at first it was confined to the efforts of the immigrant manufacturers themselves. Shops for building and repairing machinery were attached to the silk mills by the entrepreneurs, as "they find this cheaper and more convenient than to have their machinery all made outside."[51] Imported machinery was both adapted and improved by many of the immigrant manufacturers, who carried out most of the work themselves or occasionally enlisted the help of other immigrant technicians.[52] Two Lancashire-born technicians in particular made outstanding contributions to the silk machinery industry that was developing quickly. Jacquard looms were imported (at a cost of $40.00 each) until 1873, when James Jackson began manufacturing and improving them in a small Paterson shop. As late as 1878, the manufacture of such complicated weaving apparatus was regarded as the preserve of the immigrants. One report on this business stated that "the best workmen in our shops and the most skilled were foreigners."[53] Benjamin Eastwood, with long engineering experience, also began manufacturing specialized silk machinery in the 1870s. Ten years later his shop was said to produce a wide variety of products, including "winders, doublers, drawside frames, French, English and American quilling and spooling frames, ribbon blocking machines, power and hand warpers, beamers and cleaners; grosgrain and dress goods power and hand looms."[54] By the 1880s technological improvements and overall simplification of weaving machinery allowed native-American machine builders into the market, but immigrant technicians remained at the center of these improvements and continued to provide repairs and maintenance for equipment still in use.[55]

DOMESTIC WEAVING

The vast majority of the English-born silk workers in the Paterson industry failed to succeed as entrepreneurs, but for them the local mills provided a variety of skilled and semiskilled positions. The numbers of English-born who assumed skilled jobs in the Paterson silk industry rose from 20 in 1860 to 158 in 1870, and reached a total of 530 in 1880. These immigrants found the industry very similar in its organization to that which they had left behind in England. "The Civil War furnished the first real impetus in the development of the silk branch of the textile industry. From 1860 to 1880, it was still in its handicraft stages. Machinery, as well as the factory system, were little known in silk fabric production."[56] Many English immigrants were to find positions as weavers, dyers, finishers, warpers, and loom fixers.[57]

Most of the immigrant weavers found employment in the newly-established weaving sections of the Paterson silk mills. Approximately two-thirds of Paterson silk weavers in 1880 were foreign-born. The English comprised the largest group (one-fifth of all Paterson weavers), while Swiss, German, and Scottish immigrants accounted for most of the remainder.[58] In 1875 the *Paterson Weekly Press* reported that "most of the weavers at the Phoenix are men, mainly experts from England"; by 1876 it was estimated that the six local mills engaged in broad-silk weaving provided employment for approximately four hundred weavers on hand looms closely packed together in the new weaving sheds.[59]

Large numbers of immigrant silk weavers also established themselves in their new American homes as traditional "outdoor" weavers as late as the 1870s. In 1875 it was suggested, "one branch of the silk business that gives employment to whole families in various ways, is the broad-silk weaving, which is extensively carried on by men at their own homes, with the accompanying warping wheels and winding frames."[60] Based on the experiences of household textile manufacture in the Paterson cotton industry and the European silk trade, the emergence of a domestic-weaving sector at this late date was an example par excellence of the traditional attitudes toward work often found among industrial immigrants from Britain to America. As was recognized by contemporary observers, "the old hand-loom, which may be heard making its peculiar clatter in so many Paterson homes, is one of the oldest, simplest and most widely used pieces of machinery in the world."[61] Such descriptions were based on observation in the homes of the immigrant silk weavers in Paterson but were equally well suited to the traditional garrets of silk weavers in England, France, and Germany: "The upright posts, the different sets of treadles or harness depending from the cross-beams above through the loops or eyes of which the threads of the warp are passed; the roller moved by a crank, around which the warp is wound, and a second roller to receive the woven goods; the shuttle, which with its bobbins the thread of the weft or filling; the swinging bar, the reed which brings each thread home—'beats it up'—and the treadle which depresses alternatively the sets of harness—who has not witnessed the operation of this simple machinery?"[62]

The weavers who established themselves in this way in Paterson were from England, Switzerland or Germany. The looms they installed in their new homes were either brought with them from Europe or rented from the local Paterson entrepreneurs. Relying chiefly on immigrant labor, the New Jersey silk mills reintroduced the European system of putting-out work to domestic weavers as an extension of their own weaving operations. The *Paterson Weekly Press* described such a scheme organized by the Phoenix mill in 1875: "In addition to the large number of hand looms running in the mill, the company employs quite a number of weavers who work at their own homes, some of them owning their own looms—which cost about $15 each—and others being furnished with a loom. The silk is furnished from the mill, and the same price per yard is paid for weaving as for that that is done at the mill."[63] The domestic weavers of Paterson by the mid-1870s had completely reintroduced a system of outdoor weaving based upon the traditional European pattern.[64] In 1876 Brockett described the activities of the newly arrived "master weavers" from England and France: "These men individually own several looms, which in many instances they have brought with them. They carry on the weaving at their homes, one or more rooms being fitted up for this purpose. As business increases," Brockett continued, "they employ so-called journeymen weavers, who in turn will become master weavers and loom owners, and thus build up a valuable though independent auxiliary to the great factories."[65]

Unfortunately, the federal population census manuscripts failed to differentiate between the factory and the domestic silk weaver, and contemporary estimates of the number of household units remained rather vague: "In the east district of the fifth ward alone there are perhaps 100 houses at which these looms are continually rattling away, in many cases giving plenty to do to all the children in the household . . . just how many people are sustained thus it would be difficult to tell, but that they are very numerous through-out the city any person who is accustomed to travelling the less public streets, especially in the Second, Third, Fifth and Eighth wards can bear witness."[66]

The Paterson Board of Trade estimated in 1876 that there were a total of 150 households with domestic looms, a figure that would suggest that domestic weaving accounted for one-third of the total hand-weaving capacity of the industry at that date. Though the relative proportion of English-born silk workers involved in skilled positions declined continually during the 1860–80 period as the industry became increasingly mechanized, the hand-loom weaving portion in both factory and domestic sectors continued to expand, and by the early 1880s the domestic industry had grown to its maximum size of approximately 500 units.[67]

The remainder of the English-born silk workers enumerated in the Paterson industry worked in positions that could be classed as semi-

Table 3

Age Structure by Occupational Branch: Male and Female English-Born Silk Workers, Paterson, 1880. Percentage Distribution

Age Structure	Entrepreneurial M[a] no.	M %	F[a] no.	F %	Supervisory M no.	M %	F no.	F %	Skilled M no.	M %	F no.	F %	Semiskilled M no.	M %	F no.	F %	Totals M no.	M %	F no.	F %
0–9	—	—	—	—	—	—	—	—	—	—	—	—	—	—	1	0.3	—	—	1	0.2
10–19	—	—	—	—	—	—	—	—	56	12.3	30	40.5	120	25.6	207	52.3	176	17.8	237	50.4
20–29	4	9.5	—	—	8	42.1	—	—	126	27.6	19	25.7	118	25.2	111	28.0	256	26.0	130	27.7
30–39	13	31.0	—	—	4	21.1	—	—	84	18.4	13	17.6	89	19.0	43	10.9	190	19.3	56	11.9
40–49	12	28.6	—	—	3	15.8	—	—	94	20.6	11	14.9	73	15.6	20	5.1	182	18.5	31	6.6
50–59	6	14.3	—	—	2	10.5	—	—	63	13.8	—	—	49	10.4	8	2.0	120	12.2	8	1.7
60+	7	16.7	—	—	2	10.5	—	—	33	7.2	1	1.4	20	4.3	6	1.5	62	6.3	7	1.5
Totals	42	100.1	—	—	19	100.0	—	—	456	99.9	74	100.1	469	100.1	396	100.1	986	100.1	470	100.0

Source: U.S. Department of the Interior, Census Office, MSS., Population, Paterson, N.J., 1880. Percentages have been rounded.

[a]M = Males; F = Females.

skilled. [68] Immigrant representation among this group in 1880 was considerably less than for skilled workers in the industry. Almost half the employees of Paterson silk mills were born in New Jersey, while only one third of the total were foreign-born. The English nevertheless constituted the largest group of immigrant mill workers, with other British, Dutch, German, and Swiss immigrants comprising the remainder. [69]

Most of the semiskilled positions were filled by women and children. During the 1860–80 period, the relative proportion of all English-born in this category increased as developments in technology, first in the throwing side of the industry, then later weaving, acted to dilute the level of skills required in the industry. The role of women also began to change during the period. Barred by tradition from holding skilled occupations such as silk weaving in England, women were also subject to discrimination initially in Paterson. However, the development of semiautomatic looms, the weakness of male organized labor in resisting change, and the encouragement of the employers all acted to open the occupation of silk weaver to women. (See table 1.) [70]

Finally, the age structure of the English-born silk-working population in 1880 provides further insights into this group of immigrants. In that year, a quarter of the male skilled workers were in their twenties (27.6 percent), but by far the largest proportion (60.0 percent) were mature industrial craftsmen aged thirty and over. Almost all the manufacturers (90.5 percent) were aged thirty and over, while two-thirds (63.2 percent) of the supervisory class were aged twenty to thirty-nine. Only in the semiskilled branches of the industry were a large proportion (50.8 percent) of the male English-born silk workers under thirty. (See table 3.)

The situation among female English-born silk workers differed significantly. Women workers in the Paterson industry were considerably younger than their male counterparts, with over half the total female workers (50.6 percent) aged under twenty years and three-quarters (78.3 percent) under thirty. The handful of women who were recorded as holding skilled positions in the industry in 1880 were also relatively young, mostly (66.2 percent) aged between ten and twenty-nine. By far the greatest majority of the women worked in the semiskilled occupations and of this group, the overwhelming majority (80.6 percent) were aged under thirty years of age. (See table 3.)

This detailed analysis of the English-born in nineteenth-century Paterson has confirmed the importance of immigrant skills to the expanding local silk industry. Discrete flows of information—a network of exchange for ideas, skills, entrepreneurial knowledge, market intelligence, technological advances, modifications, and developments—were in existence for a period between Paterson and such old English silk centers as Macclesfield. Growth in the American silk industry at a time of drastic decline in the British industry created conditions that led to the transfer of skills and technologies westward across the Atlantic. The eventual high concentration of English-born immigrants who owned silk businesses in the New Jersey city was perhaps the most pronounced example of systematic entrepreneurial involvement in any later nineteenth-century American manufacturing industry by members of this ethnic group.

Resettlement in the Paterson silk industry was achieved to a remarkable extent during the 1860–80 period by the English-born silk workers and their families, but the process of economic adaptation required more than the presence of comparable working conditions. Issues of primary concern included relative wage rates, comparative living costs, and the extent of labor organization, as well as housing conditions, social and familial structure, and popular culture. Although not as strong or long-lasting as the sense of cultural identity maintained by the Germans in Milwaukee, nevertheless a community with a distinctly northern-English orientation did develop in Paterson. [71]

Rapid change by the turn of the century, which included the adoption of new technologies, a subsequent transfer of the silk industry toward the southern United States, the arrival of vast numbers of "new" immigrants from Southern Europe, allied with a pronounced fall in the number of English-born newcomers, served to dilute the strength of the English in Paterson in both the economic and social sense. Yet their lasting contribution to the history of Paterson was a legacy of imported skills and expertise that helped Paterson to maintain a reputation as the leading center for silk manufacture in the United States well into the early twentieth century.

NOTES

[1] Poem dated November 22, 1872, written by "A Macclesfield Weaver" resident in Paterson and reproduced in the *Paterson Weekly Press*, December 12, 1872, 3.

THE SILK WEAVERS

Aw'm a poor silk-weaver, it's plain
  To be seen by my coat an' my hat;
For a ghost aw mat easy be ta'en
  For aw'm very near equally fat.

Aw'm known by my swarthy complexion;
  By my nose an' my chin bein' sharp;
An' can think about nowt o'th d'rection
  Aw maun get when aw have my next warp.

One hawf o'my time's spent awaiting
  Or sitting me down o' th' floor.
In a job that's nee'r paid for, ca'd 'gaiting'
  Or we'vin sum new patterns o'er.

What wi' waiting, an' gaiting, an batin'
  My wages are often so smaw
That there isna much left for me atin'
  An' sometimes there's nothing at aw.

When aw take my work in very offt,
  Aw'm other too heavy or leet;
O'er spirited, short rubbed, or too soft,
  It's seldom, if ever, aw'm reet.

When my loom-rent, my gas, an' my late's paid,
  My twisting, an' turning, warp on,
An' a trifle been gen to the trade,
  There is not much left to take whoam.

It's hard work to live where there's weaving;
  But where there is none it is worse;
Aw should think that a mon was gone raving
  If he offered me much for my purse.

But there's one thing of which we have plenty,
  That's debts that we hardly can pay,
And when a man's pockets are empty,
  His wants will get more every day.

Yet these middle-class folks they all tell us
  We're a drunken, disorderly set,
Of extravagant, dissolute fellows,
  And more than we merit, we get.

If a workingman's share is aw labour
  When other folks sit an' enjoy,
Aw'm sorry I ee'r was a weaver,
  An' to be something else aw will troy.

[2]The literature on this topic is voluminous. For an introduction, see Marcus Hansen, *The Atlantic Migration* (Cambridge, Mass., 1940); Maldwyn Jones, *American Immigration* (Chicago, 1960); Philip Taylor, *The Distant Magnet: European Emigration to the U.S.A.* (London, 1971).

[3]A fine introduction to the emigration of British citizens during the nineteenth century is provided by Maldwyn Jones, "The Background to Emigration from Great Britain in the Nineteenth Century," *Perspectives in American History*, 7 (1973):3–92. For the English alone, see C. J. Erickson, "English," in *Harvard Encyclopedia of American Ethnic Groups*, ed., Stephan Thernstrom (Cambridge, Mass., 1980), 319–36. The more specific study of industrial migrants and technology transference may be introduced by Rowland T. Berthoff, *British Immigrants in Industrial America, 1790–1950* (Cambridge, Mass., 1953); David J. Jeremy, *Transatlantic Industrial Revolution: The Diffusion of Textile Technologies between Britain and America, 1790–1830* (Cambridge, Mass., 1981).

[4]For full details see Richard D. Margrave, "The Emigration of Silk Workers from England to the United States of America in the Nineteenth Century" (Ph.D. diss., University of London, 1981), 20–73.

[5]The source for the percentages given is the U.S. Department of the Interior, Census Office, MSS., Population, Paterson, Passaic County, N.J., 1850. Numbers do not add up to 100 percent because of rounding. For further information on the categories used, see Charlotte Erickson, "Who Were the English and Scots Emigrants to the United States in the Late Nineteenth Century?" in *Population and Social Change*, ed., David Glass and Roger Revelle (London, 1972), 357–59, 378.

[6]Berthoff, *British Immigrants,* passim.

[7]Margrave, "Emigration of Silk Workers," 40–73.

[8]Ibid., 70–71.

[9]Ibid., 121–61.

[10]Ibid., 74–120.

[11]Berthoff, *British Immigrants,* 37ff; C. K. Yearley, *Enterprise and Anthracite* (Baltimore, Md., 1961), 67–68, 110.

[12]*Paterson Weekly Call,* September 13, 1888, 4.

[13]Ibid., March 18, 1886, 7.

[14]*Paterson Weekly Press,* September 30, 1880, 2.

[15]*Paterson Weekly Call,* September 13, 1888, 4. This was the opinion of Edward B. Haines, the editor of the *Paterson Weekly Call,* who had visited Macclesfield. For similar contemporary support for the notion of upward mobility, see Paterson, N.J., Board of Trade, *Sixteenth Annual Report* (Paterson, N.J., 1889), 40; *Paterson Weekly Press,* December 16, 1869, 3; *Paterson Pencillings,* 1, no. 7 (November 7, 1891), 13.

[16]W. Woodford Clayton and William Nelson, *The History of Bergen and Passaic Counties* (Philadelphia, 1882), 478.

[17]Edward B. Haines, comp., *Paterson, New Jersey, 1792–1892: Centennial Edition of the Paterson Evening News* (Paterson, N.J., 1892), 134. The birth certificates of both men are to be found in the records of births, marriages, and deaths, Registrar General, London. Doherty was born February 6, 1850, and Wadsworth, March 9, 1849. Both births were recorded in the sub-district of Macclesfield West. Their fathers' occupations were found in this source.

[18]Charles A. Shriner, *Paterson, New Jersey* (Paterson, N.J., 1890), 204.

[19]The success of these two weavers from Macclesfield attracted a great deal of contemporary comment. See, for example, Clayton and Nelson, *Bergen and Passaic,* 478; Shriner, *Paterson, New Jersey,* 204; Haines, *Centennial Edition,* 134–35; L. R. Trumbull, *A History of Industrial Paterson* (Paterson, N.J., 1882), 224; William Nelson and Charles A. Shriner, *History of Paterson and Its Environs: The Silk City* (New York, 1920), 1:347.

[20]Over fifty English-born silk workers from a variety of textile backgrounds and locations succeeded in Paterson business. Detailed descriptions of their careers appeared in contemporary local histories and biographical compilations and remain compelling reading. For further details, see Margrave, "Emigration," appendix A.

[21]Shichiro Matsui, *The History of the Silk Industry in the United States* (New York, 1928), 40. For a contemporary description of silk machinery leasing, see *Paterson Weekly Call,* March 4, 1886, 6.

[22]Matsui, *Silk Industry,* 40. The occupants of the third floor of the Dale mill in 1883 were Samuel Greenwood, silk throwster; Thomas Henshall, silk finisher; John Lockett, broad-silk weaver; and Fred Alcock, silk manufacturer. See Richard Edwards, ed., *Industries of New Jersey* (New York, 1883), 947, 953, 955, 960. For a comparison with English silk mills, see *Berisfords, The Ribbon People* (York, England, 1958), 20.

[23]Matsui, *Silk Industry,* 40.

[24]For a comparison with the Paterson metal industries, see Herbert G. Gutman,

"The Reality of the Rags-to-Riches 'Myth': The Case of the Paterson, New Jersey, Locomotive, Iron, and Machinery Manufacturers, 1830–1880," in *Work, Culture and Society in Industrializing America* (New York, 1976), 221.

[25]Matsui, *Silk Industry*, 40.

[26]For details of Riley's new company, see Trumbull, *Industrial Paterson*, 293. John Ryle's recommendations are contained in John Ryle to Messrs. Laber and Stolz, March 14, 1884, Ryle Family Papers, private collection.

[27]For individual cases of failure, see for Philip Walmsley, Trumbull, *Industrial Paterson*, 189; for John Jackson Scott, ibid., 235–36, and Albert H. Heusser, ed., *The History of the Silk Dyeing Industry in the United States* (Paterson, N.J., 1927), 206; for John Lockett, *Paterson Labor Standard*, May 22, 1886, 3, and Trumbull, *Industrial Paterson*, 239–40; for John Day, ibid., 246; for Ernest Barber, Nelson and Shriner, *Paterson and Its Environs*, 3:283; for John Ryle, Trumbull, *Industrial Paterson*, 181.

[28]The only references to large numbers of failures was to this period of the so-called "silk craze," see *Paterson Weekly Call*, December 13, 1888, 2.

[29]Gutman, "The Reality of the Rags-to-Riches 'Myth'," 219.

[30]The persistence rate for the English-born silk workers in the Paterson industry equalled 26.3 percent for the period 1870–80. For a comparison, see the slightly higher rates for the English and other foreign-born in Warren and Steelton, Pennsylvania, and in South Bend, Indiana; Michael P. Weber, *Social Change in an Industrial Town* (University Park, Pa., 1976), 36; John Bodnar, *Immigration and Industrialization* (Pittsburgh, 1977), 57–58; Dean R. Esslinger, *Immigrants and the City* (Port Washington, N.Y., 1975).

[31]The primary causes of the continued decline in the importance of the manager, supervisor, foreman, and overseer in the Paterson industry were the small scale of the industrial units and the degree of personal involvement of entrepreneurs in the everyday operation of their companies. See *Paterson Silk Herald* 2, no. 10 (October 1893): 394. See also *Paterson Weekly Press*, November 23, 1876, 3; Clayton and Nelson, *Bergen and Passaic*, 482–83.

[32]John Ryle to sons, July 25, 1887, Ryle Family Papers.

[33]Nelson and Shriner, *Paterson and Its Environs*, 2:116–17.

[34]*Macclesfield: The Silk Centre of Great Britain* (Cheltenham, England, 1920), 21. Other sources, however, attest to the difficulties of such upward mobility in the Macclesfield and Coventry trades. See *Berisfords*, 16; John Prest, *The Industrial Revolution in Coventry* (Oxford, 1960), 49–52. For more general comments on this topic, see E. J. Hobsbawm, *The Age of Revolution*, rev. ed. (London, 1973), 224–38; William Miller, ed., *Men in Business* (New York, 1962), 193–211.

[35]*Paterson Weekly Press*, December 16, 1869, 3.

[36]For limited evidence that the English-born assumed some entrepreneurial positions in American industry, see Berthoff, *British Immigrants*, 37, 39, 40, 42, 66, 72; Yearley, *Enterprise*, 67–68, 110. More recent research, however, has suggested that few workers in any of the contemporary cities studied in the United States moved up into the ranks of management or became wealthy entrepreneurs. See Weber, *Social Change*, chap. 4; Bodnar, *Immigration and Industrialization*, chap. 4; Esslinger, *Immigrants and the City*, chap. 5; Stephan Thernstrom, *Poverty and Progress: Social Mobility in a Nineteenth-Century City* (Cambridge, Mass., 1964); Peter R. Knights, *The Plain People of Boston, 1830–1860* (New York, 1971), chap. 5; Sidney Goldstein, *Patterns of Mobility, 1910–1950* (Philadelphia, 1958), chap. 9; Stephan Thernstrom, "Immigrants and WASPS: Ethnic Differences in Occupational Mobility in Boston, 1890–1940," in *Nineteenth Century Cities*, eds., Stephan Thernstrom and Richard

Sennett (New Haven, Conn., 1969). Certainly the situation in the silk industry and the metal trades of Paterson was, as Gutman found, in complete contrast with the experience of the "unsuccessful" craftsmen of contemporary Poughkeepsie, New York. See Clyde Griffen, "The 'Old' Immigration and Industrialization: A Case Study," in *Immigrants in Industrial America, 1850–1920*, ed., Richard L. Ehrlich (Charlottesville, Va., 1977), 194.

[37]*Paterson Weekly Press*, August 15, 1872, 3; August 21, 1879, 3; March 18, 1880, 3.

[38]Ibid., September 30, 1880, 2.

[39]For a full description of American silk-manufacturing methods at this time, see Trumbull, *Industrial Paterson*, 152–57, 253–54; Heusser, *Silk Dyeing Industry*, vi; Matsui, *Silk Industry*, 123–30; L. P. Brockett, *The Silk Industry in America* (New York, 1876), chaps. 16–19; Silk Association of America, *Third Annual Report* (Paterson, N.J., 1875), 70; *Paterson Weekly Press*, August 15, 1872, 3; April 22, 1875, 1. Similar English methods are described in D. C. Coleman, *Courtaulds: An Economic and Social History* (Oxford, 1969), 1:9–23. An outline of the minor differences between Macclesfield and Paterson silk operations in 1888 is to be found in *Paterson Weekly Call*, September 28, 1888, 4.

[40]Brockett, *Silk Industry of America*, 129. Stearns's purchase is reported in ibid., 19; and by Ryle in *Paterson Weekly Press*, October 21, 1869, 3; Trumbull, *Industrial Paterson*, 181. Dexter, Lambert and Company purchased ribbon looms and other silk machinery in Coventry in 1858, before the Cobden treaty; Nelson and Shriner, *Paterson and Its Environs*, 1:343.

[41]Details of the Phoenix Manufacturing Company's purchase are in *Paterson Weekly Press*, April 22, 1875, 1. For Lambert's trip, see Trumbull, *Industrial Paterson*, 200.

[42]Bill of lading, Messrs. Guion and Company to Philip Hayes, January 4, 1875, Ryle Family Papers. W. B. Cochran's purchase is described in Trumbull, *Industrial Paterson* , 258; Claude Greppo's, in Clayton and Nelson, *Bergen and Passaic*, 484; Crew and Henshall's, in Trumbull, *Industrial Paterson*, 254; and Pfeffer and Wells's, in ibid., 247.

[43]The contents of the Henshall mill are detailed in Haines, *Centennial Edition*, 121, and the purchase of imported wooden machines is in *Paterson Weekly Call*, April 15, 1886, 7. See also, the purchase of velvet looms in England by James Jackson, *Paterson Weekly Press*, November 23, 1882, 3, and of silk-finishing machinery by Alfred Crew, *Paterson Weekly Call*, March 25, 1886, 7; August 12, 1886, 6; September 9, 1886, 8. Purchases of European machinery were not confined to Paterson. See, for example, a case of silk machinery purchased in England for a new mill in Leeds, Massachusetts, in *Textile Manufacturer*, 6 (May 15, 1880), 176. Compare this also with the importation of machinery from Dundee, Scotland, for the Paterson jute mills, *Paterson Weekly Call*, October 4, 1888, 4.

[44]*Paterson Weekly Press*, January 31, 1884, 3.

[45]John Ryle to sons, July 25, 1887, Ryle Family Papers.

[46]Ibid.

[47]James Atkinson, son of a Halifax woolen manufacturer, arrived in Paterson in 1848 to work as a mechanic in several local machine shops before establishing his own company to manufacture bobbins and spools for the cotton, woolen, flax and, later, silk industries. See Nelson and Shriner, *Paterson and Its Environs*, 3:439. Similar cases were those of the brothers Thomas and John Wrigley in Edwards, *Industries of New Jersey*, 953; and Clayton and Nelson, *Bergen and Passaic*, 486. For the Buckley family, see *Paterson Weekly Press*, September 29, 1880, 4; for Robert Atherton, son of English-born immigrants, see Clayton and Nelson, *Bergen and*

Passaic, 486; and for Preston-born John R. Daggers, see Shriner, *Paterson, New Jersey*, 209–10. See also the report of the small-scale manufacture of silk machinery in Paterson, *Paterson Weekly Press*, March 11, 1869, 3.

[48]Ibid., April 22, 1875, 1. For details of the switch to silk machinery by locomotive and metal companies, see ibid., May 21, 1874, 1; November 18, 1875, 3; September 4, 1879, 3.

[49]See ibid., June 1, 1876, 1, for the full report on the machine room at the Exposition.

[50]William Strange thought English spinning frames were less than half as fast as these frames. See *Paterson Weekly Press*, January 20, 1876, 3. A visiting Macclesfield manufacturer thought them "beautiful" in 1876; ibid., November 23, 1876, 3. For a further comparison, see ibid., April 22, 1875, 1. The extent of purchases of this equipment by the immigrant silk manufacturers is described in Clayton and Nelson, *Bergen and Passaic*, 477; *Paterson Weekly Press*, September 24, 1874, 3; July 22, 1875, 3; April 6, 1876, 3.

[51]Ibid., August 21, 1879, 3; Trumbull, *Industrial Paterson*, 90–93; Clayton and Nelson, *Bergen and Passaic*, 471. For other examples of machine building in mills, at an earlier date, see George Sweet Gibb, *The Saco-Lowell Shops* (Cambridge, Mass., 1950), passim; John L. Bishop, *History of American Manufactures, 1608–1860* (Philadelphia, 1864; 3d ed., New York, 1966), 3:48. The first looms manufactured in Paterson attracted considerable controversy as to their relative merits in comparison with those manufactured in Coventry. *Paterson Weekly Press*, May 18, 1876, 3.

[52]Examples of the contribution of the immigrant entrepreneurs to the developing technology of the industry are numerous. For example, see *Paterson Weekly Press*, July 27, 1871, p 3; April 29, 1875, 2; September 9, 1880, 3; *Paterson Weekly Call*, October 4, 1888, 4; Trumbull, *Industrial Paterson*, 242, 244.

[53]*Paterson Weekly Press*, March 14, 1878, 3. Details of Jackson's career, his machinery improvements, and inventions are in Clayton and Nelson, *Bergen and Passaic*, 485–86; *Paterson Weekly Call*, November 25, 1886, 1.

[54]Haines, *Centennial Edition*, 116. Further details of Eastwood's career can be found in William Nelson, *Biographical Cyclopedia of New Jersey* (New York, 1913), 183; *Paterson Weekly Call*, October 4, 1888, 4.

[55]William Strange pointed out the importance of the local machine-building and repair industry in 1886, in Paterson, N.J., Board of Trade, *Thirteenth Annual Report* (Paterson, N.J., 1886), 32. For the opinions of English-born machinist James Fryer as to the differences between working in an English and an American machine shop, see *Paterson Weekly Press*, September 20, 1888, 4. A full listing of weavers' supplies appears in Trumbull, *Industrial Paterson*, 256–60. John Ryle bought looms from two American companies in the early 1880s. See an agreement signed for the purchase of ten looms between the Pioneer Silk Company and the Danforth Locomotive and Machine Company, Paterson, November 11, 1881, Ryle Family Papers; an agreement for six looms between the Pioneer Silk Company and Kek and Fischer, New York, July 9, 1884, ibid. *Paterson Weely Press*, December 14, 1871, 3; August 12, 1875, 3.

[56]Matsui, *Silk Industry*, 208; U.S. Department of the Interior, Census Office, MSS, Population, Paterson, Passaic County, New Jersey, 1860, 1870, 1880. See also table 1 for the occupational distribution of all English-born silk workers in Paterson for these dates.

[57]The immigrant silk dyers were accorded great praise for their work in the Paterson industry. "We have English and French dyers of the greatest experience," wrote the *Paterson Weekly Press*, August 15, 1872, 3. See also Heusser, *Silk Dyeing*

Industry, 185, 267, 270, 413, 510.

[58]U.S. Department of the Interior, Census Office, MSS, Population, Paterson, 1880, e.d. 146–55 (N = 480). A similar situation with regard to immigrants existed in skilled occupations in Steelton and Warren, Pennsylvania. See Bodnar, *Immigration and Industrialization,* xv; Weber, *Social Change,* 12.

[59]*Paterson Weekly Press,* April 22, 1875, 1. The estimate of the extent of factory-based hand-loom weaving is contained in Paterson, N.J., Board of Trade, *Third Annual Report* (Paterson, N.J., 1876), 3. For individual examples of mills with hand-loom weaving departments, see *Paterson Weekly Press,* November 14, 1872, 3; April 22, 1875, 1; July 29, 1875, 3.

[60]Ibid., July 29, 1875, 3. There is evidence to suggest that the construction of new houses with basement weaving rooms began at the time of the introduction of the new protective tariffs. See *Paterson Weekly Press,* May 28, 1864, 3.

[61]Trumbull, *Industrial Paterson,* 156. For domestic hand-loom weaving traditions in Paterson, see also *Paterson Evening News,* August 14, 1873, 16. English-born industrial migrants were generally found to harbor a strong desire to become independent upon arrival in America. See C. J. Erickson, *Invisible Immigrants* (London, 1972), 247–54. English weavers also attached deep importance to the values of independence. See E. P. Thompson, *The Making of the English Working Class* (London, 1963), 305. Similar craft roles were assumed by other British immigrants in contemporary Poughkeepsie, New York, and in Pennsylvania. See Griffen, "The 'Old' Immigration and Industrialization," 195; Weber, *Social Change,* 74–75.

[62]Trumbull, *Industrial Paterson,* 156.

[63]*Paterson Weekly Press,* April 22, 1875, 1. The domestic system was introduced also by European-born manufacturers in Hackensack, Hoboken, and the Schutzen Park section of North Bergen, New Jersey. See *Paterson Weekly Press,* April 6, 1876, 3; September 4, 1879, 3. See also Brockett, *Silk Industry in America,* 119. The mill owners seem to have supplied the majority of the looms in operation: "The looms are borrowed from the silk mills, and the work carried to and from them as required," *Paterson Weekly Press,* July 29, 1875, 3.

[64]For a comparison, see the descriptions of the trade in contemporary Coventry and Macclesfield in Prest, *Industrial Revolution in Coventry,* chap. 3; C. Stella Davies, ed., *A History of Macclesfield* (Manchester, England, 1961), 130, 133, 135–39, 143, 145, 168–69, 191–93, 195–96, 230; James Chesworth to John Ryle, December 7, 1881, Ryle Family Papers; Duncan Bythell, *The Sweated Trades* (London, 1978), 153–88.

[65]Brockett, *Silk Industry in America,* 153. For a similar description, see *Paterson Weekly Press,* May 4, 1876, 1, and an editorial addition: "This movement meets with the approval of the employers, and good results are looked for."

[66]Ibid., July 29, 1875, 3.

[67]Paterson, N.J., Board of Trade, *Third Annual Report,* 30. There were 563 hand looms in operation in Paterson in 1876, *Paterson Weekly Press,* July 27, 1876, 3. The percentage of English-born silk workers in skilled positions declined from 72.7 in 1860 to 62.6 in 1870 and 52.4 in 1880. The estimate of numbers of domestic weavers in the early 1880s can be found in N.J. Bureau of Statistics of Labor and Industries, *Fifth Annual Report* (Trenton, N.J., 1882), 21.

[68]U.S. Department of the Interior, Census Office, MSS, Population, Paterson, 1860, 1870, 1880; see also table 1. The numbers of English-born workers in this category were 21 in 1860, 230 in 1870, and 865 in 1880.

[69]U.S. Department of the Interior, Census Office, MSS, Population, Paterson, 1880, e.d. 146–55 (N = 1,391). In contrast, in Steelton, Pennsylvania, as many as 70

percent of the English, German, and Irish immigrants were employed in unskilled occupations. See Bodnar, *Immigration and Industrialization, 65*.

[70]More information on the composition and rules of the semiskilled work force in the Paterson industry can be found in Matsui, *Silk Industry,* 188, 210.

[71]For a comparison, see Kathleen N. Conzen, *Immigrant Milwaukee, 1836–1860: Accommodation and Community in a Frontier City* (Cambridge, Mass., 1976).

2

An Exceedingly Irregular Business: Structure and Process in the Paterson Silk Industry, 1885–1910

■ PHILIP B. SCRANTON ■

O N DECEMBER 15, 1884, A Paterson hand-loom weaver produced "the first silk handkerchief ever woven in the State of Louisiana," an achievement duly reported in the next issue of the trade monthly, the *American Silk Journal.* The occasion was the opening of a silk exhibit at the World Industrial and Cotton Exposition in New Orleans, a perfect opportunity for Paterson's booming silk firms to display their prowess in luxury textiles to an appreciative and well-to-do audience. Indeed, the owners of the loom, the rapidly expanding firm of Doherty and Wadsworth, immediately received an offer of $175.00 for the handkerchief, patterned with entwined roses and forget-me-nots. Though the proposal came from John Harris, formerly a U.S. senator from Louisiana, the proprietors, enjoying their celebrity status, announced that they preferred "to retain possession of the trophy until the close of the Exposition, when it will be disposed of to the highest bidder."[1]

The hand loom and the international exposition together capture a transitional moment through which the Paterson silk industry was passing in 1885. Though over five hundred such looms had been scattered across the city a few years previously amid a flourishing putting-out system,[2] the recent development of reliable power looms for specialty silks had all but made Doherty and Wadsworth's weaver a living historical exhibit, an industrial artifact. On the other hand, the stylish product of his labors and their extravagant commercial setting indicated Paterson's ambition: leadership in domestic manufacture of the most fashion-sensitive textile fabrics. Shielded comfortably behind the tariff walls of Republican protectionism, the factory masters looked forward with nervous confidence to extending the dramatic growth and sizable profits of the past two decades. Yet their successes were seasonal rather than permanent, for they inhabited a complex, almost classically competitive industrial sector. Manifold risks surrounded their individual ventures: fluctuations in raw-silk supplies and prices; erratic credit arrangements; battles with laborers over the price of work, and the vagaries of style; not to mention fire, flood, machinery breakdowns, and ruinous competition. The air in Paterson reeked of coal fumes and unpredictability, making silk manufacture an exceedingly irregular business for all concerned.

The task undertaken in this essay is the reconstruction of the industrial structure and developmental process taking shape in Paterson during the generation between the city's emergence as a silk center and the 1913 general strike. Reviewing a number of local events in 1884 will provide an initial "feel" for the texture of enterprise in Paterson, before an analysis of the silk-production system in place there is offered. Then proceeding chronologically, the impact of labor conflicts, booms and panics, as well as company starts, failures, and relocations will be assessed, ending with a discussion of the essential continuities and changes that transpired over a quarter century of Paterson's urban industrial history.

PROPRIETARY FIRMS AND ANNEXES

At the same time as Doherty and Wadsworth were triumphing at New Orleans, the other side of the entrepreneurial coin was exposed at home in chilly Paterson, as "the effects of William Crew, the bankrupt silk finisher" were auctioned, bringing "but" $1,135.00. Crew, an English immigrant, had mortgaged both his equipment and the steam boiler which powered it to the firms that had supplied them. This effort to free his small capital for handling the everyday expenses of his business had failed. The machinery and boiler makers repurchased their devices at the sale, together assuming a $250.00 loss on their loans, not counting the additional costs of removing and reselling the equipment. Worse, "all the other creditors, including the hands, to several of whom quite large sums were owed, got nothing."[3] Clearly, Crew's staff had labored for weeks without pay before the collapse and now both were out of work and out of wages. The firm had so few collectable accounts that it took a month for the assignee, who handled the sale, to secure enough money to pay his expenses. By then, even the three appraisers, entitled to $.50 each for their task, had given up hope of payment.[4]

Yet this small, sad tale has a twist characteristic of proprietary firms linked by trade contracts, ethnicity, and family ties. Soon after the bankruptcy auction, Alfred Crew, a kinsman of William and likewise a silk finisher, purchased the equipment secured by machinist Samuel Watson at the sale and relocated it to his own shop at 62 Railroad Avenue.[5] Alfred was the grandson of another William Crew, who in 1830 had commenced a Macclesfield finishing works that became "celebrated throughout the United Kingdom." Alfred's father, Charles, succeeded William Crew as the head of the establishment and in time brought his son into the firm. The decline of Macclesfield's prospects by the 1870s,[6] however, led Alfred Crew to join the migration flow to Paterson in 1879. Evidently possessing a portion of the family's capital, he started immediately as a workshop master, rather than spending years in the employ of others accumulating sufficient funds to commence on his own account. More adept in the trade than his failed relative, Crew became a Paterson fixture for a generation, employing 120 workers by 1909 and proclaiming his firm's diverse skills in the 1913 textile directory: "Finishers and Refinishers of Gros Grains, Brocades, Millinery and Umbrella Silks, Serges, Satins, Veilings; Dyers of Habutals, Pongees, Crepes, Tussahs, Satins, etc."[7]

As the new machinery substantially expanded Alfred Crew's plant, and as some of it was "of special value, involving improvements made by [William], a gentleman of great experience in the business,"[8] it is likely that William Crew along with some of his workers were also added to the Railroad Avenue shop. In any event, the firm was soon reported to be "working nights" to keep up with its clients' orders, and within the year it leased "largely increased facilities" in the new Barnert Mill to which the firm relocated in November.[9] Observing one of the customs of English factory culture,[10] Crew "celebrated his removal, with a complimentary entertainment to his employees, in his new quarters" shortly after Thanksgiving.[11] Such festivities, along with Christmas treats, summer excursions and baseball contests among mill teams, were regular features of Paterson factory life, even in years of labor turmoil. They were an element in a loose system of industrial social relations that has been described elsewhere as "fraternal paternalism."[12]

Crew's new site was a factory specially built for tenants, a structure erected by real estate entrepreneur and former mayor, Boaz

Barnert. Given the small capital with which most silk firms began, securing rental space in subdivided factory buildings was a necessary preliminary to launching production. Only after having survived profitably for some years would such companies undertake to erect their own facilities, a step which indicated the firm's elevation in status from newcomer to veteran on the Paterson industrial scene. Before the 1880s, space could readily be rented in mills once used for the city's pioneering industries (cotton, locomotives, and firearms). The silk surge quickly reached the limits of such "adaptive re-use," however, and Barnert, who already owned an old factory filled with tenant firms, ventured to build a new one in 1885 to tap the rising demand for mill floor space. Joining Crew in these shared quarters were four other small companies, the backgrounds of which underscore the blend of risk and opportunity characteristic of the period. William D. Holmes, a weaver, had been "burned out in the Pope Mill fire" in late September, but within a month had taken the third floor of the new Barnert factory to start anew. J. Phillips Mackay had been nearly ruined the previous year, yet now had gathered sufficient resources to enable him "to re-enter the silk business as a throwster," the silk equivalent of a yarn spinner. By contrast, prosperous John Grish, another weaver, was moving from the old Barnert Mill to the new "in order to secure more room." Finally, the last section of the building was leased to "Reed and Lovett . . . a new firm of throwsters," partners commencing on their own account, having until "lately been in the employ of William Strange and Co."[13] Thus Barnert's floors soon held firms responding to fire, failure, and the need for expansion as well as the magnet of independent proprietorship.

Whereas but a small proportion of Paterson's silk workers ever made the transition that Reed and Lovett were attempting, as Richard D. Margrave notes,[14] most local new firms, were indeed headed by experienced shop veterans. Earlier in 1885 Jacob Horandt abandoned his post as superintendent for Pelgram and Meyer, ribbon manufacturers, and entered into partnership with his son.[15] Well matched and venturing forth on a rising ribbon market, the pair employed 250 workers within five years and had gained a reputation, both for product innovations and recurrent labor problems.[16] In February 1886, T. Kunz, an immigrant from the German silk-manufacturing town of Krefeld, left Eugene Vogelsang's shop to start "with thirty looms on the top floor of the Barnert Mill," perhaps replacing Grish in the older of the mayor's two buildings. Aiming to produce handkerchiefs, scarfs, "and whatever specialties may be in demand from time to time," Kunz was not to share the Horandts' good fortune. By 1890, his firm had vanished from view, Kunz likely returning to a foreman or overseer's position or perhaps, like Vogelsang, emigrating to Krefeld after the collapse of the handkerchief craze in 1887.[17]

While these small firms were busily relocating and starting up, Paterson's major silk companies were striking out in new directions, prefiguring a chronic dilemma that would attend the manufacturing of silk locally in the generation to come. The issue was the establishment of "annexes" or branch plants by the leading firms, transferring their routine throwing operations from the city to new factories well outside of Paterson. Pelgram and Meyer was one of the first to create an annex, at Boonton, some sixteen miles west of the silk center. By 1885, ominously, part of the firm's weaving capacity had been relocated there along with its entire spindlage. The logic of this relocation was plain, at least on the surface. The *American Silk Journal* reported a year's profits from one of Paterson's annexes "footed up a round $100,000, . . .which is attributed mainly to the lower wages paid in the town where it is located."[18] In 1880, as in 1920, labor costs in Paterson were the highest in the silk trades nationwide.[19] Other incentives were added by distant localities (particularly in the Pennsylvania anthracite districts), the now-classic packages including land and buildings either free or at nominal costs, tax exemptions, and low or no charges for water use. So when the Ryle family's aptly named Pioneer Silk Company announced in July 1885 that it would soon occupy a branch at Allentown, Pennsylvania, a three-storey brick factory valued at over $75,000.00, the note that it "will be built by local capitalists for the company" foreshadowed the pattern of similar deals over the next three decades.[20]

This regional outward migration seemed directly to threaten Paterson-based throwsters as well as their workers. Such firms would have to contend with falling prices for their work and could imagine few alternatives to levelling downward the rates paid to their "hands." Yet there were several mitigating aspects to the apparent problem. The first wave of annexes were spin-offs of existing partially-integrated companies (that is, those which performed both throwing and weaving in-house). The space freed in their mills by the removal of spinning machinery was filled quickly by new looms, as at Pelgram and Meyer, where fancy-velvet looms were installed in 1885, copying the most current Lyons models.[21] Here the result was the creation of jobs, though not for the displaced throwing workers. Yet other options remained for them. After establishing its annex, Dexter, Lambert, and Company, another "major" manufacturer, sold its throwing machinery to a new firm, George Frost and Son, which shortly reported that demand for its services required "running their mill day and night."[22] The proliferation of small Paterson weaving firms lacking their own spinning capacity meant new openings for throwsters to supply yarn locally. Even when a sizable complement of independent throwsters outside the city emerged, Paterson throwsters would continue to be "preferred because of the convenience of transportation, enabling any sudden demand to be supplied quickly."[23]

Nonetheless, the mid-eighties' exodus of segments of the major firms' operations led the Paterson Board of Trade to conduct an inquiry into the question of factory annexes late in 1885. In his report board member John Morris argued that the movement posed no danger at all, but instead was a "sign of [the] unusual prosperity of this one of our manufacturing interests." With regard to the availability of cheaper labor elsewhere, Morris showed that fulsome liberality toward workers, which general "prosperity" sometimes occasions: "If we cannot supply the cheaper labor, it is because our people are more profitably employed; this is no sign of decay, and whoever regrets that we cannot furnish cheaper labor, is no friend to the working people who compose the mass of our population and who are Paterson."[24] Turning to the issues of skill and technology, he observed that throwing, "being a mechanical operation requiring but rudimentary knowledge," was prone to migration, but that "dyeing, winding and weaving require skilled labor, and come to Paterson, that kind of labor being there . . . To make perfect goods at a profit, that kind of labor must be employed." Clearly aware that plain woven goods might also be transferable, Morris stressed that the city's strength lay in "the more elaborate branches." Its other assets were numerous: pure water (a dyeing essential); the smallest per-capita public debt in the state; ample cheap land; "a law abiding population of which we may well be proud"; and first-class machine shops "that will build you a locomotive or a loom or a steam engine."[25]

INFORMAL LABOR RELATIONS

Its naked boosterism aside, the board of trade's assessment was accurate on the whole. The city's economic base was not significantly threatened. Though Paterson's share of the national silk production would erode steadily as Pennsylvania's rose in the period 1890–1910, no rival center, no alternative concentration of craft skills and entrepreneurial ambition, would emerge elsewhere. Indeed in absolute terms, the number of jobs in the city's silk mills more than doubled between 1880 and 1901 (from 9,800 to 21,800) before leveling off at about the 20,000 mark for the subsequent two decades.[26] But in one respect the board's survey was disingenuous. In its tribute to the critical role of skilled labor as a Paterson mainstay, Morris and his colleagues sidestepped the perpetually troubled relations between silk workers and firm proprietors. Strikes and threats of walkouts were regular features of Paterson's industrial landscape for years before the annex issue arose.[27] Though, like Philadelphia's textile workers,[28] Paterson silk operatives were unable to maintain or were unconcerned with sustaining permanent unions, they did resolutely defend shop customs and craft practices. They resisted wage reductions in hard times, demanded raises when markets blossomed, and participated in politics, supporting the tariffs their employers favored while electing local officials the same proprietors frequently abhorred. In later years, more than one manufacturer cited the strike-prone, if talented, Paterson silk workers when threatening to transfer his operations to eastern Pennsylvania, upstate New York, or another area with a more malleable work force.[29]

A prime example of a quick, successful turnout and the rapid impact of its settlement on the rest of the Paterson trade may be taken from events in the spring of 1885. Wages in the local throwing sector had dropped on average about 10 percent during 1884. On March 23, 1885, as bulging orders were compelling some firms to run their machinery until nine at night, the winders and doublers at Louis Franke and Company "struck for an advance of seventy-five cents per week." This demand would increase their earnings from a postreduction $4.75 to $5.50, about 5 percent above the rates in force before the 1884 cuts. The same day, "after some deliberation on the part of the firm," the raise was "accorded," seting off "a general demand for higher wages by the operatives in nearly every throwing establishment in the city, with the result that in most instances wages were raised to $5, and in one or two beside Franke & Co. to $5.50 per week."[30] No evidence of a union or any formal organization surfaced during this cycle of demands; instead, the networks of information among workers, long a part of the terrain in dense industrial districts, spread the good news of a successful advance, emboldening the largest part of Paterson's fifteen hundred spinning-mill workers to call for a comparable settlement.

On the other hand, manufacturers, sensing that their season was not "panning out" as expected, were equally quick to order rate-cuts *in seriatim,* as happened in the ribbon division at Paterson in September 1885. Although ribbon and broad-silk weavers responded with a "mass meeting . . . in Germania Hall, for the purpose of organization," nothing materialized. The reductions were effected as the news spread that wholesale goods prices were down 10 percent and still falling. With the new year came fresh orders, followed immediately by workers' calls for restoration, a few test strikes, and general increases by the Ryle family, Pelgram and Meyer, and others.[31] At both Paterson and Philadelphia, the instabilities and uncertainties of markets, raw-material supplies, and workers' earnings reinforced one another to produce an ironically stable pattern of customary conflicts. Manufacturers well knew "petitions" for "rises" would flutter in soon after notice was broadcast that seasonal prospects were strong. Workers recognized that cuts followed a dull market. Strikes occurred when one of the parties "declined" to work or give out work at the prices named. Through the mid-eighties, no permanent or industry-wide organizations on either side were necessary for the functioning of this informal system, as it was another dimension of a factory culture shared by shop-trained English immigrant proprietors and workers, as well as by their German artisan colleagues from Krefeld.

Such periodic jousting was a clumsy but reliable and resourceful way of struggling through issues of power and profit in Paterson. Its significance may well be enhanced by recollecting that the explosive railroad wars of 1877 were but a few years past, that the long and violent battles of the iron molders of Troy, New York, had led to a bitter sixteen-month lockout, the end of which in 1884 brought a 20 percent wage-cut to unionized workers, and that blacklists flourished in New York, New England, and elsewhere.[32] Indeed, insofar as the pattern of conflict at Paterson in the early 1880s is contrasted with other contemporary exchanges, it seems to have had boundaries lacking in other areas. Given the substantial similarities between the Paterson and Philadelphia textile industries, it may be worth speculating that these boundaries flowed from a comparable pattern of mutual respect and obligation between factory masters and skilled workers. Yet such mutuality was ever vulnerable to betrayals of trust on either side and to externally developing changes in competition, technology, immigration, or the tariff.

With the rise of the Knights of Labor in Paterson, the customary patterns were displaced for a time. After two angry years, partially successful efforts to modify and restore them were made, only to founder on the rocks of the 1893 panic and subsequent depression. As the tariff came under attack, as rival firms multiplied inside and outside of Paterson, as the flow of immigrants brought an increasingly heterogeneous population of both workers and entrepreneurs to the city, and as pressure for both productivity and economy increased, manufacturers sought greater direct control over their operations by attempting to dislodge shop and trade customs that had been in place for a generation. Antagonisms deepened, not simply between bosses and workers but also within each group. The consequence was systemic anarchy, manifesting itself in ways ranging from strike violence to the emergence of cheap, poor-quality products that undermined the reputation of the silk industry. Social and political issues such as hostility towards Italians, repression of anarchists, and enlarging and strengthening the police force, had their economic parallels in pleas to restore trade standards or organize a silk trust to regulate competition. As Paterson entered the twentieth century, its economic and social relations became increasingly incoherent. The era when Paterson could boast of its "law abiding population" was little more than a memory by 1910. Indeed, Henry Doherty, the gentlemanly entrepreneur who had carried the day at New Orleans and who sponsored ball teams and summer excursions, would in time emerge as the chief promoter of the stretch-out four-loom system that triggered the 1913 strike.

THE SILK-PRODUCTION PROCESS

To appreciate better the transformation that Doherty personified, it is essential to have a familiarity with the sequence of production in the silk industry as it was organized in late-nineteenth-century Paterson. In sketching the steps from raw silk through marketed goods, two different processes are involved: the obvious movement of materials and the more elusive financial and credit arrangements. Both were complex; breakdowns within either channel had frightful implications for manufacturers.

Raw silk was consistently the most expensive fiber used for textile products. In years when the price of cotton fluctuated from $.06 to $.25 per pound and wools ranged from $.50 to $1.00, standard grades of reeled silk brought $3.50 to $5.50 per pound. Three sources dominated the supply line between the mid-eighties and World War I. Roughly half the silk imported to the United States was Japanese in origin; the remainder was almost equally drawn from China and Italy. Italian silk was routinely regarded as the highest in quality, with the Chinese product having the greatest whiteness or brilliance but often being damaged by rough handling. Japanese "raws" were better processed than the Chinese and more plentiful, falling in the middle price range between the topflight Piedmonts and the relatively cheap Cantons.[33]

Prior to transoceanic shipment, the cocoons that resulted from cultivating the silkworm were "reeled" (that is, the single filament on each cocoon was unwound and meshed with several other filaments, twisted very slightly, and taken up on a revolving reel). Each cocoon held one gossamer thread often several hundred yards long. Coarse grades of reeled silk ran 6,500 yards to the ounce and the finest topped 20,000 yards per ounce. Hanks of silk taken from the reels were combined into eight-pound "books," twelve of which comprised the customary bale.[34] As an animal product (like wool), the quality of the silk fiber varied widely. Hence cocoons were sorted by grade before reeling and books of the same quality were combined into bales labeled "Classical" or "Best No. 1," among other grades. For Japanese silks alone, twenty-five official grades were recognized, and dozens of additional private dealer grades (or "chops") were advertised. Were this not elaborate enough, separate systems operated in each of the three main supplying nations, and their highest grades represented the best quality for that production year only. "Now, as the merit of the cocoons . . . will vary considerably from season to season, it follows that the Extra Classical of a poor season may be no better than [a lower grade from] the preceding one." Hence manufacturers were urged to secure "a knowledge of the relative goodness of the succeeding crops of silk of the various countries."[35]

This of course was an impossible task for all but a few proprietors; thus the key role of the specialist importer endured. Though descendents of the patriarchal Ryles might set off in the summer of 1885 for China,[36] their Asian version of the grand tour would diminish only slightly the firm's reliance on New York houses like Morimura and Arai, whose principals had decades of experience in the trade. After all, the cost of raw silk alone often represented 40 to 50 percent of the total production expense for broad silks and ribbons.[37] Selection of the optimal grade of materials for the product envisioned had a critical importance if profits were to be realized. With fifty or more grades on the market and the highest qualities priced double or more than the lowest, close contact with the importers' expertise was essential. A few manufacturers focused on purchases at the extremes: some at the low end hoped that the savings on cheap silk would offset the modest returns possible on "inferior goods," while others at the top of the scale looked to establish reputations for quality that would compensate them for high input expenses. Most firms, however, practiced "the policy of opportunism," relying on middling qualities and moving to high or low grades only if prices broke sharply downward or upward respectively. Though fiscally sensible, this approach often led such firms "to buy rather too wide a variety of kinds and qualities," yielding products "irregular in character."[38] Thus before a yard of finished yarn was thrown, before a single loom was "clothed," proprietors of silk weaving firms had to make critical decisions that could make or break a season's profit.

Financing purchases of materials was managed through a fairly standard system of six-month credits extended to manufacturers by the raw-silk agencies. This arrangement allowed a firm sufficient lead time to generate and market finished products before its silk bills came due. In addition, a sizable order might be segmented into portions to be delivered over three to six months, a separate invoice being tendered for each and payments thereby staggered. For this privilege, buyers were charged 6 percent annually on the undelivered silk held in storage by their supply houses. This "forward selling" ensured to manufacturers both price and availability of materials, while it guaranteed sales plus a net 5 percent interest for importers.[39] The risks involved were clear to all; if a company could not pay a due bill for silk and were not a treasured customer for whom a deferral might be forthcoming, the supplier would quickly secure a court attachment of its assets, alerting other creditors that the manufacturer was "embarrassed." Under a shower of writs, the firm would either be liquidated or taken over by the principal creditors.

Actual production could commence when a teamster drew his wagon to a halt alongside the silk weaver's premises and unloaded its cargo of bales. The transformation of the bales' contents into finished bundles of fabric or cartons of ribbons entailed a half-dozen separate major operations, which might be carried on within the confines of a single integrated concern or through engaging the commission services of a sequence of independent partial-process firms. Both courses were adopted in Paterson. Generally the large, first-wave weaving firms founded in the years before 1880 had facilities for both throwing and weaving; a few (William Strange and Company; Dexter, Lambert, and Company) also had their own dye houses.[40] However, as their factory "graduates" (a term for employees who become proprietors, used regularly in the trade press) launched specialized firms in throwing, dyeing, and finishing, later-starting weavers tended to rely heavily on such services, thereby preserving capital for operating costs. As these independents multiplied, the major companies dropped internal dyeing almost entirely, built throwing annexes, and perhaps patronized local throwsters for "sudden demand" needs. Silk manufacturing in Paterson thus gradually evolved away from the integrated factory toward a Philadelphia-style system of interlocked and versatile specialists arrayed around central weaving shops of widely varying sizes.

The basic steps of silk production were six in number: throwing, winding and warping, weaving, dyeing, finishing, and inspection. For plain, solid-color goods, they followed one another in the above order, as dyeing and finishing of full hundred-yard pieces had to wait until the loom work was completed. On the other hand, for multicolored striped, plaid, or figured goods, yarns were dyed prior to winding and warping, with the colored effects achieved on the loom itself. If special, novelty patterns were sought, an outside designer might well be contacted. Such fancy work was principally oriented toward the infinite flexibility of the Jacquard loom, a Paterson version of which was the chief product of James Jackson and Sons' silk machinery workshop.[41] The designer's creation, laid out on a type of graph paper, was transmitted to another craftsman, the card cutter. Here each horizontal row of the design was translated into a pattern of holes punched into a sturdy cardboard rectangle, the full pattern being represented by a set of cards strung together for insertion into the control mechanism of the Jacquard loom. Returned to the mill, this set "instructed" the loom on each pass of the shuttle as to which groups of warp threads should be raised or lowered to reproduce the design encoded on the cards. Basic geometric patterns could be readily set up for weaving within the factory, but when floral, landscape, portrait, or imitation Oriental goods came into vogue, designers and card cutters could profit from the fees paid for the timely production of seasonal novelties. On the other hand, when such ornate fabrics were "not wanted," the outside specialists languished for want of commissions.[42]

Before weaving could begin, the reeled silk had to be converted into warp and filling by the throwster. In the trade, silk warps were known as "organzine," the filling as "tram." For each, two or more threads of reeled silk were joined into a sturdier filament ("doubling"). Organzine was "hard-twisted" for the greater strength and compactness basic to warps, the component threads given about twenty rotations ("twists") per inch. Tram in contrast was "kept as soft as possible, so as to make as bulky a thread as can be, for the sake of lustre and fullness in the finished article." Hence, it was soft-twisted, at two and a half to five twists per inch.[43] As the process for organzine throwing involved harder twists and had more stoppages for repairing breaks, the fees charged weavers for working it up were about double that for the simpler tram. In 1885, Paterson rates were $1.00 and $.55 a pound, respectively, though cost estimates were about a third less for the majors who had built annexes and used "cheap" labor.[44] By 1890 competition both at Paterson and with outside throwsters brought the rates down to $.75 and $.45. Though they rose with demand at times, the trend continued to decline, reaching levels of $.65 and $.35 by 1909.[45]

An important factor in the price decline was the development by Paterson machine shops of double- and triple-decker throwing frames, which economized on space and power and facilitated increasing the spindlage for which each worker was accountable. Further, the speed at which the frames were run was dramatically raised through improvements in gearing and spindle design.[46] The pressure from Pennsylvania independents was routinely reported as sounding the death knell of Paterson throwing, but no such collapse occurred. Productivity increases, fairly stable wage levels, together with their locational advantage, sustained a core of city throwsters into the new century. Indeed, coming out of the long depression of the 1890s, throwing activity in Paterson expanded, from eleven firms and 833 workers in 1898 to eighteen firms and 1,141 employees in 1901.[47]

Manufacturers engaging commission throwsters sent off bales of very expensive material and received back yarn in quantities that could not be known in advance. As fees dropped, the temptation could become intense for throwsters to "embezzle" a portion of each lot and sell it directly. One such case reached the Paterson courts in 1887, when C. E. Meding documented the theft of silk by throwsters Palmer and Chinn. The *Paterson Daily Guardian's* reporter noted that a dishonest throwster could retain from 2 to 5 percent of the raw silk sent to him with little fear of detection. In the Meding case this may have reached 800 to 2,000 pounds from the twenty tons forwarded to Palmer and Chinn over four years. The stolen silk was worth between $4,000.00 and $10,000.00. How was this skimming possible?

A local manufacturer explained that when a throwster shipped back the product of a hundred-pound bale, he might be "even five pounds over and yet have embezzeled several pounds; he may return two or three pounds less and yet be quite honest." The delivered weight rose a bit in processing, for an indeterminate amount of the soap and oil used in preparation for throwing remained in the material. On the other hand, the *Paterson Daily Guardian* noted in 1887, "there is always more or less waste resulting from the frequent manipulation of the fibre . . . the amount depending on the quality of the raw silk, the perfection of the machinery, the carefulness and dexterity of the hands, the condition of the atmosphere, and perhaps several other causes. Here we have a variable increment and a variable decrement, and it will readily be seen how easily the owner of the material can be victimized."[48] The extent to which this sort of fraud had been perpetrated would "amaze the uninitiated," as a more skillful throwster than Palmer could limit his "take" to ten pounds a month and thereby add $600.00 a year to his balances, a sum equal to fees for throwing tram for two weeks in a mid-sized firm with a weekly capacity of six hundred pounds. So the capital savings realized by employing an independent throwster carried with them subtle risks, as did almost all decisions in the silk trade.

Silk weaving at Paterson had two principal divisions, broad goods and ribbons. Among leading firms such as the Pioneer Silk Company and William Strange and Company, it was not uncommon to produce both varieties, but several of the veterans and nearly all the companies founded after 1885 specialized in one sector or the other. Two central technical developments enhanced a weaver's output volume late in the nineteenth century. As in throwing, the speeds at which looms were run increased as innovations from cotton weaving were adapted to silk work, yielding machines that were "simpler, lighter, swifter, steadier, and more efficient" than earlier European imports. Paterson machine shops like those of Benjamin Eastwood, John Royle, and the Machinists Association became experts in this regard, copying and adapting the most promising products of their counterparts in Lyon or Krefeld. The second major trend in machine development was a gradual widening of looms, from the customary nineteen to twenty-three inches for broad goods in the 1880s to an increasingly standard forty-two to fifty-four inches by 1910. In ribbons, where each loom simultaneously wove multiple bands of narrow fabric, double-deckers were introduced to hike volume and save space. When used with automatic stop-motions, which shut off any section of the loom where a thread had broken, the new technology reduced the need for labor up to 50 percent, while adding substantially to production figures.[49]

As was clear from the bankruptcy sale at William Crew's shop, machinery builders were another regular source of credit in Paterson, particularly for the newly starting firm. Frequently the terms were 10 percent cash on installation of their products and 10 percent of the balance per month thereafter. Even among firms that folded quickly, three or four payments could be expected, and machinery recovered after bankruptcy could be "repaint[ed]" and perhaps sold as new. If the firm prospered, frames or looms for expansion would be ordered from the same builder "for the sake of uniformity." So, the long-term prospects outweighed the short-term risks, and machinery "mortgages" were common.[50]

Following the weaving, piece goods would be sent out for dyeing to another commission specialist. Whether handling yarns or fabrics, Paterson dyers charged for their services according to elaborate tables of the price of work. The rates were calculated by the pound for yarn and by the yard for fabrics according to width, varying according to the price of dyes and the difficulty involved in processing the goods.[51] Given the tremendous variety of silks manufactured in Paterson, price lists often stretched over several pages of small print, an indirect testimony to the flexibility and skill built into this fashion-sensitive trade. Whereas dyers worked with color effects, finishers addressed the physical appearance of the fabrics, being charged with "stiffening or softening . . . the goods, making them thinner or fuller to the hand, the smoothing, stretching, polishing, singeing, . . . embossing, etc., etc."[52] Finishing thus did not refer to completing the production process, but to the "feel" or finish of the goods. Again versatility was the rule, as a 1913 finishers' price list provided the standard charges for thirty-three separate classes of goods and processes. Vivid, stylish colors were an essential element in successful sales, and "the difference between a first class finish and an inferior one [meant] a difference of 10% in the selling price."[53]

Commission throwsters, dyers, and finishers expected to be paid on delivery or, with regular clients, on monthly intervals. That more extended credit arrangements did emerge is clear however. At bankruptcy hearings for firms which collapsed after the 1893 panic, unpaid bills of dyers and throwsters running as high as $3,500.00 were submitted to the receivers.[54] Moreover, a degree of legal protection for commission specialists had been provided by the New Jersey legislature through statutes enacted in 1888 and 1889. Under their terms, the three sectors of service firms were guaranteed "a first claim on silk in their hands belonging to parties for whom they had done work" and who had gone bankrupt.[55] Still, if the accounts due had accumulated for some time, the value of the work on hand when a client folded might cover only a fraction of the sum owing.

MARKETING

Having been inspected and packed in bundles and cartons, completed broad silks and ribbons made their way to the market largely through commission-sales agencies in New York City. The most prestigious houses, such as F. Vietor and Achelis Company, had substantial showrooms for display as well as salesmen who made rounds with samples. For their services, a fairly standard 7 percent of the price realized was assessed, broken down as 1 percent for insurance of the goods, 3 percent for selling expenses, and 3 percent as a fee to guarantee payment for fabrics delivered to users in the apparel, upholstery, drapery, or millinery trades. Despite their importance, commission agents were the subjects of endemic complaints, focusing on favoritism, cancellations, and selling prices. Small firms feared being forgotten should they consign their goods to houses which handled accounts of major firms like the Pioneer Silk Company or Pelgram and Meyer. Moreover, the agents' willingness to allow their larger buyers to back out of confirmed orders was viewed as a "colossal evil" by manufacturers, who had to stand the loss of the entire sale while the agent gave up only the 7 percent commission in order to retain a customer's good offices. Cutting the prices asked by the mill was equally ruinous: "A quick easy sale of a lot of goods at fifty cents a yard," wrote James Chittick in 1913, "would suit the agents much better than the slow and laborious peddling of them at sixty cents as all that they would lose would be their commission on the difference, while the difference in the price obtained would be a matter of life or death to the mill."[56]

Why then did Paterson manufacturers not sell their products on their own? Apart from not having the networks of contacts possessed by selling houses, two main reasons may be offered. First, as is evident from the employment of outside specialists in production, silk-weaving companies generally started with limited capital that was wholly committed to paying wages, rent, machinery installments, insurance, and other expenses. (Note that initially distinctions between fixed and working capital were fuzzy.) To add the expense of a New York City office or a full-time salesman was out of the question. Having once engaged an agent, successful firms grew accustomed to working with the house; in addition, the manufacturers were offered, and at times accepted, advisory hints as to the colors, patterns or styles that were expected to sell well. For important mills, agencies would announce "openings" at which the firms' new seasonal lines would be first displayed for buyers and the trade press. Often proprietors would deal with a single staff member who handled their accounts, enlarging the personal dimension of selling. When account managers changed agencies, such relationships could produce a prompt transfer of the manufacturer's patronage from the former to the new house. For example, when Charles Hayes left Megroz, Portier, Grose, and Company in the fall of 1885 to join Spielmann and Company, he brought with him the Doherty and Wadsworth ribbon account. Spielmann's had earlier acquired Doherty's dress silks account when the company hired Mr. Runyon from Megroz.[57] Thus firms initially impelled toward selling agents by their small amount of capital might develop lasting relations with them (together with loyalties toward particular individuals who long handled their accounts), and perhaps gain a measure of protection against cancellations and hasty price cutting.

The second reason for the powerful presence of commission sellers in the silk trades is less complex—they provided mill owners with cash advances against goods delivered to them for marketing. These sums eased the entire credit network, for they supplied the money for proprietors to redeem the notes given to silk merchants for their bales, to keep them reasonably current with throwsters and dyers, and to cover a fair portion of the costs of wages, rent, and other ordinary expenses. Generally, from 60 percent to 75 percent of the estimated value of the fabrics was advanced. For orders which required fabrication, rather than being filled from the house's stock, similar advances were standard. Once goods were sold and paid for, the balance, less the commission, was remitted to the firm. Without these regular infusions, few infant firms would have survived long; for the delay between the shipping of finished goods and the closing of the balances ranged from two to six months and beyond. Only firms with substantial working funds could have continued to operate with these lags, had there been no cash advances from the New York City agencies.[58]

Yet this system was fraught with perils as well as benefits. Companies were clearly "in the hands" of their selling houses insofar as they relied on advances as their sole sources for working capital. First, to keep the cash flowing, they had to continue production even when markets looked less than promising. Second, pressure to accept direction from agents over the course of the firm's development could be exerted readily. Worse, if stocks were ultimately sold below the estimated prices that had set the advance, the balance due a manufacturer could drop near to zero, undermining profitability and perhaps even destroying the firm. Finally, should rumors of a feared "embarrassment" reach agents who already had doubts about a company's prospects, the refusal of further advances signaled that the end had come. These undesirable features of manufacturers' relations with commission houses account well for the deep ambivalence toward them. Advances supported the entry of undercapitalized "mushroom" weavers, thus helping to intensify competition and the demand for skilled labor, thereby risking both elevated wage rates and overproduction. Yet, few firms, even the "majors," could do without them, leading to frustrations that burst forth in horror stories told and retold among the factory masters.[59]

Two alternatives to the agencies were readily available, selling directly or consigning goods to the auction room. The former course involved direct employment of travelers and New York City offices, as well as forswearing any advances except those that could be negotiated directly with eager buyers. In Paterson, only very solid companies could venture in this direction. Unlike Philadelphia, where selling directly was a tradition sustained by the tours of jobbers circulating among the factories in the city's several textile districts, Paterson's proximity to New York City commanded that firms be visible there. With millions of yards of every description available at Manhattan's Greene Street agencies, the firm that expected its clients to hasten to Paterson occupied, briefly, a dream world. Even by 1913, only about forty of over three hundred local mills had followed the lead of Pelgram and Meyer, listing offices in New York City as the sites from which their products were sold "direct."[60]

For most firms the auction room was also to be avoided. One's agent might send damaged or out-of-fashion lots to be sold there anonymously, charging only a half-commission on the proceeds.[61] But as a regular practice, shipping directly from the mill to the bidding floor was thought to be utter madness. Still, the Tilt family's Phoenix Manufacturing Company did this with staggering frequency, enraging its competitors by glutting markets with thousands of cartons of ribbons and pieces of silk, establishing prices that became those at which the others' customers expected to buy.[62] Why the Phoenix had regular clients as well, who purchased the same or similar goods from their agents at higher prices, when its auctions operated "to the utter demoralization of business generally," baffled contemporaries.[63] Yet the firm's market strategy was not a great deal different from that of others who sought to cover basic expenses by making staple goods (black broad silks) on some of their looms and used the rest for weaving novelties which might "catch" and realize spectacular profits.

The Phoenix ran at full capacity most of the time, regardless of others, shipping everything beyond what was taken by regular buyers to the auction house several times a year. The orders of regular buyers set the market price for new and popular styles; any surplus of these would sell at auction for only a bit less, with the added benefit that the firm received full cash payment from the auctioneer, less an 8 percent charge, within ten days,[64] thus avoiding the long settlement delays that agent-based sales often involved. If goods that had not struck the trade's fancy brought their cost of production, the firm evaded the dead loss that such items might become if they rested in an agent's storage rooms. Phoenix had developed an optimization strategy that allowed the firm to spread its fixed costs across a broad spectrum of products, setting prices for its leaders and taking prices for its surplus. For many years, no other major firm was either bold or foolish enough, depending on one's point of view, to adopt such an approach. Such caution helped assure the Phoenix's success, for it is plausible that had a dozen major firms pushed millions of yards into the auction rooms, the collective effect on demand

and prices would have been catastrophic. Daring, despised, and solitary, the Phoenix Manufacturing Company prospered, outlasting all but a few of its competitors in the first wave of Paterson silk mills.

This then was the dynamic environment of silk manufacturing at the close of the nineteenth century. In proceeding from the structure of production and marketing to examine the process of transformation which materialized during the post-1885 generation, it may be worth highlighting the emerging troubles by noting the silk entrepreneurs' diminishing expectations for capital turnover (and hence returns to investment) from 1889 to 1913. At the earlier date, a Paterson manufacturer noted, "We should turn our capital over at least three times a year," with his anticipated profit of 4 to 6 percent of output representing a 12 to 18 percent return to capital. In the rapid-growth years before the mid-1880s, he observed that "there were small manufacturers making twenty per cent" on sales or 60 percent return to capital on the same basis. [65] Those heady days had vanished by 1889, but twenty-four years later, silk-industry consultant James Chittick would admit, "most mills will not turn their capital more than one-and-a-half to one-and-two-thirds times each year, and if they turn it twice they are doing exceptionally well." [66] Assuming the same profit expectations, which may be generous given the multiplication of competing producers, the rate of return to capital expected had fallen by one half, to a level of 6 to 9 percent. Only an exceptional company might secure as much as 12 percent if it made 6 percent clear on two turns of its investment. By 1913, the glory days were over.

Furious at the state of the silk industry, Chittick asked glumly, "What do we see year by year? Why, in the last twenty-five years the failures in the textile manufacturing trades have been appalling, both in number and in size, and how many mills make real money, that is, money that can be withdrawn from the business? Who are the gentlemen who can buy expensive yachts, and purchase New York City property . . .; who buy large interests in banks, railways, mines or what not? Are the names of silk or woolen manufacturers among them? To ask the question answers it. Manufacturers as a class are not fools, and there is something wrong with underlying causes when a great industry has to be conducted without adequate profit." [67] The industry was becoming increasingly troubled. Yet a search to find a few "fools" and place the blame on them would be fruitless. The economic, cultural, and political environment that had fed Paterson's expectations in 1885 had been largely destroyed. But the unhappy situation that Chittick bemoaned was the ironic consequence of individually rational actions by proprietors, workers, agents, and consumers, aggregating to a collective irrationality that damaged all parties to varying degrees.

Writing of the technological thread in this many-sided contradiction, Thorstein Veblen touched as well on the cultural theme in 1904: "The growth of business enterprise rests on the machine technology as its material foundation. The machine industry is indispensible to it, it cannot get along without the machine process. But the discipline of the machine process cuts away the spiritual, institutional foundation of business enterprise; the machine industry is incompatible with its continued growth; it cannot, in the long run, get along with the machine process."[68] Veblen judged that these cultural costs of material improvements were substantial, that the dispiriting of work and enterprise was taking place before his eyes, and that the dissemination of the "machine process," with its impersonal discipline and standardization, lay near the roots of the problem. For Paterson, such economic and technological shifts (for example, the proliferation of competition and new and faster machines) played a role in the cultural fragmentation that unfolded after 1885. Market pressure and productivity demands butted against a pattern of social relations rooted in the factory culture of proprietary capitalism. The decay of those relations, and of expectations of unbounded opportunity and bounded conflict, was speeded by staggering events (such as the 1893 crash), and more gradual shifts in the context surrounding the mills (deaths of the first-wave entrepreneurs, the "new" immigration). The consequence was a long-term loss of coherence, an estrangement between masters and workers, together with sharp divisions among the members of each group. In the wake of this deterioration, one is tempted to read the 1913 strike in part as a desperate effort at bonding by both labor and business, as if crisis solidarity could provide the foundation for a revitalized, coherent vision that would at least weld the fractures that divided colleagues in each camp. The mid-1880s may not have been a "golden age" in Paterson, but the texture of experience then was a world apart from the raw antagonisms and sporadic violence that were regular features of the city's life in the new century.

ESCALATING LABOR PROBLEMS

To chronicle exhaustively a quarter-century of movement in the Paterson silk industry, a larger canvas than available here would be necessary. Within the confines of this essay, a selective review of what seem to be the central lines of change will be undertaken. First, the development of increasingly volatile relations between workers and owners will be sketched, with some attention to related issues, such as shop customs, the politicization of conflicts, and rising violence. Then, the growing fault lines that surfaced among workers and within the group of manufacturers will be exposed. Finally, the market disorientation that attended the rising production of "cheap trash" silks and ribbons will be evaluated as a component of the momentum of ruinous competition. By the close, the contradictory fruits of Paterson's great success will be evident. For while the trend was for employment in the local silk trades to climb upward from the 1880s through the turn of the century (see table 1), the environment within which labor was expended and goods were finished and sold became ever more contentious and disquieting.

Paterson's unfolding relationships between labor and capital have occasioned little comment outside the context of the heralded 1913 strike. During the generation preceding that event, however, they evolved, in a direction contrary to the lines that conform with any notion of progress toward orderly collective bargaining. Instead the customary patterns of 1880s factory culture eroded without the appearance of a more "modern" replacement. When contrasted with those basic industries in which stable unions ultimately emerged, the silk trades retained major elements of instability, which were successfully displaced in the mass-production sectors of merged, giant American corporations, such as steel and electrical equipment. The latter gained ready access to financial markets, readily engaged unskilled labor, achieved significant productive integration, raised entry costs for competitive new businesses to prohibitive levels, and succeeded in channeling demand toward long runs of standard items. But the silk industry, by contrast, made no such headway. In 1910, as in 1885, it was dependent on credit and advances from suppliers and agents, relied heavily on skilled weavers, dyers, and others, as well as upon a productive network of specialist firms, had immoderately small entry costs, and responded to erratic demand rather than shaping it. These continuities were as central to the burgeoning crisis as were the scores of minor and major strikes from 1886 through 1913.

In February 1886, with weaving mills again running into the evening hours, Paterson silk workers in several factories petitioned their bosses for rate increases to offset reductions made in dull times during the previous summer. Advances were granted at John Ryle and Company, Pelgram and Meyer, and two other firms, but when similar requests were refused at Andre Cardinal and Doherty's mills, the following week, strikes involving 230 broad-silk weavers commenced. [69] Following the throwsters' pattern of 1885, walkouts were numerous and brief, or prevented by compromises and acceptance of workers' demands. There was nothing exceptional in any of this; it represented merely another of the customary and spontaneous eruptions which led to individual settlements at each firm. Something quite different followed in March 1886.

Dyers, organized in a local assembly of the Knights of Labor, held a series of meetings and collectively drafted a set of "regulations and scale of prices" for their work. This common schedule was "presented . . . for adoption" to the masters of both independent dye

Table 1
SILK EMPLOYMENT, PATERSON, 1890–1901

Year	Firms	M^a	%M	F^a	T^a
1890	83[b]	5,935	47.5	6,550	12,485
1892	88	7,129	50.4	7,006	14,135
1894	58[c]	6,489	51.2	6,133	12,622
1896	91	8,543	53.6	7,379	15,922
1898	125	9,531	53.2	8,376	17,907
1901	174	12,078[d]	55.3	9,749	21,827

Sources: Compiled from individual firm listings in the eighth through the nineteenth annual reports of the Inspector of Factories and Workshops, State of New Jersey (Trenton, N.J., 1890–1901).

[a]M = Males; F = Females; T = Total.

[b]No dyeing firms were recorded in the 1890 report; thereafter, they were included. Other textile manufacturing and machinery-building firms are not included here.

[c]The figures reflect operating enterprises; many were closed but not bankrupt in the 1893–95 period.

[d]Of the overall increase in the 1892–1901 period, excluding the initial year when dye works were omitted, male employment rose by 69 percent and female employment by 39 percent. This indicated (1) the continuing development of the all-male dyeing sector; and (2) the spatial dimension of deskilling (that is, that substantial replacement of male by female labor was occurring largely outside of Paterson). The city retained its role as a center for specialty, skill-demanding work; throwing and plain-silk weaving relocated to Pennsylvania and elsewhere. Breakdowns of dye works for three illustrative years are as follows:

Year	Firms	M	F	T
1892	5	738	4	742
1896	11	1,136	28	1,164
1901	24	2,383	71	2,454

houses and major firms with their own dyeing capacity, such as William Strange and Company. When their proposal was refused, strikes spread throughout the city, with over a thousand dyers and helpers shutting down at least a dozen plants. [70] As dyeing was essential to the completion of the production sequence, layoffs of weavers commenced within a week. By early May, William Strange was threatening to relocate outside of Paterson—he would stay but close his dyeing facility—and other manufacturers reportedly shared a similar intention. The strike ended with agreement to a price scale for labor well short of the workers' demands, to take effect June 1 and run for eight months. The day after it expired, February 1, 1887, a new and higher schedule was presented and again refused, triggering the second major citywide dyers' strike within a year. [71]

What had happened? Why had one of the most skilled divisions of the Paterson work force set off a sectorwide confrontation, joined the most feared national union of the era, and broken with the old pattern? Clues to the environment that engendered such a strategy lie in the proffered 1886 regulations and scale. First, the strikers were concerned with stretch-out; in fact, their document began by affirming, "That dyers shall not be required to run more than one box. . . ." This trade custom assured the spreading out of work to all qualified dyers, each of whom would tend "his" dye box with the same proprietary care with which skilled weavers operated and adjusted "their" Jacquard looms. Given the general expansion of the silk industry, the pressure of orders and opportunities had led firm owners to add boxes without increasing their numbers of full-fledged dyers, with superintendents and proprietors also running multiple boxes on occasion. The one-box regulation was also to apply to them. Second, dyers wanted to end the pattern of rushed work followed by idle, unpaid days; so they called for payment of "three dollars per day, *work or play,* not including holidays or days lost on their own account." Third, the proliferation of apprentices and loose regulation of the work assigned them threatened the foundations of craftsmen's control over the supply of skilled labor. Detailed rules for apprenticeship were presented, most notably delaying "binding" apprentices until they were eighteen years of age and allowing only one apprentice per hundred men employed. [72]

Technology, in the sense of innovative machinery, was not at issue here; pay rates were secondary. The core of the demands had to do with control of the work process, a fact manufacturers quickly recognized. Seeking to take advantage of their position at the production center of an expanding American silk industry, some dye-works masters were disregarding shop customs and enticing others to do likewise. Pressed to conform to the rules of the trade, they would readily point to the competition offered by the violators, whose double boxes and multiplying apprentices allowed them to handle increased volume at lower charges. The solution was to standardize working rules across the board. Paterson's mysteriously special water and its concentration of skilled labor indicated to the workers that dyeing was unlikely to migrate elsewhere. As proprietors could or would not enter into regulating one another's practices, it remained for dyers to take the initiative citywide through organization and a general walkout. The irony of course was that this response to the competition that undermined craft traditions necessitated formal collective actions which further undercut the old patterns. [73]

The compromise settlement established as of June 1, 1886, failed to specify the work-control demands put forward by the strikers and won them only a small pay increase, a time-and-a-half provision for overtime, and shorter Saturday workdays. [74] Yet the proprietors seem to have taken little comfort from the modest concessions that had ended the stoppage. The Knights of Labor had surfaced as a new force in the city, disrupting their ability individually to run their firms as they saw fit. Events in the summer and fall proved to be more unsettling. The Saturday "half-holiday" won by dyers was requested and secured by workers in other sectors. In the wake of the annual "excursions" for workers sponsored by William Strange, Henry Doherty, and other major mill owners, the Knights of Labor announced for early October a "parade and monster picnic" together with an "entertainment." When the date arrived, "the mills were quite generally closed," as thousands added "Labor's great holiday" to the traditional group of work-free celebration days. Worse, one of the struck dye houses declared bankruptcy during the strike, the first case of a firm removing "entirely" from Paterson was recorded, and dyers struck successfully to force an employer to rehire one of their number fired for an "irregularity in charging up his time." Another had to lay off three new helpers until they joined the Knights of Labor. [75] The Paterson Board of Trade suggested experimenting with arbitration for future disputes, but as workers pushed their advantage, manufacturers girded for another confrontation.

In late September 1886, Thomas Ryle of the Pioneer Silk Manufacturing Company hired a nonunion broad-goods weaver to run a ribbon loom. Having been notified that the man was "under the ban" for refusing to join the Knights of Labor, Ryle reportedly gave his ribbon weavers "several days" to "furnish the idle loom with a competent weaver." When none was forthcoming, he brought in the banned weaver, whereupon all eighty of his union ribbon workers walked out.

Ryle fired the lot and advertised for new help.

Strikebreakers who took over the abandoned looms were jeered by crowds that followed them home. Some evidently quit, and the firm escalated its challenge by shipping a number of looms to its annex at Allentown, Pennsylvania. After more than three months the struggle ended in early January, the Ryles agreeing to reemploy immediately "a portion" of the defiant eighty, the rest to be rehired "as fast as the business would warrant taking them on." Female learners had been engaged to replace the male strikers. Intimidated by the crowds and lacking the skills of experienced weavers, they had been of little use, for the firm estimated its losses at $5,000.00 per week for the duration.[76] Crowd harassment of "scabs" was a traditional component of Victorian factory culture, but the occasion for the dispute—the attempt to enforce a Knights of Labor union shop—was not. Ryle may have forced the issue by doubly antagonizing his ribbon weavers, hiring an outsider to both the union and the craft, but could claim he had been fair in waiting a few days for them to produce a substitute. After that, further interference with a proprietors' treasured prerogative to hire and fire was insupportable.

The incidents scattered through the second half of 1886 closing with the Ryle lockout demonstrated the "arrogance" of the Knights of Labor, and were much discussed in Paterson. Manufacturers were clearly angered or frightened or both. Apocalyptic visions abounded of the Paterson silk industry's death and of workers taking over the mills. Proprietors claimed the leaders of the Knights of Labor were "paid secret agents of large French and English manufacturers," and began booking orders only if delivery dates could be extended in case of strikes.[77] The promulgation of the dyers' new schedule for the manufacturers' adoption, February 1, 1887, brought the crisis to a head.

The new proposal contained several references to regulating the work process and provisions for a $1.00 per week raise, a fifty-five-hour week, and overtime at double pay. During eight days of efforts to "arbitrate the matter," the owners agreed to all of these, but refused to accept the clause that headed the document: "This shall be a union shop, and no man shall be employed in it unless he is a member of the Knights of Labor in good standing." Sixteen hundred dyers struck on February 9, 1887, as the manufacturers vowed to resist this "obnoxious demand." A local paper quickly announced that the principles of the Knights of Labor "are incompatible with the American idea of each man minding his own business. Either the Knights of Labor or the Constitution of the United States must go."[78] The *Paterson Daily Press* added that the employers recognized "this question of control of the mills has to be fought out sometime" and this was the time. [79]

Seven weeks later, the strike ended with victory for the proprietors. Their determination had been reinforced by a sense of betrayal occasioned on the first day when workers abandoned "silk in the process of manufacture." The employing dyers (owners of independent dye houses) claimed that their workers had promised to finish the work on hand before going out. The strikers had instead "put the silk in such condition that it could not perish for want of further work, but they did not finish the work. The silk manufacturers look upon this as a violation of a pledge, and it only increases the feeling of hostility against the dyers." [80] The manufacturers' terms, accepted at the end of March, included none of the provisions that would have gone into effect had the union-shop clause been abandoned earlier by the Knights of Labor. In addition, while averring that they would "not discriminate against members of any labor organization," the owners were quite explicit: "We will employ and discharge whom we please." The workers' defeat was nearly total. [81]

Both protracted and enormous, idling an estimated twelve thousand Paterson workers at the peak of related layoffs, the conflict was equally noteworthy for its orderliness. Rowdy street scenes were not recorded; none of the firms broke ranks with any attempt to engage strikebreakers. Still the new "system" of standard rates set by sectorwide committees had no staying power. The allied manufacturers' price schedule was to run for one year; no notice of collective action to renew or alter it appeared in 1888. The Knights of Labor announced in defeat a grand plan for uniting all silk laborers into a general union; this too came to nothing. [82] Instead, the Knights' organization foundered; other rival unions developed among the ribbon weavers, loom fixers, and other craftsmen; and scattered one-firm wage demands resumed their erratic rhythm. [83] As James D. Osborne has commented: "Trade unionism never made much impact among Paterson's mill hands; largely limited to a minority of highly skilled workers, it flourished among the mass of silkworkers only at moments of crisis, and then only briefly." [84]

Through 1890, a continuing boom in the ribbon trades kept local shops busy. Though unsettled by the dye works battles, the customary factory culture was revived or adapted slightly to deal with the shifting environment. On his birthday in 1889, for example, Alfred Crew received the gift of a gold-headed cane from his workers. When the ribbon-weavers' union chartered thirty passenger cars for its summer excursion, many manufacturers planned to attend, "thus gaining the good will of their employees." [85] The market pressure of prosperous times, however, brought attacks on those aspects of customary shop practice that bore directly on production. Thus when Paterson workers left their mills at noon for the annual firemen's parade, September 17, 1889, proprietors complained vocally that these frequent "holidays" were an obstacle to meeting deadlines in the busy season.

Workers had also devised means to defeat the faster machine-speeds that boosted productivity by intensifying their labor. Two of these mill-floor "tricks" were reported in 1890: "soaping the [leather drive] belt so that it would slip and the machinery run slower"; and "to oil the bobbins, by which their speed is retarded, production curtailed, and the labor of tending them lessened." On one occasion when supervisors detected the soap tactic and set things aright, "the hands wanted more pay. The firm refused and a short strike followed, but the matter was adjusted."[86] The "question of control" thus had persisted, but had returned from the arena of mass organizations to the work place. Among the various "control" issues which vexed proprietors, none was potentially more volatile than the craftsmen's efforts to regulate the supply of skilled labor. The manufacturers' attempts to bring in women learners inflamed the ribbon sector in 1890 and after. Their recruitment of immigrant strikebreaking "Turks" and "Armenians" through a New York agency "where imported help is taught the rudiments of silk ribbon weaving"[87] only aggravated the gradual deterioration of Paterson's labor–capital relations.

Lines hardened and tempers flared. Jacob Weidmann, president of the city's largest dye works, moved to break a revival of the dyers' union in 1890 by firing a number of leaders. Announcing that he would take back none of the 250 men who struck in protest, "save as non-unionists," and denouncing one of them as a "Schweinhund," he was assaulted by a striker. The same month, Joseph Bamford, partner in a major weaving plant, was arrested and charged with assault and battery against Antonia Fischer, a young employee. The girl had been ill and away from his mill for several days. When she returned, Bamford fired her, "seized her by the arm roughly and told her to get out." When she asked for her back pay, "Bamford again took hold of her and threw her bodily out of the mill, tearing her clothing after which he threw her working dress into the street."[88] Following his trial and conviction, other women reported that "assaults were committed on other occasions, but that the girls were afraid to make complaints before the courts." In December, Bamford's mill and "handsome Queen Anne residence . . . near the factory" burned to the ground, and his nervous insurers delayed through mid-1891 before settling his claims. His superintendent and a foreman both departed to form their own firms. Chastened, early in 1891 the errant manufacturer donated $1,000.00 to the city hospital fund and $100.00 to the pickets' fund of female ribbon weavers at Levy Brothers. Most of them had been his employees before the fire, and had struck at Levy Brothers against being "required to turn off as many yards as a male weaver at about half the male weavers pay." They won their strike, which included "some wild work in the vicinity of the mill," as "one female 'scab' was nearly disrobed, piecemeal, on the street, and chased, en deshabille across Arch Street Bridge by a howling mob."[89] Bamford's "uncommon" support for strikers at a rival firm, the earlier pair of physical assaults, and the blacklisting of a hundred dyers among Weidmann's discharged unionists, all signaled that earlier boundaries of labor-management conflict were fragmenting.

While the pattern of excursions, gift presentations, and the like, prevalent in the early 1880s did not expire all at once, only scattered traces survived the depression and struggles of the mid-1890s. In the wake of serial bankruptcies during 1893, Paterson dyers and ribbon and broad-silk weavers launched in 1894 a series of sectorwide strikes which shook the city. For the first time, major property damage occurred, after a rumor circulated among Weidmann's workers that the dye works they had idled was having its contract work done by other Paterson firms. Determining to "have every man out from every shop in the city," they launched a raid on other mills, "making a football rush from shop to shop." As working dyers joined the tide, havoc was wrought inside the works: "The faucets were opened so that costly dyes ran out over the floor, hot steam was turned on at a tremendous pressure, and the valuable silks in process were scattered about, trampled under foot and destroyed. . . ."[90] Years of frustration seem to have exploded in a few riotous hours; as the police were helpless or hiding, employing dyers "capitulated almost immediately" to demands for wage hikes and a fifty-five-hour week. Comparable advances were gained at many of the weaving firms as strikes and threats of strikes multiplied. Owners who refused to grant increases, William Strange, the Bamfords, and the Ryles, were "hissed . . . threatened and insulted." Indeed, in Strange's case, the threats matured into a failed attempt to bomb his residence, for which crime several "anarchists" went to prison after one of the bombers informed on the rest.[91]

Paterson manufacturers soon lodged bitter protests concerning the city government's expressed sympathy for the strikers, setting in motion the long process through which business interests came to power in local politics. Strange resigned in anger from his post on the

Paterson City Parks Commission and within a year moved to New York.[92] Three years later, when Henry Doherty, after settling the first strike in a dozen years at his mill, treated his returning workers to "ice-cream and other refreshments,"[93] the gesture was an anachronism. More characteristic of the bubbling chaos gradually engulfing Paterson's labor relations were the twenty-odd other walkouts that spring, and tales of scab recruiting that dotted the local and trade press. When a series of disorders in 1901 brought the first use of anti-labor injunctions to Paterson and a second "wholesale wrecking of dye shops" in 1902 brought the first involvement of the state militia in local factory struggles,[94] the chasm of mutual bitterness between masters and workers had become unbridgeable.

The mutualities of a shared factory culture had set limits to and rituals for conflict in the Paterson of the post–Civil War years. Their degeneration was accompanied by the emergence of internal divisions within the groups of workers and proprietors. The disintegration of worker unity which has been suggested above, has been investigated by others[95] and needs only a brief mention here. Essentially, the potential for labor unity was obstructed by antagonisms along lines of ethnicity, sex, skill, and ideology, all features familiar to social historians. The appeal of the Knights of Labor for a universal silk-trades union withered when ethnic and skill issues surfaced. "English speaking" ribbon weavers let it be known that they would "never join any body that includes the German, French and Italian weavers" and that "weavers in general" were "averse to being joined to several thousands of inferior workers." As their numbers grew, Paterson's Italian workers denounced such bigotry and the attempts of ribbon weavers to exclude them from the trade. They were welcome however at Weidmann's dye works (where the lowest rates in the city were paid) until they led the 1894 strike. At that point the trade press labelled them "the very worst and most dangerous foreign element in the ranks of American labor."[96] In the ideological arena, though the anarchist bomb-maker who menaced William Strange was German, Italians were widely accused of being anarchists and radicals. Well before the turn of the century, rival groups of socialist, anarchist, and craft-unionist silk workers battled one another over the proper tactics for reforming or replacing capitalism.

Though women workers were often valiant strikers, as the conflict at Levy Brothers illustrated, they were voteless, excluded from political debate, and generally ignored by union organizers. When manufacturers, like the Levys and Bamfords, tried to take advantage of a labor market divided by gender by opening skilled jobs to women at half the rates paid men, male workers acted to prevent this incursion.

On one occasion they made the simple and crippling demand that women's pay be the same as theirs. Far more frequent were strikes to exclude women entirely or, if that did not succeed, harassment and intimidation were used to force them to quit. Such tactics bred strikebreakers among the "despised Italians," other immigrant groups, and women, because during walkouts such workers might secure places and learn skills denied them in "normal" times. The harassment of strikebreakers, which included "the constant banging of tin pans during the dead hours of the night," drove further wedges between component groups of the Paterson working class. [97]

INDUSTRIAL FRAGMENTATION

The rigors of competition made unity among local manufacturers rather difficult. Their formal associations were crisis-inspired and generally short-lived, from the allied dyers who offered common terms to the 1887 strikers, to the ribbon association forged by eight firms in 1895, and citywide efforts begun in 1897 and renewed in 1900 and 1906. [98] Two business associations did persist, the Paterson Board of Trade and the Hamilton Club, but the former was derided in the trade press as a "notoriously somnolent body" and the latter rarely welcomed the new Jewish and Italian proprietors whose fledgling concerns began appearing in the 1890s. [99] The Silk Association of America was a national organization, which Patersonians often headed, but its members represented large companies and importers determined to defend their tariff barriers. Attempts to form silk "trusts" before and during the merger era surfaced repeatedly, but all foundered. As one Paterson manufacturer noted, "the products are so varied and the conditions so involved, it would be found difficult, if not impossible to arrive at any uniform basis of advance [for prices]." When a 1900 plan for a combination was broached at a meeting of the Silk Manufacturers Association of Paterson, it "created only smiles from those present. The matter was not regarded as worthy of discussion." [100]

Since the industrial structure of the trade prevented effective price management or common labor policies, individualism was the rule. As the labor climate sharpened, as profitability waxed and waned, public denunciations of manufacturers were recorded. Other employing dyers blamed the 1894 explosion on Jacob Weidmann, who "incites to disturbance by his arbitrary and unequal treatment of his hands." Earlier, another angry proprietor had thundered, "the average manufacturer is a coward and an idiot." His fellow ribbon men were reluctant to push up prices in a high-demand market, even though "wages have been advanced from ten to twenty percent."[101]

Newly begun small firms were a special source of difficulty. A popular foreman starting his own firm not infrequently took with him his best workers to become his first employees. Eager for a share of the market, small firms threatened the profits of other companies by cutting prices, sometimes to levels that destroyed their own enterprises, and revealed a financial ineptitude that far surpassed their technical expertise. The bankruptcy review that followed a silk-braid manufacturer's failure in 1890, for example, showed that he had been pricing his goods below the cost of their raw materials and had sunk himself and his creditors within a year of opening shop. Equally aggravating to trade veterans were New York financiers who started Paterson mills despite being "entire strangers" to silk production. Thus when a New York stockbroker and his banker partner lasted less than a year in their 1895 Paterson venture, few were surprised. Tiny firms in desperate straits might prove a more direct threat to other companies. Early in June 1906 the American Silk Manufacturing Company was burglarized, and silks worth $1800.00 were stolen. The men arrested shortly were Harry Kaufman and Joseph Koransky, operators of "a silk plant in the old Pope Mill."[102] The enormous gap separating such men from Paterson's millionaire proprietors like William Strange and Catholina Lambert, and the economic conditions that permitted the proliferation of small firms made efforts at building common policies among owners quite futile.

Finally, such leadership as had been exercised in industrial affairs by the founders of Paterson's hallmark firms withered as significant deaths and business failures mounted even before the new century opened. Between 1885 and 1900, John Ryle, Albert Tilt, Charles Pelgram, Isaias Meyer, James Booth, William Strange, Peter Ryle, and John Booth all died. In the latter year, both the Pioneer Silk Manufacturing Company and the Hamil and Booth Silk Company were forced into liquidation. Henry Doherty and Catholina Lambert were the sole survivors of the first generation. In 1913 Doherty provided the spark for yet another tumultuous strike and Lambert's firm failed in its aftermath.[103] Interdependent within the scheme of production, Paterson silk men, ethnically diverse by 1910, occupied radically varied positions in scale and financial terms and faced a shifting market whose troubles reflected their individualistic strategies.

The proliferation of small companies and a technological development in dye chemistry during the 1890s together brought a market crisis, reaching critical proportions after 1900. Productive flexibility, the key to survival in a fashion-sensitive trade, enabled weaving firms to shift rapidly to manufacturing styles and varieties that sold well in a particular season. In the 1886 surge in demand for silk handkerchiefs and mufflers, Paterson's adaptability led to concern that production would be "overdone, everybody having gone into this line, greatly to the neglect of dress fabrics, which are not in especially brisk demand." And so it happened. Within two years, handkerchiefs were out of style, "the country is heartily sick of them." However, 1888 was a presidential election year; dozens of firms shifted to making "campaign novelties," and soon that market was likewise "swamped." By 1889 the long ribbon boom had stimulated both intense price competition and the first reference to the threat that "reducing qualities" posed. The role of small companies in this was clear: "almost every day produces new competitors in the shape of newly-starting small concerns.[104] Their use of low-grade raw materials to secure a price advantage soon led to complaints that "too many cheap and trashy ribbons are being made, . . . devoid of any real merit, with no richness or wear in them." Known in the apparel trades as "knock-offs," such cheap imitations were intended to broaden the silk market to those less prosperous women who might seek to follow fashion if stylish facsimiles were available in lower price ranges. Though scores of companies taking this pathway failed, they were rapidly replaced, suggesting the widening demand for inferior goods.[105]

The increasing range of qualities added confusion to complexity in a market in which thousands of varieties of pattern and color were sold annually. Moreover, what had started in ribbons soon spread to broad silks as the chemical means to "weight" the raw fiber with "tin crystals" came into general use. Introduced to Paterson by Constant Dordoni of the Enterprise Silk Dyeing Company, this innovation involved compensating for thrown silk's 20 to 25 percent loss (during the process of "boiling off," which preceded dyeing) by the addition of tin salts, which restored the yarn to its original fullness. "Boiling off" thinned the yarn; weighting fattened it back up. A pound of thrown silk, unweighted, after dyeing might tip the scales at twelve ounces. Another pound, weighted and dyed, would come in at a full sixteen ounces, or even more depending on the volume of adulterants added and absorbed. The production implications were plain. Due to its greater fullness, a length of weighted yarn yielded more yardage on the loom than a similar length of pure (dyed but unweighted) silk. It thus "stretched" the raw material's output and spread the cost, allowing manufacturers to charge lower prices for finished goods. The negative implications were severe, however. The tin salts weakened the fiber, a deterioration accelerated by exposure to sunlight and perspiration. Thus weighted silks "rotted"; the more heavily they were "loaded," the faster they decayed. Weighting's market implications were chaotic, as a production variation of Gresham's Law came into play. Inferior fabrics undercut sales of pure, high-quality, durable silks. The faster fashion turned, the less durability was valued even by affluent buyers. Hence, frontline major firms commenced making weighted yardage, leading small companies to run more-heavily loaded goods in order to retain earlier price advantage. [106]

By 1906 the consolidated buying power of mass retailers had further shaped and energized the erosion of quality. The *American Silk Journal* deplored "the almost insane competition in retail merchandising which has swept over the country like a wave during the last decade. In order to supply the cheap silks and ribbons now demanded . . . , chemicals and minerals are made use of in silk manufacture to lessen the cost, which methods, if persisted in, will do much to shake the faith of consumers." The *American Silk Journal* that year launched a "crusade for better silks," attempting to persuade retailers to avoid "trashy fabrics which are unsuitable from every point of view." It failed. James Chittick observed ruefully in 1913, that the manufacturer "who offers a cloth, grossly overweighted, but which looks and feels all right, and which suits the customers' ideas of price . . . walks off with the business." [107] The individual firm's drive for profitability in this context had increased the risks and tensions all around. Overproduction, the degradation of quality, and the increasing need to calculate costs and lower them intensified pressures on the mill floor to speed up and stretch out, even for veteran paternalists like Henry Doherty. Over the previous quarter century, the silk manufacture had been gradually transformed from an irregular business into a sick industry.

Fluctuating raw-silk prices, fashion, the credit system, and other continuities of unpredictability had been reinforced by changes that added to the trade's volatility. Technical advance, immigration, hordes of small companies, and escalating strike violence, all contributed to the battering of once-vital trade standards and customs. Yet was not this to be expected, as market rationality progressed steadily through all aspects of business practice, supplanting earlier relations and traditions? The pressure for close-costing forced manufacturers to view workers as substitutable inputs who should accept the dictates of political economy and technical innovation. Labor's resistance then as now was a species of cultural refusal, episodic and lacking coherence. Yet it highlighted the central contradictions of the "machine process," which "cuts away the spiritual, institutional foundations of business enterprise."[108] Capitalism and the logic of entrepreneurship had ultimately flourished at Paterson in a near-classic fashion. Innovations and competition had proceeded in response to market signals. Mountains of materials were transformed into useful forms, in increasing volume and variety. On profits and wages rested the expansion of the city and the industry. Yet prosperity had not benefited all. In equally classic patterns, technological and market development made production work more intense. Debt-driven individualist proprietors poured their goods onto glutted markets. The fever to lower prices savaged the quality and reputation of silks. Untrammeled antagonisms in mill and market involved a large part of the population. By 1910, for its industrial success and international standing, for its generations of achievement, Paterson was beginning to pay a terrible price.

NOTES

[1]*American Silk Journal* 18 (1885): 7.

[2]*Paterson Weekly Press,* July 27, 1876.

[3]*American Silk Journal* 4 (1885): 12.

[4]Ibid., 27.

[5]Ibid., 12.

[6]See Richard D. Margrave, "The Emigration of Silk Workers from England to the United States of America in the Nineteenth Century" (Ph.D. diss., University of London, 1981).

[7]N.J. Bureau of Statistics, *The Industrial Directory of New Jersey* (Camden, N.J., 1909), 343; *Official American Textile Directory: 1913* (Boston, 1913), 196.

[8]*American Silk Journal* 4 (1885): 12.

[9]Ibid., 55, 177.

[10]Patrick Joyce, *Work, Politics and Society: The Culture of the Factory in Later Victorian England* (Brighton, England, 1980), Ch. 4, 5.

[11]*American Silk Journal* 4 (1885): 177.

[12]Philip B. Scranton, "Varieties of Paternalism: Industrial Structures and the Social Relations of Production in American Textiles," *American Quarterly* 36 (1984); 235–57.

[13]*American Silk Journal* 4 (1885): 145.

[14]See chapter 1.

[15]*American Silk Journal* 4 (1885): 41.

[16]N.J. Inspector of Factories and Workshops, *Eighth Annual Report* (Trenton, N.J. 1890), 75 (hereafter, *8th Report, Factory Inspector.*)

[17]*American Silk Journal* 5 (1886): 30.

[18]Ibid., 4 (1885): 12, 69.

[19]U.S. Tariff Commission, *Broad Silk Manufacture and the Tariff* (Washington, D.C., 1926), 22.

[20]*American Silk Journal* 4 (1885): 98.

[21]Ibid., 55.

[22]Ibid., 99, 115. On annexes, see also Morris W. Garber, "The Silk Industry of Paterson, New Jersey, 1840–1913: Technology and the Origins, Development, and

Changes in an Industry" (Ph.D. diss., Rutgers University, 1968), 200–201.

[23]*American Silk Journal* 4 (1885): 42.

[24]Ibid., 5 (1886): 22.

[25]Ibid., 22–23.

[26]U.S. Department of the Interior, Census Office, *Tenth Census of the United States: 1880*, Vol. 2: *Report on Manufactures* (Washington, D.C., 1883), 420; *Nineteenth Annual Report of the Inspector of Factories and Workshops, State of New Jersey* (Somerville, N.J., 1901), 236–51; Garber, "The Silk Industry," 201–11. Garber reported from census tables that Paterson's silk employment in 1909 was somewhat over 18,000; in 1919 it had risen again to 21,800.

[27]N.J. Bureau of Statistics of Labor and Industries, *Sixth Annual Report* (Trenton, N.J., 1883), 157.

[28]See Philip B. Scranton, *Proprietary Capitalism: The Textile Manufacture at Philadelphia, 1800–1885* (New York, 1983), chap. 10.

[29]*American Silk Journal* 5 (1886): 63, 81. Seven strikes in Paterson were reported in the first half of 1886 by the *American Silk Journal* which quoted the *Paterson Daily Guardian* in July to the effect that manufacturers expected "the latter part of the season will show better results than the first half, in which the business was much disturbed by strikes." Ibid., 111.

[30]*American Silk Journal* 4 (1885): 55.

[31]Ibid., 83, 115, 131; 5 (1886): 30, 45.

[32]See Jeremy Brecher, *Strike!* (San Francisco, 1976): Daniel Walkowitz, *Worker City, Company Town: Iron–Cotton Worker Protest in Troy and Cohoes, New York, 1855–84* (Urbana, Illinois, 1978), chap. 6 and 7. My view of social relations in Paterson silk manufacturing differs in some respects from that put forward in Herbert G. Gutman's seminal article, "Class, Status, and Community Power in Nineteenth-Century American Industrial Cities: Paterson, New Jersey: A Case Study," in *Work, Culture and Society in Industrializing America* (New York, 1976), 234–60. Professor Gutman related two strike chronicles in illustrating the paucity of community support for major local manufacturers in the late 1870s. His study, however, is not specifically oriented either toward relationships within the mill setting or the larger silk industry. The gradual, erratic deterioration of customary relations suggested in this essay is analogous to the pattern documented for New York craft shop workers, ca. 1815–1830, in Sean Wilentz, *Chants Democratic: New York City and the Rise of the American Working Class, 1788–1850* (New York, 1984), chap. 1 and 3.

[33]*American Silk Journal* 5 (1886): 82; Garber, "The Silk Industry," 180.

[34]Hollins Rayner, *Silk Throwing and Waste Silk Spinning* (London, 1903), 12–18.

[35]James Chittick, *Silk Manufacturing and Its Problems* (New York, 1913), 13–15.

[36]*American Silk Journal* 4 (1885): 98.

[37]Chittick, *Silk Manufacturing*, 172, 176.

[38]Ibid., 16–17.

[39]Ibid., 389–90. Chittick reported that credits on Italian silks were often extended for only sixty to ninety days, making firms with "limited capital" far more likely to buy Asiatic chops.

[40]*American Silk Journal* 5 (1886): 192; 6 (1887): 30, 33–34.

[41]*8th Report, Factory Inspector*, 75.

[42]*American Silk Journal* 4 (1885): 83; 5 (1886): 96; 8 (1889): 35, 164.

[43]Rayner, *Silk Throwing and Waste Silk Spinning*, 29–30.

[44]*American Silk Journal* 4 (1885): 41.

[45]Ibid., 7 (1888): 180; 9 (1890): 292; Chittick, *Silk Manufacturing*, 176.

[46]Garber, "The Silk Industry," 172–75; *American Silk Journal* 5 (1886): 177; 7 (1888): 45.

[47] N.J. Inspector of Factories and Workshops, *Sixteenth Annual Report* (Trenton, N.J., 1898), 138; *19th Report, Factory Inspector,* 248.

[48] *Paterson Daily Guardian,* May 25, 1887.

[49] Garber "The Silk Industry," 180–82, 184–87. Garber noted that the increased use of high-quality Italian silk was related to these technical developments, as faster machine speeds could be reliably introduced when more durable silks were thrown and woven.

[50] Chittick, *Silk Manufacturing,* 389.

[51] Ibid., 96–108. However, it should not be imagined that a great deal of production cost accounting went into the establishment of the list prices. Chittick noted that the lists "just grow up and convenient gradations were made . . . in which the measure of the cost was modified by the willingness of the customers to pay." Ibid., 96.

[52] Ibid., 85.

[53] Ibid., 92–94.

[54] *American Silk Journal* 12 (1893): 181.

[55] Ibid., 9 (1890): 250.

[56] Chittick, *Silk Manufacturing,* 248.

[57] *American Silk Journal* 4 (1885): 131.

[58] Chittick, *Silk Manufacturing,* 243–65, 390.

[59] Ibid., 246–47, 251–52.

[60] *Official American Textile Directory: 1913* (Boston, 1913), 193–201.

[61] Chittick, *Silk Manufacturing,* 259, 313–19.

[62] For details on the Phoenix's massive sales and their impact on markets, see *American Silk Journal* 6 (1887): 30; 7 (1888): 91; 10 (1891): 126; 11 (1892): 109; 12 (1893): 210.

[63] Ibid., 10 (1891): 126.

[64] Chittick, *Silk Manufacturing,* 318. For large sales, special, lower rates were arranged, making it likely that the Tilt family paid fees for auctions comparable to or less than those charged by selling agents.

[65] *Paterson Daily Guardian,* January 19, 1889.

[66] Chittick, *Silk Manufacturing,* 244.

[67] Ibid., 246.

[68] Thorstein Veblen, *The Theory of Business Enterprise* (New York, 1904), 375.

[69] *American Silk Journal* 4 (1885): 115; 5 (1886): 30.

[70] Ibid., 5 (1886): 49.

[71] Ibid., 5 (1886): 63, 192; 6 (1887): 18.

[72] Ibid., 5 (1886): 49.

[73] Technological developments were, however, an indirect presence in this and later dye works conflicts. As faster machine speeds in throwing and weaving were achieved and joined with wider broad-silk and larger multiple-ribbon looms, the sheer product volume might threaten to engulf dye works, which were more slowly mechanized. This potential bottleneck was evaded in part through the multiplication of dye works, and their enlargement. But pressure to strectch out workers and ignore apprenticeship restrictions was perennial.

[74] *American Silk Journal* 6 (1887): 18.

[75] Ibid., 5 (1886): 45, 81, 96, 111, 128, 144, 160, 161. The traditional holidays included Memorial Day, Pfingster Monday (a Dutch custom in June), the Fourth of July, and any day a circus came to Paterson. In addition, mills generally closed between Christmas Day and New Year's Day and during the last days of June preceding Independence Day for a semiannual inventory.

[76] Ibid., 161, 177, 193; 6 (1887): 12.

[77]*Paterson Daily Guardian*, November 30, 1886.

[78]*American Silk Journal* 6 (1887): 18–19.

[79]*Paterson Daily Press*, February 14, 1887.

[80]*American Silk Journal* 6 (1887): 30.

[81]*Textile Colorist* 9 (1887): 81–82. Two small firms had conceded the workers' demands after two weeks, but ten major companies, comprising 90 percent of local dye works employment, stood fast until their counterproposal, issued March 5, 1887, was accepted.

[82]*American Silk Journal* 6 (1887): 140, 158; 7 (1888): 15.

[83]On other unions, see ibid., 6 (1887): 99, 119, 139; on wage and hours requests later in 1887, see ibid., 124; 7 (1888): 46.

[84]James D. Osborne, "Italian Immigrants and the Working Class in Paterson: The Strike of 1913 in Ethnic Perspective," in *New Jersey's Ethnic Heritage*, ed., Paul A. Stellhorn (Trenton, N.J., 1978), 13.

[85]*American Silk Journal* 8 (1889): 67; 6 (1887): 119, 139.

[86]Ibid., 8 (1889): 148; 9 (1890): 123.

[87]Ibid., 9 (1890): 99–100, 110; for another similar incident, see ibid., 10 (1891): 21.

[88]Ibid., 250.

[89]Ibid., 9 (1890): 295; 10 (1891): 64, 66, 91.

[90]Ibid., 13 (1894): 48–51. The presence of scattered trade-union activism and the recurrence of riotous, insurrectionary explosions in Paterson after the early 1890s suggests labor's search for an "identity," as defined by William Reddy in his evocative treatment of French textile workers during the same era, *The Rise of Market Culture: The Textile Trades and French Society, 1750–1900* (New York 1984), chap. 10. A much fuller investigation of the penetration of the market culture into Paterson shop relations than has been possible here might well reveal startling shared experiences, though Reddy's work focused on the woolen and cotton region of northern France rather than the Lyon silk industry.

[91]Ibid., 82, 128, 179, 181.

[92]*American Silk Journal* 13 (1894): 118, 14 (April 1895): 23. In 1895, the *American Silk Journal* began using separate pagination for each issue.

[93]Ibid., 16 (March 1897): 31.

[94]Osborne, "Italian Immigrants," 18–19.

[95]Ibid.; Delight W. Dodyk, "Mill to Marriage: The Work of Girls and Young Women in the Paterson Silk Industry," unpublished manuscript, New Jersey Historical Society, 1984; Delight W. Dodyk, "Winders, Warpers, and Girls on the Loom: A Study of Women in the Paterson Silk Industry and their Participation in the General Strike of 1913" (M.A. thesis, Sarah Lawrence College, 1979); John A. Herbst and Catherine Keene, *Life and Times in Silk City* (Haledon, N.J., 1984).

[96]*American Silk Journal* 6 (1887): 140; 9 (1890): 186, 213; 13, (1894): 48.

[97]Ibid., 9 (1890): 48–49; 11 (1892): 173; 13 (1894): 101.

[98]Ibid., 16 (April 1897): 20; 19 (January 1900): 20; 25 (August 1906): 49.

[99]Ibid., 16 (April 1897): 19.

[100]On the Silk Association, see its "Minute Book, 1879–1905," Archives, Pastore Library, Philadelphia College of Textiles and Science. On trusts, see *American Silk Journal* 6 (1887): 13; 11 (1892): 71; 19 (January 1900): 21, 32, 38.

[101]Ibid., 13 (1894): 49, 83, 11 (1892): 84.

[102]Ibid., 9 (1890): 294; 12 (1893): 83; 14 (October 1895): 44; 15 (June 1896): 35; 25 (July 1906): 47.

[103]Ibid., 16 (December 1897): 19; (June 1900): 406; 19 (August 1900): 31; 19

(December 1900): 41–42.

[104]Ibid., 5 (1886): 144; 7 (1888): 131, 164; 8 (1889): 35.

[105]Ibid., 9 (1890): 184; on making silks for women with "flat pocketbooks," see ibid., 25 (July 1906): 31.

[106]Chittick, *Silk Manufacturing*, 32–39.

[107]*American Silk Journal* 25 (February 1906): 48–49; 25 (June 1906): 34; Chittick, *Silk Manufacturing*, 37. The problem of silk-weighting excesses would only abate during the 1920s with the intervention of the Federal Trade Commission, which set maximum standards which dyers embraced and advertised widely. See, for example, *Silk Digest Weekly* 16 (January 12, 1929): 2, 16.

[108]Veblen, *Theory of Business Enterprise*, 375.

3

The Unity and Strategy of the Paterson Silk Manufacturers during the 1913 Strike

■ STEVE GOLIN ■

FOR YEARS ENGLISH-BORN manufacturer Henry Doherty had been trying to induce his broad-silk weavers to work four looms instead of two, in the new mill that he had built expressly for this purpose. For years the weavers in the Doherty mill had refused to accept the four-loom system. In January 1913 Doherty's attempts to press ahead with his plan resulted in yet another walkout at his mill. This time, however, the strike quickly spread to encompass all the branches of the Paterson silk industry as well as a variety of issues; for both the silk workers and the manufacturers, the 1913 strike was in fact the culmination of years of struggle in Paterson. Each side had learned from past defeats and grown stronger. The silk workers had learned the necessity of solidarity between different ethnic groups and branches of the industry; they had also learned that larger loom assignments led to increased unemployment and lower wages, whereas shorter hours and a two-loom system led to decreased unemployment and higher wages. In 1913 the broad-silk weavers, ribbon weavers, and dyers' helpers showed unprecedented unity in resisting the four-loom system for broad silks and demanding the eight-hour day for all.

The silk manufacturers, on the other hand, had learned from experience to fear both the militance of Paterson's workers and the neutrality of Paterson's police. In the decades preceding the 1913 strike the manufacturers had succeeded both in restructuring local government, so as to make it more responsive to their needs, and in moving as much of their business as possible out of Paterson.[1] The manufacturers entered the 1913 strike with the police under their control and with factory annexes flourishing in Pennsylvania, beyond the reach of the strikers. In 1913 they successfully matched the unity and determination of the strikers with unity and determination of their own. This essay explores the nature of the manufacturers' unity in 1913 and examines their strategies for winning the strike.

THE SOLIDARITY OF THE BOSSES

In 1913, after years of disappointing experiences with unions, the Paterson silk workers found a union as militant as they were, the radical IWW. Together they constituted a formidable force. In 1913 the silk workers, backed by the IWW, shut down the mills and dye houses in Paterson and kept them closed. For nearly five months, from late February to mid-July, the manufacturers were unable to separate the workers from the IWW, to divide them from each other, or to force them back to work. But the manufacturers themselves, during this time, refused concessions, maintained unity in their own camp, rejected all attempts by third parties at mediation, and continued to insist that they would never deal in any way with the IWW or with the strikers as a body.

The unity and intransigence of the manufacturers surprised and bewildered the strikers, who knew that they had timed their strike perfectly. Nineteen thirteen was a prosperous year for silk, and March was the busiest time of year. "There is a large volume of business to be had at the present moment, and buyers are much in need of the best spring fabrics, but manufacturers are not in a position to accept this business which could be obtained with practically little or no efforts, due to the strike."[2] After two mediocre years, silk was back in fashion. The strikers knew that the buyers in New York were clamoring for silk goods, that the idled mills had lost their spring season and that, while the demand for silk ribbons and dress goods continued high through April, May, and June, they were gradually forfeiting their fall orders as well.[3] In the past, strikes in February and March, when the spring fashions were being dyed and woven, usually had been successful, because the manufacturers had not been willing to remain closed for long during their busiest months. Then why, during such a good year for silk, did the manufacturers refuse to make concessions or even to negotiate? How were they able to prevent breaks in their own camp? Anxiously, the strikers and their supporters studied the owners' united front and wondered if it would last.

Throughout the strike there were rumors of splits developing between the smaller and larger silk firms. According to these rumors, the smaller manufacturers were eager to settle the strike, while the larger manufacturers wanted to continue to hold out. At the end of the first month, the *Paterson Evening News* printed a report that some large firms hoped the strike would last another month and squeeze most of the small firms out of business.[4] Three weeks later the Socialist *New York Call* suggested hopefully that the smaller manufacturers, seeing that they had been "made the cat's paw of the Silk Trust, have signified their intention of breaking away and of dealing with the workers. Many have declared openly that should they continue to strike for any length of time, they would be forced to the wall, and, rather than go into bankruptcy, they will probably deal with the workers."[5] But nothing came of it. Reports and rumors continued to circulate; in early May, it was said that about fifty smaller silk manufacturers and several dye firms were going to break ranks with their colleagues, but when the small manufacturers met separately a week later, a spokesman told the press that "we can do nothing. . . ."[6] The rumored break never came.

This solidarity of the bosses was as remarkable in its way as the solidarity of the silk workers. As the probusiness press speculated about the hold of the IWW agitators on the strikers, so the socialist and IWW press theorized about the hold of the large manufacturers on the smaller ones.[7] The "silk trust" (conceived on the model of the woolen trust in Lawrence, Massachusetts) was blamed for forcing the smaller firms to refrain from settling with the workers. A widely disseminated article, published in *Solidarity* and the *New York Call* and printed as a strike leaflet in Paterson by IWW Local 152, argued that outside capitalists controlled the Paterson manufacturers. Pointing to "concentrated and giant capital in the hands of a few," the article detailed the national and international connections of firms like Doherty and Wadsworth; Dexter, Lambert, and Company; Ashley and Bailey Silk Manufacturing Company; National Silk Dyeing Company; and Weidmann Silk Dyeing Company. These companies dominated the Silk Manufacturers Association and the Master Dyers' Association. "Through these combined associations they control the local situation." How did the big firms prevent the little ones from settling? "The big corporations threaten the small firms who accede to the strikers' demands. They will make slow delivery or no delivery when silks are to be dyed; and give poor ratings when raw silks are purchased."[8] In short, according to the socialist press, the apparent unity of the employers was entirely artificial, the result of force and threats by giant capitalists.

This analysis was self-serving and incorrect. Like most conspiratorial theories, including the manufacturers' theory that outside agitators kept the workers on strike by force and threats, the socialist explanation of the solidarity of the bosses was a way of denying more disturbing realities. The fact was that there was no "silk trust" or "giant capital" in Paterson, no huge company or companies that offered the key to the situation, as the American Woolen Company had at Lawrence. All the manufacturers in Paterson were small firms by the national standards of 1913. In their attitudes toward competition, workers, and unions, even Henry Doherty and the managers of the Weidmann Silk Dyeing Company had more in common with nineteenth-century entrepreneurs than with twentieth-century trusts. Socialists and IWW theorists might pretend that the answer to the question "Who has Paterson by the throat?" was "simple—a few big capitalists," namely, "the same brand of capitalists who have got the country by the throat."[9] The truth was that silk was and would remain a genuinely competitive industry, and that the Paterson manufacturers could not agree among themselves to fix prices. Moreover, practically the only thing that they could agree on (all three hundred of them) in addition to the importance of a high tariff, was the necessity of retaining complete control of their own businesses and of keeping them free of interference from unions. On the issue of the strike, but on little else, the solidarity of the bosses was real.

In terms of where and how they lived and of whether or not they hired managers to run their shops, the larger and smaller manufacturers formed quite distinct groups; in wealth, status, and power they had little in common. Most of the larger, older manufacturers were English-born; many of the smaller and newer ones were Jewish. The English-born proprietors of large firms had gradually achieved acceptance into Paterson's social and political elite, though some preferred living in New York, nearer to the market.[10] But the English-born manufacturers too had originally worked their way up in the trade.

Henry Doherty, for instance, had been a young weaver in Macclesfield, like his father before him. Coming to Paterson in 1868, Doherty had worked as a weaver before entering into partnership in 1879 with another Macclesfield emigrant; at that time they owned a single loom between them. Joseph Bamford, who was also the son of a Macclesfield silk weaver, similarly built up his business in Paterson from nothing but his skill and his knowledge of the trade. Catholina Lambert began work as a ten-year-old in a Yorkshire cotton mill; at seventeen he was an office boy in a Boston silk firm; two years later he purchased a partnership in the firm, renaming it Dexter, Lambert, and Company and eventually relocated it in Paterson. There he made enough money from his five mills (including two in Pennsylvania) to pay for his English-style castle that he built on Garret Mountain—"his head full of castles," wrote William Carlos Williams in his epic poem *Paterson*, Lambert "built himself a Balmoral on the alluvial silt, the rock-fall skirting the volcanic upthrust of the 'Mountain'"—and also for his collections of some four hundred original paintings by Renoir, Monet, Courbet, Rembrandt, and others. Doherty, Bamford, Lambert, and other English-born manufacturers had founded in the nineteenth century, and continued to dominate in the early twentieth century, the Silk Association of America and the Paterson Board of Trade.[11]

It was these manufacturers who had led the fight against the Knights of Labor in Paterson and against every other union that had tried to organize among the weavers and dyers' helpers there. In 1886, responding to a proposal for establishing a labor arbitration board in Paterson with Knights of Labor representation, one manufacturer insisted that "he would sooner sell at auction than be compelled to argue with his employees, not one of whom has any practical knowledge of the business." Another declared that "the silk manufacturers were not in harmony with any project that would allow of argument as to what was right and what was wrong in matters relating to employers and employed."[12] Over the years, the manufacturers were remarkably consistent in fighting against workers' interference in the running of their businesses. Each manufacturer fought for the power to decide by himself the number of looms worked, the hours of work, the piece rates, the schedule of fines, and the ultimate question of who got fired. In 1913, the silk association's mid-year report declared, "The very life of the individual manufacturer depends upon running his own mill without interference on the part of his operatives. It is a basic principle of hiring and service that there must be a master and a servant. The master must direct and success must depend upon skilled directions based upon justice."[13]

If the manufacturers were extremely opposed to the 1913 strike, it was because this strike was the most determined effort ever made by the silk workers to organize themselves in a union. The fact that this union was openly revolutionary in its aims, repudiating the whole distinction between master and servant, only served to clarify the issue from the owners' point of view and to make it easier for them to intimidate deviants within their ranks and to mobilize public support. During the strike, a number of manufacturers were interviewed by John Fitch for the national magazine *Survey*. "It is not alone against the IWW that the employers have set their faces," he concluded. "Unionism, organization, under whatever name, is opposed whether its aim to be 'reasonable' or 'revolutionary,' because it 'interferes with business.'" Fitch noted that the Paterson manufacturers had previously opposed the American Federation of Labor (AFL) as strongly as they now opposed the IWW. Though they complained about the IWW, "the employers, if pinned down, admit that they are opposed to unionism as such, and not to the IWW alone."[14]

Unable to prevent their Paterson employees from arguing with them about what was right and what was wrong, the large firms had led the exodus to Pennsylvania. In 1891 the mills in Paterson averaged 151 workers; by 1914, the average was down to 58.[15] As the large manufacturers moved their less skilled work out of Paterson, new small mills specializing in plain work took their place. In 1913 it was still possible for an ambitious weaver to start a mill in Paterson with a few hundred dollars, employ his family members and close friends, and carry the product under his arm to the market in New York, making the best deal he could. Such newcomers were already known, in 1913, as "cockroach manufacturers," and to them (despite socialist theory, which dismissed them as "the relics of a fast disappearing class") belonged the future.[16] Between these newcomers, who were generally Jewish, and the veteran English-born manufacturers who still dominated the trade, there was an impassable gulf. Yet although it would not have occurred to either group to stress it, the Jewish and the English-born manufacturers shared a tendency to rely on themselves and to be fiercely competitive and independent. Some proprietors, remembering their origins, tried to treat their employees fairly and were personally respected by them.[17] But none would brook interference, by a labor organization, with his own right to run his business as he saw fit.[18]

Thus the rumored tensions in the bosses' camp, while real, never affected the outcome of the strike. In fact, the unity of the strikers tended to force the manufacturers together. By mid-March the broad-silk manufacturers, ribbon manufacturers, and silk dyers' associations were meeting together and taking common action, in contrast to the squabbling that had usually divided them. Within the combined associations, the large mill owners spoke for all the manufacturers, and dominated their discussions.[19] A number of small mills did indeed go bankrupt.[20] They had no capital reserves and no annexes in Pennsylvania to sustain them. To avoid bankruptcy, by ending the long strike, some small manufacturers would have agreed temporarily to anything, even an eight-hour day. But in addition to the pressure from the larger firms, there were two compelling reasons why these small manufacturers could not reach a settlement with their employees. First, the strikers did not trust them. In the 1912 strike, seventeen smaller firms, with orders begging to be filled, agreed to the conditions of the Socialist Labor Party union. "As soon as the strike was settled and the slow season was on, these manufacturers repudiated their contracts."[21] To an ally of the big firms, the behavior of these small manufacturers was typical: "I will tell you frankly from past experience the employers—I am speaking of the smaller ones—they will make agreements with these [labor] organizations, and they will be breaking them the next morning; in fact, before they get downstairs they are trying to find a way to break them."[22] To the manufacturers there was nothing sacred about an agreement. Like the IWW itself, they regarded the breaking of an agreement as a legitimate tactic in their struggle with the strikers. Therefore the tentative overtures that some of them made in 1913 were not taken seriously by the strikers, except as signs of weakness in the opposing camp.

The second and more important reason why even those smaller manufacturers who wanted to reach agreement could not have done so is that the silk workers were no longer making separate agreements with individual mills. As a result of their experience in 1912, and guided by IWW strategy, the 1913 strikers had decided not to settle with any firm until the overwhelming majority of the manufacturers agreed to terms. This hostility to piecemeal shop settlements was intended to maintain unity in the strikers' camp, which it did. It also, however, cemented the unity of the bosses. With nowhere to turn, the individual manufacturer was practically forced to fight on to the end.

Arthur Price, who employed about fifty workers in his mill on Broadway, tried several times to work out an arrangement with his weavers. In March he offered to concede to their hour and wage demands, pending the outcome of the strike, when they would receive the benefits of a general settlement. His workers rejected the offer and the manufacturers' association denounced him. In May he made a similar offer; this time his now-hungry weavers agreed to return to work. The strikers picketed the Price mill *en masse*. The police, to Price's evident distress, attacked the crowd of pickets with clubs and arrested eighty-five of them in one day.[23] For Arthur Price and the other manufacturers, large or small, there would be no separate peace. Defectors would be treated roughly by both sides; the solidarity of the workers and the solidarity of the bosses, which reinforced each other, left little or no ground for maneuvering. Fighting to preserve his business autonomy, each manufacturer had to merge his interests with the general interests of other mill owners, even if by doing so he might go out of business.

Some of the larger manufacturers, too, despite their superior resources, paid a price for not dealing with the strikers. Lambert was apparently one of these. At the beginning of the strike, the manager of his Straight Street mill moved to divide the weavers and intimidate the English-speaking into remaining at work. "The 'boss' went around to all the 'foreigners' and told them not to come in . . . until the trouble was over." On the following afternoon, with the Jews and the Italians locked out, "the power was stopped and a shop meeting called by the boss to determine whether the remaining weavers wanted to go on strike or not. Seventy-five voted 'no strike' and forty-one voted 'strike,' the boss taking tally. This was a rather remarkable showing in the face of the circumstances, and it must have required a considerable amount of courage on the part of that forty-one to stand up and vote as they did."[24]

Refusing to be intimidated, Lambert's English-speaking weavers soon joined the other strikers. (Attempts by the manufacturers to divide American-born workers from recent immigrants continued throughout the strike, with generally disappointing results.) Also refusing to weaken, Lambert himself stood firm with the other manufacturers. But though they won, he lost. Despite his vast private wealth, or perhaps because of it—so much of his income had been spent in economically nonproductive ways—Lambert could not recover from the strike and was finally forced to declare bankruptcy and to sell his famous collection of paintings.[25]

Stubborn and willful, self-made men like Lambert preferred to risk their life savings rather than to compromise with a union. In this they typified the attitude of the National Association of Manufacturers (NAM), to which many of them belonged. The NAM stood for militant opposition to all labor unions and for the open shop. By contrast, the more sophisticated National Civic Federation recognized conservative trade unions as a possible means of integrating workers into large corporations. Many of the largest corporations in the nation, especially those which enjoyed some protection from market conditions, supported the National Civic Federation position, whereas relatively small and middling manufacturers belonged to the NAM and identified with its anti-union hard line.[26] Essentially provincial, Paterson silk manufacturers had nothing in common with National Civic Federation employers. They did business in the old ways. As Bill Haywood understood, "Paterson manufacturers have an absolute monopoly on the finer grades of silk, like brocades, that are made on the Jacquard loom, and it would be easy for them to raise prices to meet wage increases, but because of the cut-throat competition among them, silk is cheaper, on the whole, than it was 15 years ago."[27]

In contrast to the national trend represented by trusts and the National Civic Federation, Paterson manufacturers preferred direct meetings with each other, and their workers. In the summer of 1913, after turning briefly to the AFL in the hope of breaking the strike, the Paterson employers returned to their starting point. Sensing victory in July, "eighty-six of the Paterson manufacturers, all of whom are members of the National Association of Manufacturers, issued what they called an ultimatum . . . No union of any kind will be recognized, the shops to remain wide open."[28]

This picture of the small-scale, self-reliant entrepreneur, almost equally opposed to combination with other manufacturers as to combination among his workers, must be modified to fit the dyeing sector of the silk industry. Doherty and Wadsworth was not the largest employer in Paterson's silk industry in 1913. The Weidmann Silk Dyeing Company and the National Silk Dyeing Company were each larger, and they operated on a somewhat different basis. Silk dyeing, under separate ownership from the mills, had taken root in Paterson later than broad-silk or ribbon manufacturing, and from the beginning it tended to be big business. Jacob Weidmann was born in Switzerland, where his father already ran a silk-dyeing plant. Coming to Paterson in the 1870s to manage the dye works of a large silk manufacturer, Weidmann stayed to build his own dyeing company, relying on the capital and connections of such prominent Patersonians as Garret A. Hobart (vice president of the United States under Pres. William McKinley) and John W. Griggs (former governor of New Jersey and McKinley's attorney general), both of whom became officers of Weidmann's corporation. In 1909, ready to retire, Weidmann sold his company to French capitalists.[29] The National Silk Dyeing Company, second in number of Paterson employees only to Weidmann's, was even larger nationwide. Formed by a merger in 1908 between four Paterson-based dyeing companies and one Allentown plant, the firm immediately purchased a larger dyeing plant in East Paterson and continued to expand aggressively, buying three more plants, one each in Paterson, Pennsylvania, and Virginia.[30]

But the greater wealth, power, and readiness to combine of the larger dye works were not reflected in greater tolerance of their workers' attempts to organize. On the contrary, their profits came from the exploitation of immigrant labor—from paying their Italian helpers a fraction of what master dyers were paid, subjecting them to unsafe conditions, and employing them sporadically, according to the amount of work on hand. Under these circumstances, unions could only limit the dye works' flexibility and lessen their profits. "We are ready to treat with our men at any time, but we will not treat with their union . . . ," said Jacob Weidmann during the 1902 dyers' strike. "We say that the men must come to work again before we can do anything for them."[31] In 1913 the dye-house employers took an identical stand, and backed it up by force.

THE STRATEGY OF FORCE

The methods used to control Italian workers in the dyeing sector of the silk industry were exemplified by the hated O'Brien detectives employed by the Weidmann Silk Dyeing Company throughout the strike. The O'Brien Detective Agency of Newark supplied men at $5.00 a man per day or night to guard the plant and the homes of the employing dyers and foremen. Hired to enforce the claims of French and American investors, the "special detectives" were troubled by none of the mixed feelings about hurting local people, which many local policemen had. In Paterson, it can be argued, the O'Brien detectives were the real "outside agitators." "We realize that the detectives were a despised body of men by the workers," said police Capt. Andrew J. McBride. "Even our own policemen despised them. . . ."[32] The battle between the O'Brien detectives and the dyers' helpers, fought out daily in Paterson's Riverside section, epitomized the fierceness of labor strife in Paterson in 1913.

On April 17, at 6:30 P.M., an O'Brien detective guarding the Weidmann plant shot and killed Valentino Modestino. The special detective, Joseph Cutherton, was putting a group of strikebreakers on a trolley car after they finished work, as an angry crowd of dyers' helpers watched and booed. Modestino, who had just come home from the file works where he was employed, was sitting on the front stoop of his home in the Riverside section watching the now-familiar confrontation developing between the special detectives and the dyers' helpers. Shots rang out, fired by the detectives to intimidate the crowd. Modestino was hit in the back. In Paterson General Hospital that night he told police: "Those bums at Weidmann's shot me."[33] Three days later he died. "We never expected things like that—to be killed—shot," said a female striker.[34]

No one, not even the O'Brien detective, claimed that the pickets had fired or even possessed guns when Modestino was shot, and six witnesses in the recorder's court while Modestino was dying in the hospital identified Cutherton as the man who had shot him. Although Cutherton, represented by John W. Griggs, Weidmann's attorney, was arrested after the shooting, he was never indicted.[35] Amazed at Cutherton going free despite the evidence against him, State Supreme Court Justice James F. Minturn asked, "What power is there in this community that is greater than the power of the law?"[36] The answer, of course, was the power of the manufacturers.

As a result of their successful campaign for structural reform of local government after the destructive 1902 strike, the silk manufacturers and dye-works owners in 1913 were able to anticipate a level of police support previously never enjoyed. One of the prominent silk manufacturers sat as a member on the police board, which had been created in 1907 to give Police Chief John Bimson a free hand. During the strike, the National Silk Dyeing Company lent its car to the police, to be used on patrol. Moses Strauss, manager of two large ribbon mills, directed the police to arrest specific pickets outside one of the mills. O'Brien detectives were authorized to serve as "special policemen" by Chief Bimson, and as "deputies" by the county. Outsiders were shocked at this open collaboration between manufacturers and police. Two federal investigators noted in 1914 that sixty specials had been "clothed with the authority of the police and sheriff" and used "as a private army of the mill owners."[37]

The manufacturers also appeared to have the active support of the local courts. In New Jersey, where all judges were appointed, whoever controlled the local political authorities also controlled the courts. Recorder James Carroll had been chosen by municipal authorities who were the open allies of the mill owners. Carroll routinely imposed sentences of $10.00 or ten days on strikers for peaceful picketing. On the day Adolph Lessig, silk weaver and local IWW leader, was sentenced by the recorder to six months in prison, he saw a silk manufacturer leaving the recorder's office.[38] The Passaic County grand juries that indicted pickets and IWW speakers, but refused to indict the O'Brien detective who shot Modestino, were appointed by the sheriff. Decisions in the recorder's court and in county court were so flagrantly partisan that conservative New York newspapers were frequently driven to protest against them. But again, what mattered to the manufacturers was that they received support when they needed it. Appeals to higher courts were slow and costly. For all practical purposes, during the period of the strike, the law belonged to the manufacturers.

Mayor Andrew F. McBride was a Democrat, whereas the manufacturers preferred Republicans; he was an Irish Catholic, whereas they preferred Englishmen or Scots. He was also, however, a trustee of the Paterson Board of Trade, which existed to represent and promote the interests of the business community and especially manufacturers. For a while the strikers of 1913 seemed to hope that McBride would at least make a show of neutrality, in the tradition of earlier mayors and aldermen. Previously in Paterson, the police had refrained from interfering with peaceful picketing, and this tolerance had reflected the determination of the aldermen and mayors not to take sides in labor disputes. But the 1907 change to a commission form of government, backed by the mill owners, had deliberately taken away the power of the aldermen to control the size of the police force and had turned over direction of the police to a commission, appointed by the mayor, on which silk manufacturers were well represented. In 1913 the assaults of the regular and special police on the pickets were authorized and encouraged by the mayor and his police commission, as the strikers soon realized. When in late March McBride personally offered them $2.00 for their relief committee, they returned the money to him, insisting instead that he curb the police. Speaking for the strikers, Elizabeth Gurley Flynn explained that they wanted justice from the major, not charity.[39]

In the suburb of Haledon, when a silk manufacturer cursed pickets in front of his mill late in the strike, Haledon Mayor William Brueckmann, a socialist, had him arrested for using profanity, and the Haledon court convicted and fined him.[40] Nothing like this ever happened in McBride's Paterson. As the two federal investigators concluded, legal authority in Paterson was, "in effect, turned over to the mill owners."[41] Throughout the strike, the Paterson silk and dye manufacturers were very successful in using both the forces of public authority and of private detectives against the strikers. Still they could not break the strike. As a strategy, force failed. It failed in the first days of the strike, when the police arrested the IWW out-of-town speakers and tried to club the broad-silk weavers back to work; in response to these actions, the ribbon weavers joined the broad-silk weavers on strike. Force similarly failed in March when the arrests of Haywood and Lessig on absurd charges, which Minturn later dismissed, led to renewed activity on the picket lines and in the halls. The murder of Modestino in April resulted in the largest and most impressive demonstration of solidarity by the strikers and their families, as they marched silently through Paterson from the Catholic church on East 19th Street to the Laurel Grove Cemetery. Force fared somewhat better in May, when Bimson finally closed the strikers' halls, thereby depriving them of an opportunity to meet together and combat rumors of breaks. But the strikers and the IWW fought back by meeting more frequently in nearby Haledon, and the mills remained closed. On balance, the strategy of force proved to be counterproductive.[42]

STRATEGIES OF MANIPULATION

From time to time the manufacturers employed strategies other than force. But the tendency of the mill owners to underestimate their employees similarly hampered the effectiveness of the other strategies. Weidmann's futilely gave frankfurters to the dyers' helpers as a bribe to stay at work at the beginning of the 1913 strike. The National Silk Dyeing Company similarly wasted its money when it hired Rodney Miller of New York as an "organization engineer." Employed from February to August 1913, Miller was supposed to find out what was bothering the men, as he had done previously in labor conflicts in Brooklyn's clothing industry and Boston's shipping industry. If hiring him represented a gesture from within the Paterson silk industry toward the fashionable concept of scientific management, Miller was no efficiency expert, as he made clear, and he made no time-motion studies in Paterson. On the basis of his investigations, Miller predictably concluded that the IWW was symptomatic of a problem, of which immigrant labor was the cause.[43]

The problem, as the mill and dye-house owners conceived it, was how to separate their impressionable employees from the militant IWW leadership. After Police Chief Bimson's initial attempt to drive the IWW leaders out of town resulted in an increase of union support, the manufacturers decided to arouse a spirit of patriotism. Hanging large American flags over their mills, and inviting the town's tradesmen to do likewise, the manufacturers urged their workers to come back on Monday, March 17, which they designated "flag day." The stage had been set by the local press, which stressed how un-American the IWW was and luridly featured Bill Haywood's reference to the red flag in his first Haledon speech. The theme of flag day was the necessity of choosing between the flag of socialist revolution and the American flag. Across Market Street a large American flag pointedly proclaimed: "We live under this flag, we work under this flag, we will defend this flag." A similar strategy had been effective at McKees Rocks, Pennsylvania, in 1909 in separating the American-born workers from the foreign-born and the IWW; and it had even succeeded at Lawrence in 1912. The Paterson silk manufacturers believed that patriotism might achieve what Bimson's scare tactics had failed to accomplish.

On Monday morning hopes were high: "With flags flying and the city decked out in gala garb, the great silk mills of Paterson reopened their doors. . . ." According to the *Newark Star*, "The ending of the gigantic labor war was beautifully planned. The factory owners were going to forgive their erring workmen. Mayor McBride and the police saw the end of their trouble approaching. The ministers who had urged the workers to return understood that their exhortations were to be obeyed. It was a very successful end of the strike, marred by only one thing—none of the strikers went back."[44] Throughout the city on that day strikers wore a card in their lapels designed and paid for by local socialists, picturing an American flag and explaining: "We wove the flag. We dyed the flag. We won't scab under the flag." At Turn Hall that morning, Flynn met the charge of un-Americanism by pointing to the workers of different nationalities supporting the strike. "The IWW in Paterson has done what no other institution in this city can do. It has brought together men and women of all nationalities. . . . The IWW represents the ideal spirit of America."[45] As Flynn tried to explain the meaning of the red flag, a striking dyers' helper jumped to his feet, exclaiming "I know! Here is the red flag!" and holding up his right hand, stained blood red from years of working with dyes. "For an instant there was silence, and then the hall was rent by cries from the husky throats as all realized that this humble dyer indeed knew the meaning of the red badge of his class."[46]

Flag day failed miserably. The assumption behind it, like that behind the force used repeatedly against the IWW, was that the majority of silk workers were passive people. The manufacturers perceived the strike by their employees as the result of manipulation by the IWW and therefore believed that some countermanipulation of their own could get their employees back on the job. Intelligent as they were in practical matters, they never understood the anger of the dyer's helper with the stained hand, of the broad-silk weaver forced to work four looms, of the ribbon weaver threatened with dismissal if he or she complained about a piece rate. The managers and owners of the dye works and mills normally were protected from that anger by their power at the work place and could only explain the collective behavior of their workers in 1913 as an aberration, a result of outside influence. In the search of a way to return the majority of workers to their former ways, the manufacturers discarded unsuccessful stratagems without learning why they had failed; therefore they repeated their mistakes. By Monday, March 24, they had begun to take down the useless flags from the mills, and to prepare for the next round.[47] In April they appealed to the AFL.

John Golden of the AFL was in Paterson on flag day and saw it fail. As president of the United Textile Workers of the AFL, Golden had intervened already against the IWW and on behalf of the manufacturers in Lawrence in 1912 and in the Hazleton, Pennsylvania, silk strike in 1913.[48] Encouraged by the Paterson proprietors, he launched an all-out campaign in April to separate the Paterson silk workers from the IWW and end the strike. The *American Silk Journal,* the organ of the Silk Association of America, was enthusiastic: "The latest phase in the situation, and one which it is thought may possibly lead to a change for the better, has been the arrival in Paterson of representatives of the American Federation of Labor. . . . The strikers, divided, may be more inclined to mediate with the manufacturers."[49]

But Golden made few recruits among the strikers. Broad-silk weavers remembered Golden as the union leader who had collaborated with Henry Doherty in introducing the four-loom system in 1910.[50] Within Paterson's silk industry, the AFL had aligned itself historically with the highly skilled loom fixers known in the mills as the "bosses' men."[51] Despite sporadic efforts, the AFL had been unable to organize the weavers or dyers' helpers; AFL officials in Paterson complained especially about the Italian and Jewish weavers, whose readiness to strike made them difficult to control.[52] Nationally, the AFL stood for restricted entrance into trades and restricted immigration. Locally, E. O. White, secretary treasurer of the AFL's Central Labor Council, explained that the AFL in Paterson "has always been willing to play fair with the manufacturers." If the AFL gains control of the strike, White volunteered, "it will not try to take possession of the mills." On the contrary, the constant aim of the AFL in Paterson was only "to establish a reasonable wage." In the case of the silk industry, "lots of men now on strike were getting plenty good enough wages before the strike." If the AFL settles the strike, "I don't think there will be any demand for general increase over the top notch wages before the strike."[53] The willingness of Golden and White to impose their own notion on the workers of what was good for them recommended the AFL to the manufacturers, who were opposed to all unions. This stance, however, alienated the AFL spokesmen from the silk workers, who would not support a union that would not support them. As a weapon aimed by the manufacturers at the strikers, the appeal to the AFL was even less successful than their appeal to patriotism.

The climax of Golden's drive to break the strike came on Monday, April 21, five weeks after flag day. The critical event was a mass meeting called by the AFL to discuss its plan for settling the strike; it took place in Paterson's largest hall, the Fifth Regiment Armory, which the manufacturers had persuaded the state government to provide free of charge to the AFL for the evening. The meeting had been well publicized; even the *Paterson Evening News,* the only local newspaper that did not openly support the AFL against the IWW, had contributed to the feeling that the meeting would be decisive: "It now remains to be seen whether the claim that has so often been made that the majority of the silk strikers are held out by coercion and fear is correct. Monday night will tell the story and the outcome will make history for Paterson."[54] When the doors opened at 7:30 P.M., over ten thousand strikers filled the armory, with thousands more left waiting outside: "While waiting for the A.F. of L. speakers the crowd amused themselves by cheering for the I.W.W., until one worker took out his membership book and holding it up in the air called for three cheers for the I.W.W. In a few minutes, you could see thousands of the little red books waved over the heads of the crowd and the cheering for the I.W.W. shook the building. . . . When Big Bill, Gurley Flynn, Tresca and Lessig entered the big hall . . . the crowd opened up before them and they walked all around the hall, the crowd closing again after them amid wild cheering. It looked like a motor boat plowing its way through the waves opening up in front and immediately closing after them."[55] From this point the AFL was unable to influence the meeting. At 8:30 P.M. the crowd was still cheering for the IWW and waving red cards and red handkerchiefs. To obtain order the chairman, representing the Paterson Labor Council, was forced to ask Evald Koettgen, organizer of IWW Local 152, to quiet the crowd. Obtaining silence, Koettgen announced briefly that the meeting's organizers would not allow the IWW to speak. "So, let us all go home."[56] Koettgen and perhaps five thousand strikers then left the hall, but others immediately rushed in to take their places. The crowd booed and jeered at the AFL organizers, who still could not start the meeting.

Some strikers had apparently hoped, until the last moment, that a real debate between the AFL and IWW was going to take place: Louis Magnet, the spokesman of the ribbon weavers, had called publicly for such a debate several days earlier.[57] Once the AFL officials had made clear there would be no debate they forfeited any chance of controlling the meeting. Sarah Conboy, an organizer for the United Textile Workers, tried to speak over the heckling: taking a large American flag from the speakers' table, she waved it in front of the crowd. Instead of abating, the jeers were changed to cheers. Giving up, the meeting's organizers sent for Police Chief Bimson, who entered the armory with about fifty policemen and used force to drive ten thousand men and women out of the hall.

By 9:10 P.M. the Fifth Regiment Armory was empty and the police, still anxious to help the AFL, began readmitting strikers who wore no red. Even then, with about four thousand strikers allowed to reenter the hall and the police watching closely, the meeting did not go smoothly. When Conboy made personal attacks on Flynn and Haywood, strikers shouted out objections, and had to be escorted outside by the police. When Golden rose to speak, denying that he was a strikebreaker, more people left the hall. Conboy defended the settlement in Hazleton, Pennsylvania; a girl, one of a group from Hazleton who had come to the armory, tried to rebut Conboy from the floor but was ejected by the police. An AFL official from Scranton, Pennsylvania, claiming that "Waving red flags doesn't get you anything," argued that the strikers would not be relinquishing their rights if the AFL was allowed to set up a meeting between a committee of strikers and a committee of manufacturers.[58]

But most of the strikers thought otherwise. No committee of strikers was ever appointed under AFL auspices to negotiate with the manufacturers. Though Golden tried to recruit silk workers in the weeks after the meeting before finally admitting defeat, it was apparent on April 21 that the manufacturers' attempt to separate the silk strikers from the IWW was actually strengthening the IWW. Those silk workers who had not joined the IWW were alienated completely by the AFL intervention.[59] Given their experience in Paterson, the broad-silk weavers, ribbon weavers and dyers' helpers overwhelmingly preferred the IWW, with its openness, its bias toward direct action, and its emphasis on democratic control of the union and the shop, to the AFL, with its restrictiveness, its bias toward legislative action, and its emphasis on controlling the workers.

The weavers and dyers' helpers had transformed the AFL meeting in the armory into the most dramatic demonstration of support for the IWW up to that point in the strike. For the manufacturers, it was a serious setback. Recapitulating as it did their appeals to the force of the policeman's club in February, to the American flag in March, and to the AFL in April, the armory meeting underscored the limits of the power of manufacturers. They could not get the strikers to abandon the IWW or the strike. Not even reluctantly overcoming their own distaste for dealing with a labor union had been able to accomplish that.

PENNSYLVANIA: THE KEY TO VICTORY

What finally won the strike, for the manufacturers, was their ability to outlast the strikers. Their dramatic efforts to break the strike usually backfired, since they were rooted in the owners' misconception of the silk workers as easily led and misled by radical labor agitators. Quieter efforts, like the manufacturers' sustained campaign to win public opinion in Paterson, were more successful. By May, the manufacturers had gained the support of the press, the clergy, and the small businessmen of Paterson for extreme measures, such as closing the strikers' halls. But what sealed the employers' victory, more than any strategic efforts to break the strike, was their capacity simply to hold out longer than their employees. The strikers succumbed to hunger after five months and returned to work under the old conditions. The most effective strategy, in the end, was endurance.

Two factors enabled the manufacturers to endure the strike. The minor factor, which was fortuitous, was that their fierce competitiveness and lack of monopolistic control had created a market glut in previous years. These surplus goods were sold during the strike. Normally, companies shipped goods to commission agents who warehoused them for sale, the firms being able to draw cash on account at interest against the future sale of these goods, frequently 60 percent of the expected market price. Having accumulated large surpluses as a result of competition in the industry, the commission houses were able to unload them during the strike, to their profit and that of the silk manufacturers. As the *American Silk Journal* noted, "The labor troubles and a scarcity of many lines in quick demand have, in a way, been a boon to the selling houses having stocks of goods to move. As a direct result of this situation and the demand for stock goods the market is cleaner, and with less jobs being available buyers have shown a willingness to pay prices to secure anything like what is desired."[60] The strike, in that sense, proved a "blessing in disguise for the producer," by cleaning out inventories and transforming the market "from a buyer's to a seller's market."[61] Though their mills were closed, Paterson manufacturers could still make some money when their middlemen sold, at high prices, goods that were otherwise going to waste.

The losses in Paterson were nevertheless tremendous. But here the major factor, which was by no means fortuitous, came into play. Those Paterson manufacturers who had moved much of their business out of Paterson before the strike were able to keep operating in the outlying areas, albeit at reduced capacity. Particularly in Pennsylvania, the Paterson silk strikers and the IWW proved unable to close the mills, or at least to keep them closed. Paterson manufacturers with annexes in Pennsylvania were able to limp through the strike. Decentralization of their operations had become a conscious policy in the years before the strike. At the beginning of 1913, just prior to the strike, the *American Silk Journal* approvingly quoted advice which had been given at the cotton manufacturers' convention: "Those corporations which have divided their mills among different localities have avoided the dangers of over-concentration by the operatives, so

Seal of SUM. The origins of Paterson as a planned industrial community date back to 1792, when the SUM purchased land at the Great Falls of the Passaic River to develop as mill sites. This private corporation had the backing of Alexander Hamilton, who saw the SUM as a means of promoting the development of industry in the United States. Although it discontinued manufacturing directly in 1796, the SUM played an important role in Paterson as an energy broker and real-estate developer until World War II. [*Paterson Museum*]

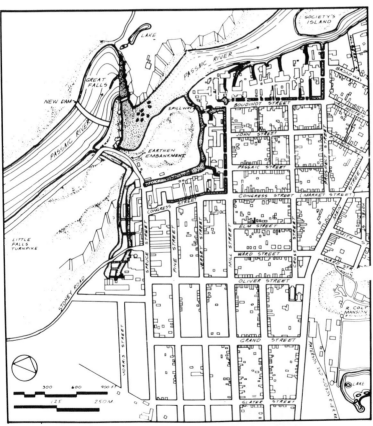

Paterson raceways. The SUM engaged Pierre Charles L'Enfant to engineer a system of raceways to bring waterpower to the proposed mills. The raceways were altered many times before they reached their fullest extent in about 1838. [*Great Falls Development Corporation*]

Plate 1

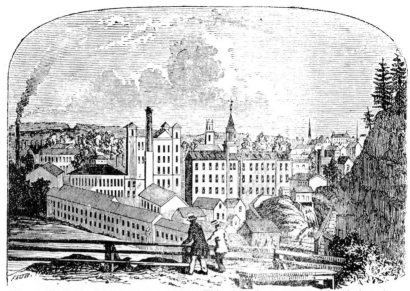

View of industrial Paterson, 1868. This view shows some of the city's early manufacturing establishments. At the time, an essayist wrote, "The advantages which Paterson possesses for a manufacturing town are obvious. An abundant and steady supply of water; a healthy, pleasant, and fruitful country, supplying its markets fully with excellent meats and vegetables; its proximity to New York, where it obtains the raw material, and sale for manufactured goods; and with which it is connected by the sloop navigation of the Passaic, by the Morris Canal, by a turnpike-road, and by a railroad—tender it one of the most desirable sites in the Union." Such conditions fostered the silk industry as well as other textile manufactures and machine and locomotive shops. By 1875 there were thirty-two silk manufacturing companies and five dyeing establishments in the city, employing a total of nearly eight thousand people. In John W. Barber and Henry Howe, *Historical Collections of the State of New Jersey . . .* (New Haven, Conn., 1868), 407.

John Ryle, 1882. The father of the Paterson silk industry, Ryle is shown here in his maturity. A silk weaver from Macclesfield in the English Midlands, Ryle immigrated to Northampton, Massachusetts, where he worked for silk manufacturer George W. Murray. In L. R. Trumbull, *A History of Industrial Paterson* (Paterson, N.J., 1882), facing 171.

Plate 2

John Ryle's letterhead. When George W. Murray purchased the small Paterson silk venture of Christopher Colt, Jr., in 1839, John Ryle was put in charge and moved to Paterson. In 1843 Ryle became Murray's partner and then in 1846 bought out Murray's portion of the business, which was located in the Gun Mill pictured in his letterhead. Ryle's Paterson enterprise is an early example of the ways in which Paterson's developing silk industry drew on the flow of ideas, technology, and skilled workers from the textile centers of Europe. After experimenting with silk weaving and finding it unprofitable, Ryle settled into the production of tram (warp thread), and organzine (weft thread), spool silks, and trimmings. [*Ryle Family Papers*]

Murray Mill. In the 1850s John Ryle built his first mill on Ward and Mill streets. When that structure burned in 1869, he built a new mill of a more modern design. Pictured here, it was a one-storey brick building with roof skylights of northern exposure, brick partitions, and flagstone floors. Photograph by Reid Photos, Paterson. [*Ryle Family Papers*]

Plate 3

Catholina Lambert and partners, 1885. Among the early companies to prosper after the Civil War and the establishment of protective tariffs was Dexter, Lambert, and Company, organized in Boston in 1855. It relocated its operations to Paterson in 1867 under the direction of Catholina Lambert, a Yorkshire immigrant. In 1885 the firm included Lambert (*seated*) and (*left to right*) William Suydam, his son-in-law; Walter Lambert, his son; Henry Wilson; and Charles Sterret, a former partner of Sterret, Ryle and Murphy. [*Passaic County Historical Society*]

Plate 4

Handkerchiefs

TWILLS
and
JACQUARDS.

Dress Silks.
"BELLEMONTE" BRAND.
BLACK & COLORED GROS
GRAIN SILKS; BLACK and
COLORED BROCADE
SILKS; SURAHS, BLACK and
and RHADAMES, SERGES

Millinery Goods.
NOVELTIES IN
PIECE SILKS,
GAUZES AND
GAUZE EFFECTS.

RIBBONS.

"DOUBLE WARP" GROS
GRAIN.

"L" SATIN AND GROS
GRAIN.

Extra Quality
DOUBLE WARP
D.L.&Co.
GROS GRAIN

SATIN FAILLE
SUPERIOR QUALITY

OFFICE and SALESROOMS 33 & 35 Greene St., cor. Grand, New York.
FACTORIES: PATERSON, N. J., AND HAWLEY AND HONESDALE, PA

Dexter, Lambert, and Company advertisement, 1893. This advertisement reflects the importance placed by Lambert on his corporate image. His elaborate Dexter mill built in 1879 on Straight Street, Paterson, was of his own design and featured a clock tower and crenelation. Lambert was a pioneer in the movement of Paterson throwing (thread-making) establishments to northeastern Pennsylvania, when he built a mill in Hawley in 1880 and another in Honesdale in 1887. Lambert was an avid art collector and built an elaborate home on Garret Mountain in 1893 to house his collection. In *American Silk Journal* 12 (October 1893):xviii.

Plate 5

y

Pelgram and Meyer Mills, 1882. One of the early silk companies to thrive in
Paterson was the firm of Pelgram and Meyer, organized in 1873 as a ribbon
manufacturer. The company soon expanded into broad-silk and Jacquard weaving,
throwing (thread-making), and dyeing. By 1881 the firm had expanded its throwing
operation annexes to Boonton and employed a total of 1,200 people. In L. R.
Trumbull, *Industrial Paterson,* facing 203.

Plate 6

Seal of the Silk Association of America, 1899. The Silk Association of America, founded around 1872, was comprised of the owners and officers of the nation's leading silk firms. This group of influential industrialists gathered in New York for meetings and social events. For decades Paterson businessmen were leaders in this organization, which sought to lessen harmful competition between manufacturers and to secure federal protective tariffs. Printed on silk. [*Passaic County Historical Society*]

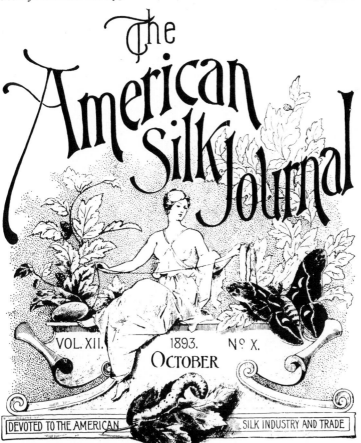

Cover of the *American Silk Journal*, October 1893 Several silk-trade publications covered the news of the domestic and foreign industries. Such journals contained advertising pertinent to the industry and provided an important communication link between manufacturers.

Plate 7

Office of the Columbia Ribbon Company, 1906. The office of the silk mill was the place where decisions were made about product patterns and designs, where employees were hired or fired, and where shift assignments, payroll schedules, and production deadlines were established. Here manufacturers placed orders for raw silk, both through New York brokers and directly with suppliers abroad. The production of raw silk was never commercially successful in the United States; it was the only part of the silk operation not represented in the Paterson industry. Raw silk was imported from northern Italy, China, and Japan. Photograph by John Reid. [*Passaic County Historical Society*]

Plate 8

Claude Greppo, 1879. French immigrant from Lyons, Greppo opened his Paterson dyeing business in 1867–68. Soon to become one of the country's foremost dye-industry entrepreneurs, he was well-known for the quality of his "brilliant and permanent" black dyes. Greppo was responsible for bringing numbers of skilled French dyers to Paterson. By the 1880s Paterson had earned the sobriquet, the "Lyons of America," reflecting its role as the center of the American silk industry. In W. Woodford Clayton and William Nelson, *The History of Bergen and Passaic Counties* (Philadelphia, 1882), 527.

Weidmann dye works, 1882. Jacob Weidmann, a Swiss immigrant, opened his dyeing business in 1872. In 1876 he was awarded a medal for excellence in dyeing at the U. S. Centennial Exposition in Philadelphia. The architecture of Weidmann's dye houses, with their banks of clerestory windows, reflects the importance of natural light to the industry at the time. In L. R. Trumbull, *Industrial Paterson,* facing 250.

Plate 11

Interior of a dye house, ca. 1900. Dyeing was considered "men's work." It involved dipping skeins of silk threads hung from cross sticks into long troughs of dye and moving the sticks back and forth to insure even coloring. The exact formulas for various colors were trade secrets, carefully worked out in the company laboratory. After dyeing, the silk was washed and dried. [*Passaic County Historical Society*]

Plate 12

Master dyer in his Paterson laboratory, ca. 1900. Master dyers, many of whom came from Lyons, France, and from Como, Italy, created the chemical formulas for the constantly changing colors ordered to accommodate the New York fashion industry. The most difficult color to achieve was black, much in demand for formal wear and mourning attire. [*American Labor Museum*]

Plate 13

Horizontal warping shop, ca. 1920. This photograph of the interior of a warping shop shows large horizontal warping mills at the left and their creels of bobbins at the right. At the rear of the room is a winding frame for winding these bobbins. Warping involves winding the desired number of threads of the proper length onto the beam, or feed, of the loom. Traditionally, hand warping was "women's work." But when the highly innovative, power-driven horizontal warping mill was introduced in the 1880s, men were hired to operate it. Within a few years, however, manufacturers again employed some female warpers to avoid dealing with unionized men. Warpers were among the most highly skilled silk workers. [*American Labor Museum*]

Plate 14

Master dyer in his Paterson laboratory, ca. 1900. Master dyers, many of whom came from Lyons, France, and from Como, Italy, created the chemical formulas for the constantly changing colors ordered to accommodate the New York fashion industry. The most difficult color to achieve was black, much in demand for formal wear and mourning attire. [*American Labor Museum*]

Plate 13

Horizontal warping shop, ca. 1920. This photograph of the interior of a warping shop shows large horizontal warping mills at the left and their creels of bobbins at the right. At the rear of the room is a winding frame for winding these bobbins. Warping involves winding the desired number of threads of the proper length onto the beam, or feed, of the loom. Traditionally, hand warping was "women's work." But when the highly innovative, power-driven horizontal warping mill was introduced in the 1880s, men were hired to operate it. Within a few years, however, manufacturers again employed some female warpers to avoid dealing with unionized men. Warpers were among the most highly skilled silk workers. [*American Labor Museum*]

Plate 14

Machine twister, 1937. As the industry developed, technical advances permitted the gradual displacement of certain categories of skilled workers. The machine twister did the work in half the time of the human "twister," whose job was to connect by hand each thread of the new warp being put on a loom to the comparable thread of the old warp. Photograph by Lewis Hine. [*National Archives*]

Plate 15

Broad-silk weaving shop, 1920. After the Civil War, Paterson silk manufacturers who had previously produced thrown silk, began to develop broad-silk and ribbon weaving capabilities. British- and European-born entrepreneurs and highly skilled weavers and other silk artisans were responsible in large part for this development. Initially, skilled male weavers worked on hand looms. But the industry quickly mechanized in the 1870s and 1880s, and the craft of weaving was opened to women also. [*American Labor Museum*]

Plate 16

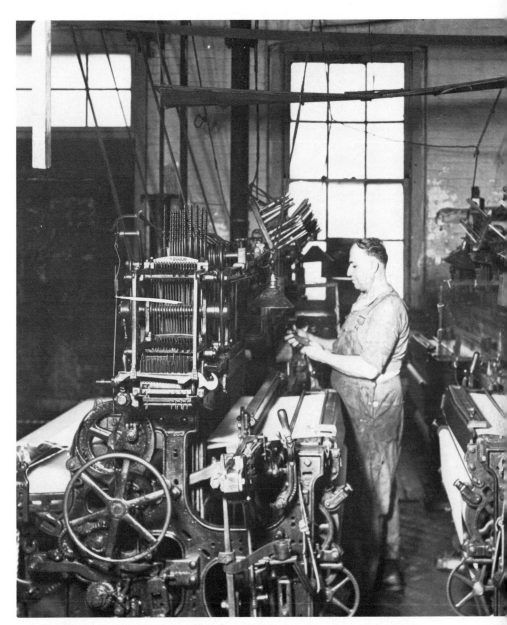

Broad-silk weaver, 1937. Technological improvements in loom design resulted in increased loom assignments for Paterson weavers. In 1883 weavers had to accept a two-loom system. By 1913 new advances made possible a four-loom assignment, and during the next two decades this system became widespread. Photograph by Lewis Hine. [*National Archives*]

Plate 17

Alexander Zukowski, ca. 1900. Many of the skilled weavers in the Paterson mills came from European textile centers. Zukowski immigrated from Lodz, Poland, in the late-nineteenth century. [*American Labor Museum*]

Plate 18

of the Paterson silk industry. Each weaver tended two looms, high-speed ribbon loom was introduced in the first years of the ng the entry of women into a sector of the labor force previously

Picking room of a silk mill, 1914. Picking was an important step in the production of silk fabrics. Before being sent for "finishing," bolts of woven cloth were carefully inspected for flaws or spots. This work was performed by skilled women, some of whom did picking at home as "outwork." Underwood and Underwood stereoscopic card. [*Paterson Museum*]

Plate 21

Jacquard loom, undated. Much of Paterson's reputation as the "Lyons of America" stemmed from its production of fancy and high-grade silks. Jacquard fabrics were an important part of this production. The Jacquard loom was developed around 1800 by a Lyonnaise silk weaver, Joseph Marie Jacquard. A special attachment above the loom allows for the weaving of minutely detailed patterns by means of pierced cards which regulate the raising of the individual warp threads. Initially, in Paterson, Jacquard looms and the skilled craftsmen to operate them were brought from Europe, especially from England and France. In 1873, James Jackson, an English immigrant and master-mechanic, began manufacturing Jacquard looms locally. [*Passaic County Historical Society*]

Plate 22

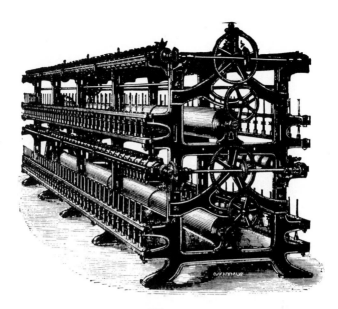

Silk-equipment advertisements, 1876, 1893. After the Civil War, Paterson machinists began to produce equipment which made silk manufacturing faster and more efficient. In 1876 the Danforth Locomotive and Machine Company exhibited various textile machines at the Philadelphia Centennial Exposition. Its three-tier spinning frames (*above*) attracted special attention and were to revolutionize the silk-throwing business. In L. P. Brockett, *The Silk Industry in America* (New York, 1876), viii. The Benjamin Eastwood Company, founded in 1872 and still in business today, was a major Paterson manufacturer of textile machinery. It first catered to the needs of the Paterson silk industry and then became a major supplier of textile machinery in its own right. By 1893 it was marketing and advertising a wide variety of machines including warpers, winders, and looms (*below*). In *American Silk Journal* 12 (October 1893): xxxi.

Plate 25

View of Paterson, looking north from Monument Heights, ca. 1895. In the late nineteenth century, much of Paterson's immigrant silk work force lived in ethnic neighborhoods within walking distance of the mills and dye houses. This photograph shows typical wood frame and brick houses surrounding several mills. The Valley of the Rocks Dye Works lies in the foreground, identified by its water tanks and tall chimney. To the right of the dye works, on the Passaic River, is the Addy Silk Mill, and in the center of the photograph, with its tall, round chimney, is the Pelgram and Meyer silk mill complex. When the first streetcar lines were completed between Paterson and outlying areas in the 1870s, those workers who were prosperous enough began moving from the crowded city to the new suburbs. [*Passaic County Historical Society*]

Plate 26

The Gallo family, Haledon, undated. The Gallo family and friends were in many ways typical of other immigrant silk-worker families. They emigrated from Biella, in the province of Piedmont, Italy, where skilled textile workers had been engaged in linen and wool weaving for many generations. Many members of the family were silk workers in Paterson and participated in anarchist and socialist organizations attractive to Paterson immigrants at this time. [*American Labor Museum*]

Plate 27

Worker gymnastic club, 1907. Social and recreational groups were a significant feature of silk-worker culture and contributed to cohesive social life. The women's division of the Arbeiter Turnverein, a German-American gymnastic club pictured here, was one of several such groups that flourished in Paterson in the late nineteenth and early twentieth centuries. The abundance of these societies and other ethnic organizations reflected the sophistication and political ideologies of the work force. [*American Labor Museum*]

Plate 28

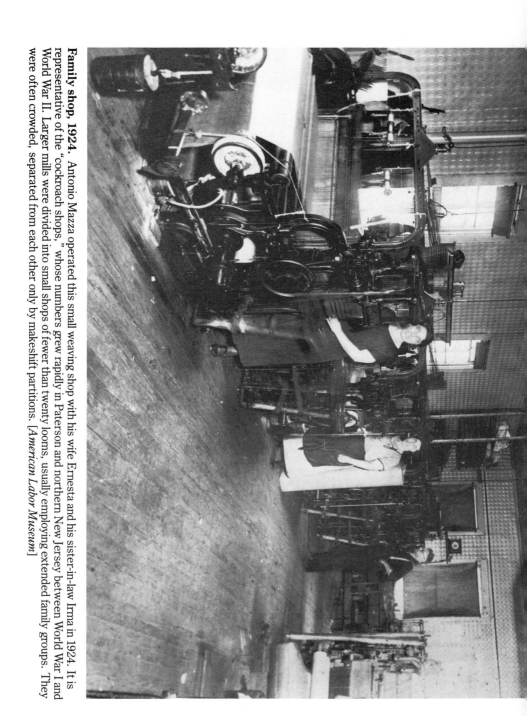

Family shop, 1924. Antonio Mazza operated this small weaving shop with his wife Ernesta and his sister-in-law Irma in 1924. It is representative of the "cockroach shops," whose numbers grew rapidly in Paterson and northern New Jersey between World War I and World War II. Larger mills were divided into small shops of fewer than twenty looms, usually employing extended family groups. They were often crowded, separated from each other only by makeshift partitions. [*American Labor Museum*]

Plate 29

IWW leaders, Haledon, 1913. In February 1913, leaders from the IWW were invited to Paterson to help organize the strike. Arturo M. Giovanitti, Elizabeth Gurley Flynn, and William D. Haywood are shown (*left to right*) standing by the Botto family's grape arbor. [*American Labor Museum*]

Strike rally, Haledon, 1913. Unlike earlier strikes during which police and city government were sympathetic to the workers, the 1913 strike was characterized by government suppression of the civil rights of the strikers and support of manufacturing interests. As a result of the denial of the strikers' right to public assembly in Paterson, huge Sunday meetings were held in nearby Haledon around the home of silk weaver Pietro Botto. Haledon's socialist mayor, William Brueckmann, guaranteed the safety of the workers, and the area around the Botto home afforded a natural amphitheater for large crowds to hear speakers. [*American Labor Museum*]

Plate 30

Paterson strikers, Cross and Ellison streets, undated. Major silk strikes in 1919, 1924, and 1926 in Paterson continued to raise the issues of the eight-hour day and uniform wages in the industry. [*Paterson Museum*]

Paterson silk dyers, Washington, D.C., 1933. The rights of workers to unionize and bargain collectively, established by the National Industrial Recovery Act, spurred the growth of unions throughout the Paterson silk industry. The Paterson CIO Dyers Local 1733 marched in Washington, D.C., in September 1933 to protest wage codes set under the act. [*American Labor Museum*]

Plate 31

Winding rayon bobbins, 1937. By the 1930s several Paterson silk manufacturers had begun production of rayon fabrics. Those manufacturers willing to turn to rayon production survived the displacement of silk by synthetic fibers. The Paterson silk industry suffered a severe setback during the Great Depression and continued to contract during the post–World War II years. Today nearly thirty textile mills remain in the Paterson area, six of which still manufacture silk products. Photograph by Lewis Hine. [*National Archives*]

Plate 32

disastrous in Lawrence and Fall River."[62] During the strike, the movement of plants from Paterson to Pennsylvania, and the opening of
annexes there, continued and accelerated.[63] This strategy worked.
Before 1913 the Paterson silk workers could succeed in their disagreements with the manufacturers. What proved decisive in the end,
was the ability of the manufacturers to keep their businesses going in
Pennsylvania. As Flynn admitted after the strike, "we were sort of
playing a game between how much they could get done in Pennsylvania balanced off with how great the demand for silk was and how close
they were to bankruptcy."[64] The winning moves, in the manufacturers' strategy, had been made before the strike ever began. The
manufacturers continually underestimated the silk workers during the
strike, suffering frequent setbacks as a result. But ironically, their
deeper respect for the militance of Paterson's silk workers had led
the manufacturers to become as independent as possible of their
employees in the years before the strike.

The victory itself was partial and temporary. In Paterson, the
future of the silk industry belonged to the small family shops. The
strike strengthened the determination of the large manufacturers to
flee from Paterson. After the strike, the *American Silk Journal*
noted prophetically, "the South is a safe haven for silk and other
textile manufacturers who want to get away from disturbing elements
which exist in the North."[65] In defeat, the Paterson strikers made
their presence felt; perhaps Pennsylvania was not far enough away.
Meanwhile, in Paterson itself, the remaining manufacturers, fearing
the "disturbing element," held back on a thorough introduction of the
four-loom system for another decade. In winning, the employers lost
also by failing to secure the increased loom assignments that had
triggered the strike. Neither side in the bitter 1913 strike would ever
be quite the same again.

NOTES

[1]On the manufacturers' exodus from Paterson prior to 1913, and on their struggle
for power in Paterson, see Steve Golin, "Bimson's Mistake: Or, How Paterson Police
Helped to Spread the 1913 Strike," *New Jersey History* 100 (Spring-Summer 1982):
66–67 and 72–73. On the silk workers' ability to learn from past defeats, and in
particular on their rejection of four looms, see ibid., 69, 73, 76–78.

[2]The New York *Daily Trade Record*, quoted in *Paterson Evening News*, March 13,
1913, 10.

[3]*Paterson Evening News*, April 23, 1913, 1, and April 25, 1913, 13; *New York Call*,
March 8, 1913, 1, and April 30, 1913, 1; James D. Osborne, "Industrialization and
the Politics of Disorder: Paterson Silk Workers, 1880–1913" (Ph.D. diss., University of Warwick, 1979), 104; *American Silk Journal* 32 (August 1913): 43.

[4]*Paterson Evening News*, March 22, 1913, 7.

[5]*New York Call*, April 15, 1913, 1. See also *New York Call*, May 3, 1913, 2.

[6]*Paterson Evening News*, May 8, 1913, 1; *New York Call*, May 2, 1913, 2. For similar rumors, see *New York Call*, March 26, 1913, 2, and April 8, 1913, 1; *Paterson Evening News*, May 21, 1913, 1.

[7]*New York Call* editorial, April 10, 1913, 6. Wilson Killingbeck wrote: "The strike has been used by the largest bosses as a means of eliminating this [small shop] element." *New York Call*, May 9, 1913, 6. See also Jacob Panken, in *New York Call*, July 26, 1913, 6; U.S. Commission on Industrial Relations, *Industrial Relations, Final Report*, Senate Executive Doc. no. 415, 64th Cong. 1st sess., 1916, 3:2526 (hereafter, *Report of CIR*); William D. Haywood, "The Rip in the Silk Industry," *International Socialist Review* 13 (May 1913): 785. "The strike undoubtedly would have ended much sooner had it not been for the desire of the richer manufacturers to see the smaller makers starved out. . . ." But Haywood understood that "the big capitalists have never tried to enter the silk trade. . . ."—as did Flynn, who complained after the strike about the lack of monopolization or concentration of the industry in Paterson. Elizabeth Gurley Flynn, "The Truth About the Paterson Strike," in *Rebel Voices: An IWW Anthology*, ed., Joyce L. Kornbluh (Ann Arbor, Mich., 1964), 216.

[8]"Who Has Paterson by the Throat?" IWW Papers, box 3, Tamiment Library, New York University; also in Chicago *Solidarity*, June 7, 1913, 1, and *New York Call*, June 19, 1913, 6, where it was signed by Justus Ebert. Patrick Quinlan, in an article in the *New York Call* in July, followed the same line and used the same research. *New York Call*, July 4, 1913, 2. Also reflecting the belief in an international capitalist conspiracy was the rumor that the strikers would "show jap bosses in IWW pageant," *New York Call*, June 5, 1913, 1.

[9]"Who Has Paterson by the Throat?" Killingbeck wrote, "Paterson is suffering from the growing pains of capitalism. It is the old battle being fought out, which has been settled in most other large industries." Killingbeck assumed, like most Socialists, that the victory of the big manufacturers over the smaller ones was inevitable. *New York Call*, May 9, 1913, 6.

[10]*Paterson Evening News*, March 14, 1913, 15; James Chittick, *Silk Manufacturing and Its Problems* (New York, 1913), 191. On the earlier difficulties of the manufacturers in winning acceptance, see Herbert G. Gutman, "Class, Status and Community Power in Nineteenth-Century American Industrial Cities: Paterson, New Jersey: A Case Study," *Work, Culture and Society in Industrializing America* (New York, 1976), 256–58.

[11]Richard D. Margrave, "The Emigration of Silk Workers from England to the United States of America in the Nineteenth Century" (Ph.D. diss., University of London, 1981), 166–68, 228–29, 340, 346, 349; William Carlos Williams, *Paterson* (New York, 1963), 122; Edward M. Graf, *Catholina Lambert: A Biographical Sketch* (Passaic County Historical Society), 1970, no. 2; Morris W. Garber, "The Silk Industry of Paterson, New Jersey, 1840–1913: Technology and the Origins, Development, and Changes in an Industry" (Ph.D. diss., Rutgers University, 1968), 216.

[12]James E. Wood, "History of Labor in the Broad-Silk Industry of Paterson, New Jersey, 1872–1940" (Ph.D. diss., University of California, 1941), 150.

[13]Ramsay Peugnet, "Six Month's Review of Trade," *American Silk Journal* 32 (October 1913):43. Peugnet was secretary of the Silk Association of America.

[14]John Fitch, "The IWW, An Outlaw Organization," *Survey* 30 (June 7, 1913): 361.Similarly, Moses Strauss complained about the IWW when testifying in 1914: "The IWW I don't consider an American organization." *Report of CIR*, 3:2492. "Their preamble says that they have nothing in common with the capitalists, and I

suppose that means the people who own the mills," but Strauss admitted that he was opposed to the Socialist Labor Party union and to the AFL as well. Ibid., 2491.

[15]Garber, "The Silk Industry," 218–19. These figures do not include the dye houses. As 1913 began, there were a total of 293 silk mills in Paterson and 473 in Pennsylvania. In 1912, Paterson had lost seven mills and Pennsylvania had gained fifty-three. *American Silk Journal* 32 (February 1913): 70.

[16]Killingbeck, in *New York Call*, May 9, 1913, 1. On the small-mill preference for plain work, see W. L. Kinkead, letter to the editor, *Survey* 30 (May 31, 1913): 315.

[17]For example, when James Mitchell of Ketterman and Mitchell Company was killed in an automobile accident in New York state on May 4, 1913, "as a mark of respect to Mr. Mitchell the operatives at the Ketterman and Mitchell Co., who were out on strike, attended the funeral in a body." *American Silk Journal* 32 (June 1913): 69. In another case, Joseph Bamford's method of holding back half the pay of the teenage girls who wove in his mill was offensive to many of the manufacturers. After Elizabeth Gurley Flynn publicized Bamford's practice as constituting contract slavery, some manufacturers wanted to expel him from the manufacturers' association. *Paterson Evening News*, April 9, 1913, 1.

[18]On the character of the manufacturers, see Garber, "The Silk Industry," 221–25; Nancy Fogelson, "They Paved the Streets with Silk: Paterson, New Jersey, Silk Workers, 1913–1924," *New Jersey History* 97 (Autumn 1979): 139. To Chittick, an industry expert and consultant, "the unwanted jealousy and mistrust" between silk manufacturers prevented necessary cooperation, even when such cooperation would have been in their common interest. Chittick, *Silk Manufacturing*, 229.

[19]F.G.R. Gordon, "A Labor Man's Story of the Paterson Strike," *National Civic Federation Review* 4 (December 1, 1913): 16; *New York Call*, March 15, 1913, 4; *Paterson Evening News*, April 25, 1913, 1; *American Silk Journal* 32 (October 1913): 60.

[20]Gregory Mason, "Industrial War in Paterson," *The Outlook* 104 (June 7, 1913): 285. See also, for example, *American Silk Journal* 32 (July 1913): 64.

[21]Philip Newman, "The First IWW Invasion of New Jersey," *Proceedings of the New Jersey Historical Society* 58 (October 1940): 279.

[22]*Report of CIR*, 3:2580. This view of the smaller manufacturers, expressed by John W. Ferguson, is supported by the experience of some strikers who returned to work in June 1913, at Berwin Company, a small concern, and found that their employer would not keep his promises. Chicago *Solidarity*, June 21, 1913, 1.

[23]*Paterson Evening News*, March 19, 1913, 12; *New York Call*, May 17, 1913, 2, and May 20, 1913, 2. The pickets were released, partly on the basis of Price's testimony. See *New York Call*, June 26, 1913, 1. For the effect of the strikers' no individual settlement policy on the manufacturers, see Philip S. Foner, *History of the Labor Movement in the United States* (New York, 1965), vol. 4, *The Industrial Workers of the World, 1905–1917*, 369. Doherty himself offered to let his employees run the mill, if they guaranteed him a 5 percent profit, but he was turned down. William D. Haywood, *Bill Haywood's Book: The Autobiography of William D. Haywood* (New York, 1929), 268.

[24]*Paterson Evening News*, March 6, 1913, 12.

[25]Graf, *Catholina Lambert*; Garber, "The Silk Industry," 216. Lambert declared bankruptcy in 1914 and sold the paintings at auction in 1916.

[26]James Weinstein, *The Corporate Ideal in the Liberal State, 1910–1918* (Boston, 1968), 4. At its May 1913 convention in Detroit, the NAM, in an addition to its original declaration of principles, called on all American citizens to rally against the IWW. *New York Call*, May 23, 1913, 3. For an application to Paterson of the Civic Federation/NAM distinction between firms, see *New York Call*, April 10, 1913, 6: "A

petty silk-mill proprietor in Paterson can easily be put out of business by a long strike, where a Steel Trust or Beef Trust could survive indefinitely. Hence the attitude of the Steel Trust magnate and the petty silk-mill proprietor toward organized labor will be essentially different in form. One will join the Civic Federation, while the other will enroll in the forlorn hope of the Manufacturers' Association." The *New York Call*, however, never quite admitted that all Paterson silk manufacturers were petty proprietors, by National Civic Federation standards. In Paterson, John W. Ferguson took the position that workers subjected to the "more conservative" unions would prove more productive than nonunion workers, a strictly "economic position" which he associated correctly with large corporations. Ferguson, an engineering and building contractor, was not speaking here for the silk manufacturers. *Report of CIR*, 3:2580.

[27]Haywood, "The Rip in the Silk Industry," 785. Fixing prices, however, would not have been as simple as Haywood made it sound, due to uncontrollable fluctuations in demand for silk, which were tied to changes in fashion. On the extreme competitiveness of the silk industry, see B. Edmund David, "The Silk Trade Conditions," *American Silk Journal* 32 (May 1913): 63.

[28]*New York Call*, July 18, 1913, 1. In a federal study, done a few years before the strike, only 8.4 percent of New Jersey's silk manufacturers approved of labor organizations in any form, though many had lived with conservative unions of loom fixers and warpers for years. *Federal Report on Woman and Child Wage Earners* (Washington, D.C., 1911), vol. 4, *Silk*, 325.

[29]Albert H. Heusser, ed., *The History of the Silk Dyeing Industry in the United States* (Paterson, N.J., 1927), 208–22. Griggs remained after 1909 as an officer of the reorganized corporation.

[30]Ibid., 257, 259. The founder of the company, Charles Auger, had been born in France. He started his own dyeing plant in Paterson in 1885, later adding a branch in Williamsport, Pennsylvania.

[31]*Paterson Morning Call*, June 24, 1902, quoted in Wood, "History of Labor," 181.

[32]*Report of CIR*, 3:2562. Captain McBride had to keep reminding his men that the special detectives also had rights. There were at least one hundred O'Brien men in Paterson during the strike at any one time, including some employed by other manufacturers. Doherty estimated in June that $100,000.00 had been spent on special detectives. *New York Call*, June 11, 1913, 6.

[33]*Paterson Evening News*, April 21, 1913, 10. For details of the shooting, see also *New York Call*, April 21, 1913, 1; James D. Osborne, "Paterson: Immigrant Strikers and the War of 1913," in *At the Point of Production: The Local History of the IWW*, ed., Joseph R. Conlin (Westport, Conn., 1981), 65–66. According to Alexander Scott, Modestino, though not a silk worker, often invited several of his fellow Italians who were picketing Weidmann's to have coffee or a little lunch. *Report of CIR*, 3:2525.

[34]Irma Lombardi, interviewed in *The Wobblies*, a film directed by Stewart Bird and Deborah Shaffer, 16 mm, 89 min., 1980. Distributed by First Run Features, New York. *Paterson Evening News*, April 18, 1913, 1. To the strikers, the Weidmann Silk Dyeing Company and the National Silk Dyeing Company were the enemy, not hesitating to use the immense financial and political power they held. The strikers blamed the large proprietors not only for much of the violence but also for blocking a settlement. From the second week of the strike, stories circulated about the readiness of the small dyeing firms to settle. In the 1902 strike, the dyers' helpers had permitted smaller firms to reopen, only to find them secretly doing work for the bigger plants. In 1913 the dyers' helpers, like the weavers, rejected the idea of separate deals with the smaller employers. Meanwhile the big dye works showed no

interest in negotiating and were popularly credited with threatening to ruin the silk of the smaller silk manufacturers if they tried to grant the weavers' demands. But the threat, if real, was unnecessary. To block a settlement all that the larger manufacturers had to do was to refuse to trade with their men. They occupied the same decisive position in the manufacturers' camp as the dyers' helpers did in the strikers' camp, and for the same reason: Silk could not be woven into ribbon and dress goods unless it had first been dyed. See Wood, "History of Labor," 180; *Paterson Evening News*, May 14, 1913, 1, and May 31, 1913, 1; Chicago *Solidarity*, March 8, 1913, 4, and May 31, 1913, 4.

[35]*Paterson Evening News*, April 18, 1913, 11; *New York Call*, April 19, 1913, 1. In jail before he was released, Cutherton got privileged treatment, according to Alexander Scott, *Report of CIR*, 3:2528. The leader of the special detectives, Edward Dyer, was present at the shooting, and was arrested with Cutherton and also never indicted. Dyer was a former Newark policeman who had been fired for excessive drinking. See the testimony of Andrew J. McBride, ibid., 3:2567, though McBride was unsure of Dyer's name. Some witnesses claimed to have seen Cutherton and another special detective emerge from a bar, apparently intoxicated, just before the shooting. Frederick Sumner Boyd, "The General Strike in the Silk Industry," in *The Pageant of the Paterson Strike*, ed., Brooks McNamara (New York, 1913), 5. Strikers had previously complained to Recorder James Carroll about violence by the O'Brien men, but the authorities did nothing, which encouraged the special detectives. See *New York Call*, April 18, 1913, 1.

[36]Quoted by Henry Marelli, *Report of CIR*, 3:2537. Marelli had written Minturn's words down at the time, after the third grand jury in a row failed to indict Cutherton.

[37]P. F. Gill and R. S. Brennan, quoted by Osborne, "Industrialization and the Politics of Disorder," 310. On the relationship between the mill owners and the police, see ibid., 269, 286; *Report of CIR*, 3: 2524; *New York Call*, May 27, 1913, 1.

[38]*Report of CIR*, 3:2463. In 1911, as a lawyer, Carroll had defended the management of a Paterson movie theater for charging blacks $.25, instead of the usual $.05. Michael B. Ebner, "Mrs. Miller and 'The Paterson Show,' A 1911 Defeat for Racial Discrimination," *New Jersey History* 86 (Summer 1968): 88–92. In 1913, as a judge, Carroll had no difficulty in understanding management's point of view against immigrant workers and the IWW. On Carroll's appointment, see Osborne, "Industrialization and the Politics of Disorder," 310–11.

[39]*Paterson Evening News*, April 1, 1913, 10–11: "We want him to call off the police if he is sincere and let him notify Chief Bimson that we are going to have free speech and free assembly." See also *New York Call*, March 29, 1913, 1. On Mayor McBride, see Richard A. Noble, "The Relation of the Middle Classes and Local Government of Paterson, New Jersey, to the Labor Movement in the Paterson Silk Industry, 1872–1913 (senior thesis, Princeton University, 1973), 84–85. On the "reform" of 1907, and the new direction of the police, see James D. Osborne, "Italian Immigrants and the Working Class in Paterson: The Strike of 1913 in Ethnic Perspective," in *New Jersey's Ethnic Heritage*, ed., Paul A. Stellhorn (Trenton, N.J., 1978), 19, 28–29.

[40]*New York Call*, July 30, 1913, 1. The Haledon manufacturer's name was Edward Spennymore. In Haledon, in March, "the anxious bosses of the Cliffside Mills hastily lined up their ten special 'guards'. . . ." The Haledon manufacturers were anxious because Breuckmann gave them no help in intimidating the pickets. *New York Call*, March 10, 1913, 1.

[41]Quoted by Osborne, "Industrialization and the Politics of Disorder," 312.

[42]For more details, see Steve Golin, "'Deadlock': The 1913 Paterson Strike as a Way of Life," *Labor in New Jersey History: Proceedings of the Fifteenth Annual New*

Jersey History Symposium, forthcoming, New Jersey Historical Commission.

[43]*Report of CIR*, 3:2494, 2497, 2512–14; on Miller generally, see ibid., 3:2494–2519. Although one of efficiency pioneer Frederick W. Taylor's associates, H. L. Gantt, was employed by a textile mill in the nearby city of Passaic from 1905 to 1908, the Paterson silk manufacturers and employing dyers remained uninterested in Taylorism. See Daniel Nelson, *Managers and Workers: Origins of the New Factory System in the United States, 1880–1920* (Madison, Wisc., 1975), 71. A 1911 article by James Chittick that praised the work of Taylor, Gantt, and others and called for the application of their time-motion studies to silk met with no response. The article was reprinted in Chittick, *Silk Manufacturing*, 411–14. On Weidmann's offer of the frankfurters, see *New York Call*, February 26, 1913.

[44]*Newark Star*, quoted by Alexander Scott, "What the Reds Are Doing in Paterson," *International Socialist Review* 13 (June 1913): 855, and by Chicago *Solidarity*, March 29, 1913, 1. On flag day, see Chicago *Solidarity*, July 19, 1913, 3; *New York Call*, March 18, 1913, 1. On McKees Rocks, see John W. Ingham, "A Strike in the Progressive Era: McKee Rocks, 1909," *Pennsylvania Magazine of History and Biography* 90 (July 1966): 371. A parade for "God and Country" was successful at Lawrence after the strike, during the general strike agitation. For example, see Elizabeth Gurley Flynn, *The Rebel Girl: An Autobiography* (New York, 1973), 151.

[45]*Paterson Evening News*, March 17, 1913, 9. For a similar vision of America, see Arturo Giovannitti's speech a few weeks later, in *Paterson Evening News*, April 3, 1913, 9.

[46]Haywood, "The Rip in the Silk Industry," 786. This incident probably took place at the Monday, March 17, meeting at Turn Hall.

[47]*New York Call*, March 25, 1913, 3.

[48]*New York Call*, March 25, 1913, 3; Wilson Killingbeck, "From Paterson to Hazleton," *New York Call*, March 29, 1913, 6; William Morris Feigenbaum, "Paterson and Lawrence—Some Inside Facts," *New York Call*, March 3, 1913, 1. On Golden in Lawrence, see Meredith Tax, *The Rising of the Women: Feminist Solidarity and Class Conflict, 1880–1917* (New York, 1980), 265–66; Weinstein, *Corporate Ideal*, 14.

[49]*American Silk Journal* 32 (May 1913): 31.

[50]Chicago *Solidarity*, December 23, 1911, 1, 4.

[51]Wood, "History of Labor," 222; Chicago *Solidarity*, December 23, 1911, 4.

[52]See the testimony of James Starr and Thomas Morgan, *Report of CIR*, 3:2612–13, 2422–23, 2430.

[53]E. B. White, quoted by Killingbeck, "The Paterson Strike Breakers," *New York Call*, May 7, 1913, 1.

[54]*Paterson Evening News*, April 19, 1913, 4.

[55]Chicago *Solidarity*, May 3, 1913, 1. Evald Koettgen wrote the article.

[56]*New York Call*, April 22, 1913, 1. James Mathews was the chairman.

[57]*Paterson Evening News*, April 19, 1913, 1. Adolph Lessig testified, "We had advised the people to keep away, but they had insisted they were going to hear . . . ." *Report of CIR*, 3:2467.

[58]*New York Call*, April 22, 1913, 4. See also the accounts of the Armory meeting in Chicago *Solidarity*, May 3, 1913, 4; Scott, "What the Reds are Doing," 855–56; William D. Haywood, "On the Paterson Picket Line," *International Socialist Review* 13, 12 (June 1913): 849–50; Boyd, "The General Strike," 7–8; Flynn, *The Rebel Girl*, 167. Some of these accounts put the number who were allowed back in by the police much lower. For the AFL version, which grants the "successful attempt for an

hour and thirty minutes" to prevent the meeting from starting, see Gordon, "A Labor Man's Story," 16.

[59] *New York Call*, May 9, 1913, 2.

[60] *American Silk Journal* 32 (April 1913): 24.

[61] Ibid., 32 (May 1913): 63, and (July 1913): 47.

[62] Ibid., 32 (January 1913): 57.

[63] Ibid., 32 (June 1913): 66, 68, 71, and (July 1913): 64.

[64] Flynn, "The Truth About the Paterson Strike," 216–17.

[65] *American Silk Journal* 32 (December 1913): 54.

4

"Fantasy and Realism Combined": The Manufacture of Silk at Pelgram and Meyer, 1872-1928

■ PATRICIA C. O'DONNELL ■

THE MOST SURPRISING oversight in all the research on the textile industry in Paterson published to date is that historians have rarely considered the processes of silk manufacturing and have never discussed the end product. The making of plain and fancy broad silks and ribbons is, in fact, a very specialized undertaking, one that lent its unique character to Paterson's image as the "Lyons of America." In this article, the examination of an important local company and its products will provide some insight into the world of manufacturers and workers, and suggest the potential for further research on silks as industrial artifacts.

PELGRAM AND MEYER

The collection of eight pattern books donated by Joseph Bamford to the Passaic County Historical Society at Lambert Castle, Paterson, New Jersey, makes possible the study of one firm, Pelgram and Meyer, to an extent that is unique in the silk industry.[1] Nevertheless, Pelgram and Meyer was hardly a typical company, for unlike many of its competitors, it operated for over fifty years and was one of a very few fully integrated firms, performing all the manufacturing processes within the confines of its own plants. Unlike others, who used commission houses to sell their goods, Pelgram and Meyer marketed its products directly, long occupying its own offices at Twenty-eighth Street and Fourth Avenue in Manhattan. When in 1919, there were 574 Paterson establishments engaged in throwing, dyeing, printing, and weaving silk, Pelgram and Meyer was one of only a half-dozen that could trace its roots back to the early days following the Civil War. [2]

The founding partners were both German immigrants. Charles Pelgram was born near Cologne in 1844, the son of a "physician of considerable eminence." Educated in Germany, France, and Britain, he also underwent "a course of technical instruction, which was added to by practical service in one or two of the large silk weaving establishments of his native land." At twenty-four, he emigrated to the United States, serving a year as bookkeeper for the Howe Sewing Machine Company in Bridgeport, Connecticut, before relocating to Paterson as a superintendent in the silk mills of William Strange and Company. [3] During this period, he developed the technical expertise necessary to monitor quality at all levels of production. After three years he commenced his own operations in Paterson's Industry Mill, having formed a partnership with the father and son, Isaias and Oscar Meyer. The elder Meyer became a special partner, the younger an active member of the firm. In 1839, Isaias Meyer had been an emigrant fresh from Landau on the Upper Rhine, aged twenty-seven. He proceeded to the South immediately, opened a dry goods store in Bayou Sara, Louisiana, adding branches, including one in New Orleans, as his business grew. When the city fell to the Union during 1862, Meyer gave up his retail operation and moved to the North, where he "entered into the real estate business and made money rapidly." It is probable that Meyer was the financial backer enabling his son to join Pelgram's manufacturing effort. [4]

After two years in their first location, the partners purchased the Heathcote Mill at the corner of Temple and Matlack streets on the north side of the Passaic River. This building was soon renovated and enlarged; by 1882, new structures were erected adjacent to this property, fronting on Temple and Lane streets. The firm imported all of its raw materials from European and Asian sources. Each raw-silk cocoon had been reeled to unravel its fine single strand, four hundred to six hundred yards long. These strands were twisted together to form silk yarns, which were remarkably strong and lightweight. Though all the steps preparatory to weaving—referred to in the trade as "throwing"—involved careful handling of precious raw materials, each task could be learned readily in a few weeks by inexperienced hands. The relocation of silk-throwing operations in 1880 to a separate plant at Boonton, sixteen miles west of Paterson, enabled the owners to take advantage of the labor force in a less competitive market, which was near convenient transportation. From Boonton, prepared yarn was shipped to Paterson.[5] Together with the Boonton mill, total flooring area had reached 162,000 square feet after the first ten years of the partnership's operation. Machinery at both sites included 310 power looms and 22,000 throwing spindles; the firm by 1882 employed twelve hundred workers with an annual payroll of $375,000.00.[6]

Over the next decade a series of problems plagued Pelgram and Meyer, but the firm survived. In 1884 the original partnership was dissolved, as Oscar Meyer withdrew and his father became an active member, with no change in style or operations. The following year, as the mill was installing its own fire-alarm box and erecting another addition, Pelgram and Meyer's superintendent departed to start in business on his own.[7] In 1886, amid a general boom in ribbon production, Pelgram and Meyer ordered the largest throwing frames ever commissioned in Paterson, each fifty-six feet long, and leased a building for its second annex in Harrisburg, Pennsylvania. The firm was well prepared for the dyers' strike early in 1887, having six to eight weeks' stock of dyed silk on hand, but not for the sudden death of Charles Pelgram from "heart trouble" and "enlargement of the liver."[8] Isaias Meyer, who became sole proprietor with very little experience in silk manufacturing, soon took into partnership two brothers, Herman and Alfred Schiffer of New York; the latter took charge of production. Within a year, the elder Meyer, then seventy-six, died of a heart attack.[9] While his family retained their interest in the firm, Meyer's new partners were charged with charting its course. As so often at Paterson and other sites where proprietary management was customary, the firm retained its original name, though a succession of new entrepreneurs succeeded one another as proprietors and partners.

The Schiffers managed well, although they had rough moments. The company's silk workers launched at least four strikes between 1890 and 1893 either for rate increases or against rate reductions; the final strike lasted nine weeks at the outset of the 1893 Panic, which ruined a dozen other Paterson silk firms. After those experiences, the Schiffers sought an alliance with other Paterson proprietors through the short-lived ribbon manufacturers association (1895–96), and persevered through the turn of the century.[10] In 1900, the heirs of Isaias Meyer sold their half-share in the firm to the Schiffers for $359,000.00, a sum that testifies to the continued prosperity of the enterprise.[11]

Within a few years, another set of new partners, Charles M. Weil and Joseph Whitehead, took over the company and continued under its widely recognized trade name, although neither a Pelgram nor a Meyer had been actively involved for nearly two decades. By 1913 the Paterson mill contained three hundred piece-goods looms and two hundred ribbon looms, operated with steam power. In addition to the plants at Boonton and Harrisburg, with well over 300,000 spindles, a third annex had been started at Hummelstown, Pennsylvania, primarily for throwing and for weaving simple broad silks.[12] With the increasing success of Pelgram and Meyer's products in the marketplace, the firm had continuously plowed back its profits into scattered silk mills for over thirty years, which guaranteed the Paterson plant adequate supplies of yarn for specialty weaving and enabled it to fill market demands for plain goods that could be woven by less-skilled workers.

SILK RIBBONS

The manufacturing processes requiring the greatest skill were still located in Paterson, where much of the work force had been trained in the silk mills of France, England, Germany, Italy, and Switzerland. From the beginning, Pelgram and Meyer had both a broad and a specialized focus, in plain and figured ribbons, as well as in plain and brocaded dress goods. Although velvets and plushes were introduced in 1881,[13] this product line may not have constituted a significant operation, for the tariffs on foreign-made plushes were soon reduced. The eight Pelgram and Meyer pattern books contain samples of original work from the firm's ribbon lines, dated from 1904 to 1928, the era of the Weil and Whitehead partnership. This invaluable source provides the textile historian with rare documentation on style and techniques of manufacture. The orders themselves, where indicated, date from 1917 to 1928; the dates of purchase of the binders, written on their outside covers, support the conclusion that this record-keeping system was begun in 1917, incorporating older designs with current work at a time when the consumption of domestic ribbons was at an all-time high.

Although today ribbons are generally regarded as plain goods, to be used for gift wrapping and other mundane purposes, ribbons had a broader visibility in the age of high ornamentation (1885–1925). Tens of millions of yards were needed annually for the decoration of hats, high-style dresses, peignoirs, and fine cloaks. Silk was the material of choice for the most ornate patterns, since the delicate fibers colored richly and could be woven into extremely intricate patterns.

Pelgram and Meyer's samples include examples of satin beauvoirs, tinsel and roman belts, taffeta warp print, gros grain, satin bayard, satin and taffeta millinery, taffeta moire, moire Jacquards, Jacquard warp prints, moire velour warp prints, and tapestry Jacquards—every style that the designer's imagination could conceive or the market demand. The ribbons themselves range from less than an inch to a foot in width, many of the latter produced on broad-silk looms.

From a 1911 taffeta warp print, one of the earliest documented ribbon series in this collection (patterns 30–33), one can appreciate the complexity and sophistication of an average fancy ribbon. Four and one-quarter inches wide, the wide taffeta or plain woven center is bordered on each edge by a narrow satin stripe. The floral design was printed directly on the warp threads before the ribbon was actually woven. To prepare this specialty warp, silk from one or two beams was fed through a gravure (or engraved-copper) printing press, with one plate cylinder for each of the eight colors, to print the pattern shades at intervals along the continuous threads. After weaving the printed warp with a yarn-dyed or uncolored weft, the design was equally apparent on both sides of the fabric. The finished ribbon was quite distinct from that which would have resulted from printing on an already-woven surface. Its soft, almost fuzzy character was far subtler than the sharp definition of pattern that fabric printing realized. Pelgram and Meyer also experimented with "duplex" printing (surface-printing both sides of an already-woven fabric to imitate the more difficult warp-printing process), but this was dropped after a few less than impressive attempts in 1912.

After printing, twenty-four ribbons of this pattern were woven together on the same loom in separate sections; narrow looms could accommodate from ten of the wide ribbons to a hundred or more of the narrower widths, but there was always at least one separate shuttle for each individual fabric width. The reed was finer than that used for broad goods; in fact, this sample is woven with over two hundred and fifty warp ends per inch, as compared with a hundred threads per inch today in very fine cotton-percale sheeting.

Pelgram and Meyer also produced particularly fine examples of work woven on the more complex Jacquard looms and many of the Lambert Castle ribbon samples are of this type. In the place of shafts, which lifted a predetermined series of warp threads to allow a filling shuttle to pass through the shed, Jacquard weaving allowed individual control of these warp threads. Punched cards carried the design, one card for each pick or pass through. Pattern 3731, a

"Jacquard Persian" (frontispiece) produced in 1922, is one example of a subtle but complex pattern that was woven on this machine. Notations on the cost of "Design" ($216.00) and "Cards" ($122.40) were made in pencil to the left of the specifications. The figure for the latter indicates that for this pattern, the 2,880 individual cards necessary for the design were punched by another company, probably a small concern which specialized in this work. It is most likely that Pelgram and Meyer purchased free-lance design work as well, in addition to that done by the company's own staff.

Pattern 3348, a "Satin Jacquard" (frontispiece) dated 1919, demonstrates the use of yarns other than silk in their narrow weaving. Appearing occasionally after 1908, cotton wefts were used in some warp-faced ribbons where the filling would not be visible. As early as 1917, metallics such as gold and silver tinsel were incorporated into fancy Jacquard designs. This particular pattern was available with or without the tinsel, and the full design was woven in 1,696 cards. Also designed and punched outside, the respective costs were noted as $63.75 and $40.80, reflecting the relative lack of complexity.

After weaving, all of the ribbons were "finished." Finishing involved the mechanical or chemical manipulation of the final product— to soften or stiffen, improve the "hand," or modify the final appearance by polishing, moireing, or embossing—to the requirements of the trade or contemporary fashion. Pattern 3076 (frontispiece), for example, a "moire velour warp print," dated 1917, had a distinct rib which, when passed through large press cylinders (and sometimes superimposed on another ribbon of the same pattern), would show the distinct "watered" or moire appearance so typical of this work.

END OF AN ERA

In 1928, Weil and Whitehead dissolved their partnership and liquidated the business.[14] According to oral tradition, the owners "saw the handwriting on the wall" and managed to find jobs for many of their senior employees.[15] Until further documentation is found, it can be assumed that this was the result of one or many of a number of conditions prevalent in the industry at that time. There is evidence that the growing use of rayon, changes in production technology, and the fickleness of contemporary fashion may have put pressure on Pelgram and Meyer. The high fixed costs for an integrated mill with multiple sites made the firm less competitive in volatile markets. Contracting specific jobs to other firms like the National Silk Design

Company and the "W.W.L. Co."[16] was attempted after 1922, but one can assume that this course met with limited success. The growth in the 1920s of family shops, small contract operations, and the gradual closing of all the integrated broad-silk mills signalled the end of the era in which Pelgram and Meyer had made its reputation and its fortune.

NOTES

[1]The Pelgram and Meyer pattern books are a very valuable resource. It is most difficult to prove American origin for many original samples currently in public collections, due to the textile manufacturers' long practice of collecting samples from other companies and countries for design and technical reference. The Joseph Bamford donation is, however, fully documented. (The author wishes to thank Catherine Keene, director of the Passaic County Historical Society, for her assistance.)

[2]*Monthly Labor Review* 29 (August 1929) 281–82; James Chittick, *Silk Manufacturing and Its Problems* (New York, 1913), 72.

[3]Charles Shriner, ed., *Paterson, New Jersey* (Paterson, N.J., 1890), 317; *American Silk Journal* 6 (1887):183.

[4]*City of Paterson, New Jersey* (Paterson, N.J., 1898), 20; L. R. Trumbull, *A History of Industrial Paterson* (Paterson, N.J., 1882), 203; *American Silk Journal* 7 (1888): 137.

[5]Trumbull, *Industrial Paterson*, 204.

[6]Ibid.

[7]*American Silk Journal* 4 (1885): 41, 83, 98.

[8]Ibid., 5 (1886): 145, 177 and 6 (1887): 30, 183.

[9]*City of Paterson, New Jersey*, 20; *American Silk Journal* 7 (1888): 137.

[10]*American Silk Journal* 9 (1890): 150, 186; 10 (1891): 231, 12 (1893): 180, 203; 15 (July 1896): 19.

[11]Ibid. 19 (June 1900): 38.

[12]*Official American Textile Directory: 1913* (Boston, 1913); *Griffith's Paterson Directory* (Paterson, N.J., 1897–1903); *Boyd's Paterson Directory* (Paterson, N.J., 1890–1904); *Paterson City Directory* (Paterson, N.J., 1905–09); *Paterson Directory* (Paterson, N.J., 1910–13). See also Pelgram and Meyer Company correspondence, October 1, 1925, June 15, and August 30, 1927, Ralph and Clara King Coll., file 74.10.5d, Paterson Museum, Paterson, N.J.

[13]Trumbull, *Industrial Paterson*, 205.

[14]*Davison's Silk Trade* (New York, 1927–29).

[15]Ralph and Clara King telephone interview with author, Ridgewood, N.J., October 2, 1984.

[16]Pelgram and Meyer pattern books, Passaic County Historical Society.

5

The Battle for Labor Supremacy in Paterson, 1916–22

■ DAVID J. GOLDBERG ■

THE LABOR MOVEMENT RE-
vived throughout the United States in 1916, as factories began to
turn out goods for the allied war effort. Workers in all parts of the
country demonstrated a new boldness and conducted more strikes in
1916 than in any year since 1900.[1] This unrest was quite evident in
Paterson, as well, as silk workers began to recover from the shock of
the 1913–14 defeats.[2] Though many Paterson firms had moved all or
part of their operations to Pennsylvania, silk remained the city's predominant industry, with almost 26,000 of the city's 41,816 wage
earners being employed in silk manufacturing or dyeing.[3] The largest
sector of the Paterson silk industry was broad silk, which employed
close to 15,000 of the city's silk workers. Well over half of these
employees were weavers, since throwing was concentrated in out-of-
town plants. Broad-silk mills varied widely in size. A large number
employed fewer than twenty persons and resembled a cottage industry, with operations often carried out in the owners' home. Over 150
mills employed from 20 to 100 workers and about 25 mills employed
100 to 400 workers. The only really large broad-silk mill was owned
by Henry Doherty, who employed six hundred workers at his main
plant.[4] These mills produced such goods as dresses, ties, umbrellas,
and taffetas. Many of the firms that produced the cheapest plain
goods had left the city, but Paterson continued to lead in the production of finer broad silk, which required Jacquard attachments.[5]

Five thousand other workers were employed in ribbon weaving. This sector provided a sharp contrast to broad silk, since most ribbon weavers were employed in mills with over one hundred employees. Significantly, of the six Paterson mills with over four hundred employees, five were devoted exclusively to the production of ribbons.[6]

Silk dyeing differed greatly from broad-silk and ribbon weaving. The vast majority of dye-works employees were unskilled dyers' helpers; their jobs required the submerging and the lifting of silk out of vats. This sector was dominated by two large firms; the Weidmann Silk Dyeing Company and the National Silk Dyeing Company. The Weidmann plant, built in 1895, was the single largest dye house in the United States and employed over eighteen hundred workers. The National's silk-dyeing works were a result of a 1912 merger of six separate firms and employed three thousand workers in its Paterson plants.[7]

Regardless of the sector in which they were employed, Paterson silk workers were determined to achieve the goals that had eluded them in 1913. The favorable economic climate during and after World War I enabled employees to score a series of significant victories, while the 1920–21 depression allowed employers to take back most of these gains. It was against this volatile backdrop that a wide variety of labor organizations competed for workers' loyalties in the period 1916–22.

THE NINE-HOUR DAY

The catalyst for the renewed labor activism was the demand for the nine-hour day. After the 1913 strike, Paterson silk manufacturers had pledged that they would grant shorter hours once workers had disavowed the IWW. In 1916, however, the ten-hour day (and the fifty-five-hour week) was still in effect, just as it had been since the early 1900s. Ideological divisions among Paterson's workers remained a major obstacle to the winning of the nine-hour day. In January 1916 four separate unions competed for workers' loyalties and spent as much time in denouncing each other as they did in formulating a positive program to combat the mill owners.

The oldest of these unions was the United Textile Workers (UTW), which had existed in Paterson since the national organization was founded in 1901. Skilled crafts formed the core of the UTW's membership, the two most important branches being the Horizontal Warpers Local and the Loomfixers and Twisters Local. These locals, which totaled approximately three hundred to four hundred members each had been led since 1903 by James Starr and Thomas Morgan respectively. The position of these crafts was strong enough that the union was able to enforce a closed shop, restrict the number of apprentices, and establish a union scale of wages. When disagreements developed with employers, Starr and Morgan usually came to the shop to aid in their settlement.[8]

Before 1916 the UTW made no effort to organize the five thousand dyers' helpers or other unskilled silk workers who labored in Paterson. But the union had made numerous efforts to reach broad-silk weavers and in 1908 had chartered a separate local for these workers. In fact, it was this branch that had signed the 1909 agreement permitting the four-loom system in the Doherty mill, a pact that had done much to discredit the UTW and to provide an opening for left-wing unionists.[9]

While the UTW's base was composed of English-speaking workers, left-wing unions had drawn their support from recent immigrants to Paterson. The Workers' International Industrial Union (WIIU), for instance, was largely composed of Jewish broad-silk weavers.[10] These weavers had migrated in massive numbers from the Polish city of Lodz after a series of lost strikes and pogroms in 1905–6.[11] In the process, they established Paterson as "the largest and best known Jewish textile city" in the United States.[12] Most of these Jewish silk workers had belonged to the General Jewish Workers Union (or the Bund as it was commonly called), which though socialist in orientation had also fought for recognition of Jewish national rights in the Russian Empire.[13] The vast majority also belonged to the Workmen's Circle, an American organization that aimed at maintaining Yiddish cultural and socialist traditions among Jewish workers. In Paterson, the Workmen's Circle printed its own books and sponsored its own schools, hospital, singing societies, and orchestra.[14] The WIIU appealed to many of these individuals because its emphasis on the necessity for both political and economic organizaation resembled the bundist program. Its leaders had split from the IWW in 1908 precisely because the latter deemphasized political action and after its founding the two organizations remained bitter rivals.[15]

The IWW had a far different base. Large numbers of its supporters were northern Italians who had resided in Paterson since the early 1890s. Many of these members had participated in the anarchist movement that had flourished in Paterson until the suppression of a violent dye-workers' strike in 1902.[16] The IWW had also won the support of many southern Italians (including Sicilians) who had emigrated to Paterson in large numbers after 1900. They responded to the IWW because leaders such as Bill Haywood, Carlo Tresca, and

Elizabeth Gurley Flynn captured so well their own hostility to the intense work regimen imposed by industrial capitalism. [17]

The strikes of 1912 and 1913 demonstrate the ideological differences that divided Jewish and Italian workers as well as the fierce rivalry that existed between the WIIU and the IWW. During the WIIU-led 1912 walkout, the leadership was determined to prevent any violence or provocation of authorities and went so far as to order a halt to picketing when three workers were arrested on the first day of the work stoppage. While emphasizing its revolutionary goals, the WIIU cautioned workers that no disorder would be tolerated and the strike was one of the most peaceful in Paterson's history. [18] By contrast, in 1913 the IWW made use of the same confrontational tactics that had been employed in McKees Rocks, Pennsylvania, in Lawrence, Massachusetts, and in other cities. Unlike the WIIU, the IWW refused to obey police rules and regulations that it considered to be unjust. Close to two thousand strikers were arrested because of their refusal to cease picketing and demonstrating. [19]

The WIIU expressed contempt for tactics of this sort and treated the IWW as if it were an atavistic organization. Tactics such as sabotage and violence allegedly advocated by the IWW were criticized as a "remnant of barbarism" that appealed to the baser instincts of workers. In keeping with this perspective, the WIIU frequently referred to Haywood as a "brute" and to the IWW as "the bummery." [20] The extent to which the different orientations of ethnic groups entered into these divisions was noted at the 1914 hearings of the U.S. Commission on Industrial Relations by a witness who commented that the 1912 walkout had been called a "Jew strike" and one in 1913 an "Italian strike." [21]

These divisions were important because both organizations remained active following the 1912–13 walkouts. The WIIU's Local 25 retained at least some of the support that had developed out of its early opposition to the four-loom system, and as late as 1918 claimed to have members in at least one hundred shops. [22] From 1912 to 1918 the Paterson local was entitled consistently to the most delegates at the WIIU conventions and two of the most prominent Paterson leaders, H. J. Rubenstein and Joseph Yannarelli, also sat on the WIIU General Executive Board. [23]

The IWW's Local 152 also continued its organizing efforts after 1913. Ironically, the IWW was more successful in establishing a permanent base in Paterson than in Lawrence, even though it won its strike in the latter city. The ability to maintain an organization in Paterson was largely due to the fact that it was impossible for employers to blacklist workers effectively from the over two hundred small silk mills and because many IWW members were skilled workers who were needed by employers. By way of contrast, the large Lawrence mills maintained a spy system that was especially effective because it was far easier to replace the largely unskilled workers in the woolen and worsted industry. [24]

The form of organization adopted by the IWW's Local 152 was based on the model advocated by the "easterners" (also known as the "industrialists") in the IWW, who favored combining elements of the AFL's business unionism with the revolutionary philosophy of the IWW. This meant establishing closed shops with well-defined work rules, the use of intermittent strikes, and the hiring of permanent organizers. The most extensive application of these tactics was on the Philadelphia waterfront, where the IWW exercised job control for a number of years. [25] Though never as powerful as on the docks, the IWW had some limited success with this same strategy in Paterson's silk industry.

Paterson represented a logical place to test the strategy of the "easterners," since it was not difficult to gain control of a small broad-silk mill that employed only twenty to thirty workers. Sporadic or intermittent strikes had long been used in Paterson and were especially effective during the busy season. As an IWW leader noted, the practice was usually to "stay in the mill and refuse to work for a couple of hours; send a committee down to see the firm; and if they cannot get any satisfaction, continue to work for a couple of days [sic] and repeat the same system the next day." [26] These tactics, on the other hand, could not be applied in the large dye works, where the IWW had no base of support after 1913.

Despite their ability to survive, the WIIU and IWW enrolled no more than a thousand of Paterson's twenty-five thousand silk and dye-house workers in 1916. [27] Both organizations continued to attract the more radical of Paterson's silk workers, but neither group had demonstrated an ability to expand beyond a narrow base. Both organizations had suffered grievously from the failure of the 1912–13 strikes and the majority of Paterson's mill workers still lacked a union to represent them on the job.

One last group had recently entered the Paterson labor scene. This was the Brotherhood of American Silk Workers (BASW), which had been founded in 1914 with the open support of the Paterson Manufacturers' Association. Its expressed purpose was to create harmony between capital and labor and to keep "outside agitators" from coming to Paterson. The preamble to its constitution spoke of the need to eliminate strikes and lockouts and to settle all disputes peacefully through arbitration, a goal that caused many union members to charge that the BASW was entirely a creation of the Paterson silk manufacturers. [28]

All of the above organizations participated in a February 1916 conference convened by the Passaic County Socialist Party. Though the party had lost a great deal of support since its near victory in the 1913 Paterson mayoral election, it still commanded respect among union members. It hoped that its status as a relatively neutral body would enable it to convince Paterson's labor unions to work jointly for shorter hours. [29] The manufacturers' initial response was to offer nine and one-half hours beginning May 1 and then nine hours on November 1. This timetable, though, was rejected by all of the groups connected with the campaign and plans were made for conducting a strike. The real initiative among workers, however, was actually taken by the hatband weavers who set their own strike date of March 27. These workers, who formed part of the ribbon sector, had been the first to call for nine hours. Their own actions left no doubt that a walkout was inevitable unless the nine-hour demand were granted. [30]

The hatband weavers forced the issue. When it became clear that much of the ribbon trade would be tied up by a strike, the ribbon manufacturers prevailed upon the broad-silk manufacturers to concede shorter hours. All mill owners feared another strike at a time when business was booming; as a result, the nine-hour day and fifty-hour week was instituted in the silk mills on April 3, 1916. In return, the UTW promised to conduct a nine-hour campaign in the runaway shop sections of Pennsylvania, and many workers pledged financial support for this effort. [31]

Though the *Paterson Evening News* reported that the participants in the conference of silk workers were "loath" to abandon the meetings, [32] the unity that marked the nine-hour campaign did not last the month of April. Soon after the nine-hour triumph, the WIIU charged that the BASW had followed a "peace-at-any-price" policy, one that it claimed had almost undermined the coalition's efforts. Soon the craft unions withdrew from the conferences altogether. The reopening of these divisions was further indicated by the announcement that the radical organizations planned a May Day jubilee while the UTW planned a massive Labor Day rally. [33] Even the radical groups were not able to maintain their organizational unity. The May Day committee was composed of the Socialist Party, WIIU, Socialist Zionists, Jewish National Workers' Alliance, and several branches of the Workmen's Circle—noticeably absent from the left-wing coalition was the IWW. The fact that the key demand of the May Day rally was the release from prison of Patrick Quinlan, a former IWW member who had joined the Socialist Party, may have hastened the split. [34]

RESURGENCE OF THE TEXTILE WORKERS

The organization that actually benefited the most from the nine-hour struggle was the UTW. Soon after its conclusion, new locals were chartered for ribbon and broad-silk weavers. In the wake of a 1918 strike by dyers' helpers, a new local was also chartered for this group of workers. By 1918 the UTW claimed to have enrolled most of the city's ribbon weavers and over fifteen hundred broad-silk weavers. [35] This dramatic change in its fortunes marked the first time since 1909–10 that a craft union had played such a leading role in Paterson.

A number of factors contributed to the renewed influence of the UTW: (1) the radical unions had not been able to recover from the lost strikes of 1912–13, while their own in-fighting alienated many workers who might otherwise have supported them; (2) the national UTW was capable of sending in experienced organizers who could offer workers a definite return for their dues; (3) craft unions appealed to many silk weavers whose status (unlike those in the cotton and wool trades) had not been reduced totally to that of machine tenders; and (4) the UTW's participation in the nine-hour conferences demonstrated that it was more willing than in the past to work with all segments of Paterson's labor movement. [36]

The UTW's position was also enhanced because many manufacturers believed that only strong unions belonging to the AFL could put an end to the shop strikes that constantly beset Paterson's silk industry. [37] The UTW was the ideal vehicle for bringing such order, as the union's constitution forbade strikes that were not authorized by the national office. To bolster its reputation as a "responsible" union, the Paterson UTW's newly reorganized Textile Council declared that it aimed to end the "small disturbances" that were constantly bedeviling manufacturers. [38] The fact that the mill owners conceded the nine-hour day without a prolonged fight vindicated the UTW's approach. It demonstrated that it was possible to make major gains without a long strike. This was to be of paramount importance in 1919 when the eight-hour issue was raised and the UTW and the left-wing unions offered alternative strategies for achieving it.

The UTW's position was further bolstered by the demise of the BASW in 1916. The entire history of this organization was shadowy, for it was never clear how much control the manufacturers exercised over it. What the BASW represented most clearly was an attempt to stabilize Paterson's labor relations through the use of arbitration. For this purpose, it was bound to fail as it was never able to remove the taint of the bosses' sponsorship. The manufacturers ultimately had more to gain by working with the UTW, since it was independent of the employers' control while sharing many of the same objectives as the BASW. By the end of 1918, peaceful negotiations between the manufacturers and the UTW appeared to present a solution to continuing labor turmoil in Paterson.

THE RIVAL EIGHT-HOUR ORGANIZATIONS

During World War I, Paterson's silk mills experienced little labor unrest. But the fight for control of Paterson's labor movement resumed in earnest at the end of the conflict. As in 1916 the issue of hours per day was the focus of the unions' organizing efforts. This time, however, the unions sought to achieve the eight-hour day in the silk mills. The initiative in the eight-hour campaign was taken by the WIIU, which convened a meeting of the radical labor organizations on November 8, 1918. This initial gathering established the Workers' Eight Hour Day Conference composed of the WIIU, IWW, Passaic County Socialist Labor Party, the Socialist Party, Paole Zion (a socialist, Zionist organization), three branches of the Workmen's Circle, and the Sons of Italy. For the past two years, the IWW had refused to participate in such meetings, but by November 1918 it had once again consented to work with other groups. [39] A separate organization, the Eight Hour Day Committee, was established by the UTW shortly afterwards. This group was set up in response to the UTW's decision to launch a national campaign for the eight-hour day on February 3, 1919. [40] In order to avoid any conflict with the UTW, the radical conference also set the first Monday in February as its strike date. Even though they were fighting for the same objective, the two groups did not cooperate on any level. Each group distributed its own literature, held its own meetings, and acted as if it was the only legitimate eight-hour organization.

Though the manufacturers rejected any idea of shortening hours, they agreed to discuss the hours issue with the UTW at a conference that was arranged by the Paterson Chamber of Commerce. This meeting, though, was upstaged by the UTW's announcement that it was now willing to accept the forty-seven-hour week—the union did not specify how the work week would be divided up under this proposal—and unlike the radicals did not demand forty-four hours. This decision was made by the UTW's Textile Council without consulting the membership and came soon after the publication of an open letter by the UTW's national president John Golden, stating that the UTW's

demand was for the forty-eight hour week.[41] This last change meant
that the strike began under the most bizarre circumstances, as rival
groups walked out for forty-seven and forty-four hours on February
3. Though both factions wore eight-hour buttons—one was colored
red, white, and blue and the other bright red. Even on the picket
lines, no attempt was made to bridge the gap between the hostile
groups, as separate lines were established by each organization.[42]

INTERVENTION BY THE WAR LABOR BOARD

Faced with a massive walkout, the manufacturers suggested that
the dispute be submitted to the War Labor Board (WLB), which was
still hearing cases in Washington. At first, the UTW rejected this idea
but relented on the condition that the WLB issue a temporary "short
hours" ruling prior to its final decision. The UTW made the proposal
amid signs that a rebellion was brewing in its ranks. The ever-militant
hatband weavers had just voted to endorse the forty-four-hour demand, and the UTW ribbon-weavers local had decided to send delegates to the radicals' forty-four-hour meetings though deferring any
endorsement of this demand.[43]

Both the mill owners and the UTW had their own reasons for
desiring to see the issue decided by the WLB. Since the board had
never granted less than the forty-eight-hour week, manufacturers
had no reason to fear that it would bestow forty-four (or even forty-
seven) hours on a permanent basis.[44] From the UTW's perspective,
the main goal was to move workers off the streets and back to the
mills, as left-wing unions had often been able to capitalize on mass
activity that accompanied strikes. In effect, the "short hours" strategy was a ploy that was designed to enlist governmental aid in order
to undercut the left-wing union movement in Paterson.

At the initial hearing, UTW representative James Starr noted that
the manufacturers and the UTW were now "playing fair together" and
that a favorable ruling was necessary "in order to kill off the element
that created so much trouble in 1913." Henry Tynan, one of the
manufacturers' representatives, concurred with this argument and
noted: "Having again returned to work, if this War Labor Board, then
within a week, two weeks, or three weeks comes out for a forty eight
hour week . . . these men and women will not again go out on strike
because there is this dictum from the Government establishing the
forty eight hours." Both sides stressed the need for the WLB to act
immediately. Starr feared that "radicals" within the UTW would "soon

get more people lined up with them" while the manufacturers' representatives predicted that if no agreement were reached by February 17, the dyers' helpers would join the seventeen thousand silk workers who were out on strike. [45] The only WLB member to object to this was Frederick Judson, who feared that the UTW and manufacturers were asking the WLB to engage in "a bit of camouflage." But other board members had no such reservations and a short hours ruling of forty-two and a half hours was handed down on February 13. [46] In Paterson the UTW called this decision "the greatest achievement in the history of Paterson silk strikes," even though nobody in the organization expected the final verdict to be forty-two and a half hours. [47]

From the very beginning of this conflict, the left-wing organizations had opposed the WLB's interference in the Paterson strike because they feared that it was a "trick" to "smuggle in the 47 hour week through the back door." [48] Despite their vehement objections, however, all attempts to prolong the strike proved to be futile. While the chief of police ordered the arrest of all those who picketed the mills, the crucial fact was that the loss of the 1913 strike had left workers with little taste for confrontations that could lead to mass arrests. By the end of the week, both the IWW and the WIIU instructed their members to return to work, since it appeared futile to remain out any longer. [49]

A serious split in the radicals' ranks further doomed all attempts to rally the unorganized silk workers. Soon after the strike began, the IWW succeeded in changing the basis of representation in the Eight Hour Conference so that shop organizations rather than Jewish and socialist groups would play the predominant role. This tactic had given the IWW the controlling hand during the first week of the strike. [50] In response to the IWW's actions, a committee of twenty Paterson workers, composed chiefly of WIIU members, traveled to New York in order to seek the support of the Amalgamated Clothing Workers of America (ACWA). [51] This union had just won a strike for the forty-four-hour week in the New York men's clothing industry—a triumph that represented the first significant postwar victory of American labor. It had a socialist ideology, a large Jewish membership, and did not belong to the AFL. All of these were elements that attracted many of Paterson's silk workers. More important, it was to expand its influence within the American labor movement, and the textile industry (which directly supplied material to the clothing industry) was a logical place to start. [52]

The ACWA immediately sent three organizers to Paterson. The IWW objected to this "interference," however, claiming that the

ACWA's involvement was a disguised attempt by the WIIU to regain control over the radical forces. [53] This opposition was to be expected since the IWW and the ACWA had long engaged in ideological disputes. Just as important, the Paterson police also rejected any interference by "outsiders" and forced the ACWA cadre to leave town. [54] Though it is unlikely that the ACWA could have stimulated mass opposition to the "short hours" ruling, these two events insured that silk workers would return to the mills on February 17, 1919.

At the actual WLB hearings, the labor representatives claimed to favor the forty-four-hour week and explained that they had made the forty-seven hour offer, at the last moment, only because of the "memories of the last strike." But the UTW's case rested almost entirely on the need to counteract the IWW who were usually referred to as the "Bolshevik element." According to Starr and Morgan, a favorable ruling from the WLB would put a "weapon" in the UTW's hands that could be used to drive this "pernicious element" from Paterson "once and for all." The manufacturers scoffed at using the threat of radicalism and argued instead that the fifty-hour week was needed on account of the danger posed by the Pennsylvania mills. According to their figures, Paterson mills produced broad silk at a cost of $.13 per yard, while the Pennsylvania cost was $.08 per yard. If Paterson's hours were reduced, this differential would only increase, and more manufacturers would choose to relocate. Talk of moving out of Paterson threatened the consensus that had brought both sides to Washington, as the UTW representatives were angry that the mill owners had raised issues that they thought would never arise. The air of amicability that characterized the beginning of the hearings had largely dissipated by the time they concluded. [55] Though the UTW and the manufacturers continued to cooperate with one another, this conflict foreshadowed the ultimate breakdown of the relationship which was to occur in the midst of the 1920–21 depression.

The final WLB decision was announced on April 9, 1919, when the WLB set the work week in the silk mills at forty-eight hours. The ruling specified that the forty-eight-hour week should remain in effect for the "duration of the war" with the proviso that either party could reopen the case at intervals of six months. [56] While the manufacturers expressed satisfaction with the edict, Starr, Morgan, and other UTW leaders were disappointed that silk workers had only been granted a two-hour reduction in the workweek. [57] On the other hand, the UTW leaders did not even contemplate taking action against the ruling because such a stance would have threatened the working relationship that had been developed with the manufacturers since 1916.

Though the left-wing unions had vowed to oppose any WLB ruling, they were incapable of mounting any opposition to it. By April the radical Eight Hour Conference had been disbanded and the rank and file showed no inclination to disobey the WLB's ruling on their own. The left's impotence was particularly striking, since the final decision confirmed their prediction as to the role that the WLB would play. The denouement vindicated the manufacturers' and the UTW's decision to take the case to the WLB, as the board proved to be the ideal instrument for defusing the Paterson situation. While the agency did much during its brief existence to frame a progressive labor code, by the spring of 1919 its members were intent on using its authority to restrain radical labor movements. It is doubtful that any locally arranged settlement could have gotten workers to accept the forty-eight-hour week as the WLB did in April 1919.

LOCAL OR NATIONAL UNIONISM

Paterson was only one of a number of textile cities that experienced labor unrest between February and April 1919—major battles also developed in West Hoboken and Passaic, New Jersey, and in Lawrence, Massachusetts. In all of these cities, the ACWA extended aid to workers who had no use for the UTW. Furthermore, at the ACWA's urging, textile workers from these centers and from Paterson met in New York on April 12–13, 1919, and founded a new organization, the Amalgamated Textile Workers of America (ATWA), which aimed to apply the ACWA's version of socialist industrial unionism to the textile industry. The ACWA's National Secretary Joseph Schlossberg played a key role at the union's initial convention and the new organization's preamble, constitution and newspaper were all modeled on the ACWA's. General Secretary A. J. Muste, a former minister, had impressed the ACWA leadership by his handling of the 1919 Lawrence strike; he was one of several college-educated persons who held leadership posts in the new union.[58]

The influence of the intellectuals in the new organization was demonstrated by the selection of Evan Thomas to head the Paterson local. Thomas, who was Norman Thomas's brother, had devoted most of his life to academic pursuits and had no previous experience in the labor movement. He had spent the last year of the war in prison as a conscientious objector and after his release had been championing the cause of political prisoners.[59] Along with Thomas, the ATWA also assigned Robert W. Dunn to Paterson. Though Dunn had written on labor matters, he had graduated recently from college and was inexperienced in the world of organized labor.[60]

On the other hand, the movement of most of Paterson's WIIU members into the ATWA's ranks placed many persons with years of experience at the union's disposal. In particular, the WIIU lost the bulk of its Jewish membership as well as the shops that they controlled. Likewise, the IWW reported the defection of "Jewish workers" from its organization.[61] The few Jewish members of the UTW also joined the new union.[62] According to both the IWW and WIIU, the Jewish branch of the Socialist Party, Paole Zion, and the Workmen's Circle were all encouraging their members to join the ATWA.[63] Most of these persons worked in broad silk, which meant that this sector served as the ATWA's base in Paterson.

The ATWA also gained some of the Socialist Party's most experienced cadre. Two of these persons, Frank Hubschmidt and William Derrick, had long been active in Socialist Party affairs and were frequent candidates for political office.[64] Fred Harwood, who served on the ATWA staff, had worked as an organizer for the UTW as well as for the Socialist Party.[65] Most of those who were recruited from Jewish and socialist organizations had actually been working together since 1916. Their fondest hope was that the ATWA would supplant the "little radical unions" and create a broad-based union. The ATWA's first organizing appeal in Paterson noted that "for over twenty five years, we have been divided against ourselves, disorganized, split up into factions and into impotent local unions" and that the time for "amalgamation" into one organization had finally arrived.[66] Over twelve hundred workers had signed the petition requesting the ATWA's aid—a further sign of the support that existed for a socialist industrial union on the ACWA model.[67]

The ATWA had a great opportunity in Paterson because practically all of the silk workers chafed under the restrictions imposed by the WLB. Much of their anger was directed at the UTW for being a party to the "short hours" maneuver. As in 1916 the first workers to take action were the five hundred hatband weavers who staged their own successful walkout for the forty-four-hour week in July 1919. These weavers, who were members of the UTW Ribbon Weavers Local 980, also won a pay increase and new work rules giving them the option of piece or day work when performing certain tasks.[68] These hatband weavers had long been known as an "independent lot."[69] Despite their small numbers, they had played an important role in the Paterson labor movement. They had been the forefront of the nine-hour agitation 1916 and in August 1918, and had conducted a successful one-week strike for a pay increase. They were proud of their separate identity and had only joined the ribbon weavers local in

1918. Many IWW members had participated in their organization; one IWW member, William Halbach, had chaired one of the shop committees during the forty-four-hour walkout.[70]

Their militancy was based on various factors. These workers were both the highest paid and the most skilled of all weavers in Paterson. Unlike other branches of the silk industry, this sector faced little outside competition. Their prior strikes had demonstrated their ability to win concessions from management, while the scarcity of skilled labor in 1919 further guaranteed that the walkout would be successful.[71] Threats by the UTW to take disciplinary action against them only spurred their movement as hatband weavers relished their reputation for independence.

The ease with which the hatband weavers won the forty-four-hour week forced the UTW to repudiate its support for the WLB settlement only three months after the forty-eight-hour ruling. The union announced that it intended to establish the shorter workweek for all silk workers on August 4. This just happened to be the date that the ATWA had set for its own forty-four-hour walkout, and the UTW's purpose was to undercut the ATWA's strike movement. However, the mill owners insisted that the WLB ruling forbade any alteration of its terms for at least six months from the date of the decision. John Golden agreed with this interpretation and he convinced (or forced) the Paterson UTW to go along with his view. Consequently, the manufacturers and the UTW jointly declared that the forty-four-hour week would begin on October 10, an agreement that the UTW hailed as further proof of its ability to win gains "without strife and struggle."[72]

Naturally, this new arrangement provoked an outcry from many segments of the Paterson labor movement. Ribbon weavers, especially, were outraged because of the "secret" manner in which this accord was negotiated and because the national UTW ordered Local 980 to expel the rebellious hatband weavers.[73] This intra-union conflict provided further impetus for the ATWA's own strike movement, and on August 4, between five thousand and ten thousand workers walked out of the shops. Strikers included members of the ATWA and the IWW, unorganized workers, as well as dissatisfied members of UTW locals 980 and 989, who were broad-silk weavers. From the perspective of many UTW members, this was a "grudge strike" against its own leadership as well as a movement for shorter hours.[74] Disgusted with the machinations of the UTW's officers, the rank and file seized the opportunity to express their dissatisfaction with the lack of democracy in the union.

For the next two weeks, workers staged a series of highly successful shop strikes. The first manufacturers to give in were the small broad-silk mill owners who could not afford to take a strike while they were backed up with orders. Other employers had no choice but to concede workers' demands, though they feared that this would only encourage further walkouts. By mid-August 1919, practically all broad-silk and ribbon shops had granted the eight-hour day and forty-four-hour week. [75] This achievement represented the culmination of a long struggle in Paterson and, more particularly, brought to a successful conclusion the eight-hour agitation that had been launched in December 1918.

The ATWA won many members by virtue of this walkout, and the UTW was left with little choice but to free itself of its commitment to the October 10 date. Using as an excuse the fact that one of the manufacturers who had signed the WLB accord had granted the forty-four-hour-week, the UTW on August 9 announced that the entire agreement had been abrogated and that UTW members were justified in now going out on strike. This last maneuver was necessary if the UTW was to have any hope of recouping its standing among Paterson silk workers. As it was, the UTW leadership was badly shaken by the ATWA's ability "to put over the forty four hour week." [76]

THE DECLINE OF THE ATWA

Despite this impressive beginning, the ATWA proved incapable of greatly expanding its base in Paterson. Though firm figures are not available, it probably enrolled more than two thousand workers, almost all of whom labored in the broad-silk sector. The ATWA's failure and the subsequent emergence of the Associated Silk Workers (ASW) is important because it reveals much about the orientation of Paterson silk workers as well as about the problems of building national unions in this era.

The ATWA's goal was to create a true industrial union and for this reason it made a determined effort to reach the five thousand dyers' helpers. These largely unorganized workers had walked out with the silk workers in August, and the ATWA immediately assumed leadership of their strike. Rather than asking for just forty-four hours, which the dye-house employees were scheduled to receive, in any case, on October 10, strikers demanded a wage increase. The slogan "44 and 25%" came to sum up the strike, and the dye-house employees emphasized their determination to stay out beyond October 10 in order to win this goal. [77]

By October, however, only a few of the smaller dye houses had granted the workers' demands as the Weidmann and the National silk-dyeing companies refused to make any concessions to the ATWA. The strike steadily lost strength so that when October 10 arrived, workers reluctantly voted to return to the tubs.[78] They had gained nothing by staying out and the ATWA had lost its one opportunity to recruit this group of workers. For various reasons, this effort ended in failure. The Weidmann and the National were large companies and far better positioned than the smaller dye houses to withstand a strike—this was especially true of the National, which operated branch plants outside of Paterson. Despite pledges of aid, the dye-house employees received little support from the other silk workers, which was not unusual, as only in 1913 had silk and dye-house workers actually fought together. Moreover, the pacifistic orientation of the strike leadership also hampered the walkout. Of all of the ATWA's intellectual cadre, Evan Thomas was the most committed to non-violent methods. The fact that he had served a sentence in military prison had only hardened his determination to show that his philosophy could be applied in the labor field, yet dye-house employees were used to conducting their battles in the streets. This had been true in 1902 and 1913, when considerable violence had been used against opponents of the strike.[79] The fact that the largely Italian and Polish work force lived and worked in the Riverside section had often enhanced their ability to intimidate scabs. In August and September 1919, dyers' helpers once again engaged in this type of activity as strike breakers were attacked, "loyal" workers' homes were stoned, and foremen were threatened. In the most serious incident, workers set upon scabs and battled police outside of the Weidmann Silk Dyeing Company.[80]

When faced with these incidents, Evan Thomas's policy was "to hold the men back from rioting."[81] On one occasion, he even refused to defend an Italian member of ATWA who had been charged with carrying a concealed weapon. Thomas read the individual out of the union, commenting that ATWA was "not in favor of such actions and did not care to have persons responsible for them as members."[82] Norman Thomas, who was active in the strike, claimed that the ATWA had shown workers "the folly of violent tactics and given outlet to their spirit by carefully organizing picketing. They have aroused the social sense," he continued, "and restrained the man who will 'fix heem' with a brick by showing him how he will not only hurt himself but the good name of his comrades."[83] Such attitudes were bound to alienate the militant dye-house workers.

Lastly, the ATWA's inability to recruit these workers was attributable to the union's lack of Italian cadre. One Italian organizer, Flavio Falatio, served on the local's staff but did not have any particular standing with the dye-house employees. The one individual who could have made a difference was Joseph Yannarelli, who had been a Detroit IWW/WIIU organizer since 1908. Yannarelli was later to be active in the 1924 strike and in 1933 spearheaded the successful organization of the Dyers' Union. In 1919 he remained loyal to the WIIU and did not join the movement of most of his comrades into ATWA.[84] Without his aid, ATWA was further limited in its ability to reach out to this group of workers.

Even in the broad-silk sector, the ATWA's membership had stagnated by January 1920 at around the 1,500–2,000 mark. In part, this was because the UTW Local 989 continued to receive concessions from management. This was most vividly demonstrated in January 1920, when forty-three UTW broad-silk shops received a 20 percent increase after a brief agitation. Some weavers even won increases of $.05–$.08 per yard, which the UTW claimed was the single largest increase ever granted in Paterson.[85] Far more important, though, was the fact that the ATWA's single greatest source of strength—its base among Jewish workers—also proved to be a weakness. This was because the silk boom of 1919–20 led to an enormous expansion of the tiny broad-silk mills, which came to be known as "cockroach shops." These shops had grown steadily in number during the war, so that in 1918 there were 385 broad-silk firms in Paterson, while in 1915 there had been 210. The increase, however, only foreshadowed the enormous expansion of the immediate postwar year, during which 170 new shops were founded, bringing the total number of Paterson's broad-silk firms in 1920 to 555.[86]

Almost all of these firms were Jewish-owned, and their establishment caused considerable conflict within the Jewish community. Most immediately affected were the various branches of the Workmen's Circle, to which most Jewish weavers belonged. One branch actually had to be "dissolved" because most of its members were "small bosses."[87] The controversy within the Workmen's Circle did not blossom fully until 1924, when the fact that some members who were employers kept their mills open during the strike became a subject for intense debate within the national organization.[88] By 1920, however, it was evident that many Jewish workers were attracted to the idea of opening their own small shops and were moving away from identification with Jewish working-class organizations.

The ATWA was concerned that it was losing potential members because the dream of business success was luring them away from the union. An article in its organ, the *New Textile Worker,* ridiculed those who consciously left the ranks of the working class in order to become "a Guggenheim" and who ended up exploiting their own families in sweat shops. [89] On a more personal level, the IWW head Adolph Lessig noted that one former "Wobbly," who had purchased a few looms, now refused to recognize him on the street. [90] Most significantly, the desire of many Jews to open their own shops restricted the ATWA's growth in the precise area where the union was strongest. This fact explains, in part, why as early as January 1920 the union had reached its maximum membership in Paterson.

THE RISE OF THE ASW

In the ribbon sector, the ATWA lost out to the ASW, which soon emerged as the key union in Paterson. The impetus for the establishment of the ASW was provided by the hatband weavers who had been expelled from the UTW for defying the WLB edict. These workers were joined by large numbers of ribbon weavers who had also been members of the UTW. A new organization was founded on August 5, 1919, when all of these disaffected UTW members met to write a constitution. [91]

There are a number of reasons why, contrary to the ATWA's expectations, [92] the ribbon weavers did not join its ranks. Foremost was the desire of these workers to form a purely local union that would be free of any outside control or influence. According to an early ASW pronouncement, "What we propose to do is organize a silk union right here in Paterson that will be independent of outside organizations, we will run it ourselves." [93] Almost all of the ASW's pronouncements that followed, stressed its desire to concentrate solely on "the problems at hand in the city, with strictly local officers." [94]

This localism was rooted in a resentment of outside leadership that had developed out of the conflicts between ribbon weavers and the UTW's national office. Many of the ASW's founders had been especially upset by the UTW's tendency to discourage strikes or other forms of militant action. This experience had bred a distrust of all national organizations. As one of the ASW's leading members, Leon Chevalier, said: "The silk workers don't need any paid leaders. The silk workers have brains enough to run their own labor organizations . . . The only thing a labor leader can do is live on the fat of the land and sell the workers out when he gets his price. No labor leader is going to sell me out. That is why I belong to the Associated Silk Workers. We have no leaders to sell us out . . . ." [95] In the eyes of the

ASW members, a belief in local autonomy and democratic control went hand in hand. Such an attitude led the ribbon weavers to look askance at the ATWA as well as the UTW.

The ribbon weavers' unique work experiences also contributed to the preference for an independent organization. While ribbon weaving still required far more skill than broad-silk weaving, these workers had suffered from dilution of their skills and the speeding up of machinery which threatened their deep-seated craft traditions. These factors contributed to a defensive psychology that colored much of their thinking. Ribbon weavers commonly referred to the deterioration of conditions since the 1890s, which were recalled as a time when weavers were "physically capable of participating in studies for self improvement and enjoyment" after working on the smaller looms. Eighteen ninety-four served as a benchmark for many ribbon weavers, for in that year they had achieved a standard price list—after that point conditions were considered to have steadily worsened.[96] Conditioned by historical memory, these workers showed little interest in an outside union that was headed by a man who had never run (or even seen) a loom.

Moreover, ribbon weavers had been prone to acting independently of all other workers' organizations. This was true in 1913 when they defied the IWW and accepted separate shop settlements[97]; in 1916, when they threatened to strike on their own; and in February 1919, when they came close to leaving the UTW's Eight Hour Committee. Ever ready to be convinced that their own interests could not be met by national unions, they were quick to take leave of organizations which they saw as insensitive to their needs and traditions.

Significantly, the ASW's ideological orientation proved to be far different than the ATWA's. For the most part, the ASW paid little attention to international or national affairs and focused almost exclusively on building a strong organization in the shops.[98] To the extent that the union had a world view, it was one that had much in common with the nineteenth-century perspective emphasizing the clash between producers and nonproducers. Typical of this attitude was the preamble to the ASW's constitution, which spoke of the "inevitable conflict between those who do the work of the world and those who live in ease and idleness from their their labor."[99] In style and content, it most closely resembled the independent shoeworkers' organizations that emerged out of conflicts with the AFL's Boot and Shoe Workers' Union in Lynn and Haverhill, Massachusetts. In all three cases, workers rebelled against the attempt of national unions to impose settlements on locals that had a strong sense of craft and local autonomy.[100]

Precisely because this new union was nonsectarian, it was able to bring together a wide variety of Paterson's labor radicals. In this connection, it is significant that a number of IWW members with extensive experience in the silk industry joined the ASW.[101] By way of contrast, though ATWA proclaimed that "silk workers must forget old factions and unite under a new banner,"[102] many workers viewed ATWA as merely the WIIU under a new name—a charge that was well founded, given the prominent role that former WIIU members played within the ATWA.

From its founding, the ASW underwent a slow but steady growth. The union first concentrated on winning over those ribbon weavers who remained within the UTW—a task that it had practically completed by 1921.[103] The ASW's efforts in this regard were actually aided by the fact that in January 1921, the Paterson manufacturers launched their own version of the open-shop campaign under the aegis of the Associated Industries.[104]

THE OPEN-SHOP MOVEMENT

The manufacturers used the open-shop movement to attack long-standing trade-union practices in Paterson. In a series of newspaper advertisements, the Associated Industries announced that henceforth it would oppose "any limitation upon the amount of work which may be accomplished in a given time"—a veiled reference to the enforcement of the one- and two-loom system by ribbon and broad-silk weavers. Management also announced its opposition to restrictions on the training of apprentices, to the collection of dues on company time, and to the participation of "outside" shop representatives in the settlement of grievances. As part of its campaign, the Associated Industries opened its own "Free Employment Bureau," which was formed for the purpose of ending union control over the hiring of workers.[105]

The launching of the open-shop campaign indicated that the mill owners had decided to end all forms of cooperation with the UTW. These steps were taken because the diminished strength of the left-wing unions had emboldened the Associated Industries, because the depression of 1920–21 had had a serious impact on their own economic fortunes, and because the national open-shop drive had spurred activity on the local level. Already in August 1920 extensive wage cutting had taken place in small as well as large mills. In many cases, the installation of a new class of work was used as an excuse to slash wages even further. As an indication of its new attitude, man-

agement failed to renew its agreement with the UTW's Ribbon Twisters and Loomfixers and refused to meet UTW shop committees that
it had previously recognized. [106]

The manufacturers' offensive discredited the strategy that the
UTW had followed since 1916. James Starr now condemned the mill
owners for conducting an "industrial war" against workers, even
though a few years earlier he had praised Paterson's bosses for being
"about as good a bunch of employers as I know anywhere." [107] Cooperation with the bosses had bred complacency within the union's
ranks while its own preoccupation with battling the left ensured that
the UTW was in no position to confront the manufacturers. In the
wake of wage cutting by the broad-silk firms, the UTW had already
lost most of its membership in that sector. [108] During the open-shop
campaign, most of its remaining weavers joined the ASW. Only the
Warpers, Ribbon Twisters and Loomfixers remained from the UTW's
organizational campaign of 1916–19, and the union never again played
such a leading role in Paterson.

As for ATWA, it was no better able than the UTW to oppose the
open-shop offensive. Not only did it lack support in the ribbon sector,
but its entire organization was greatly weakened by a merciless assault that the IWW launched against it. The primary targets for these
attacks were Muste, Evan Thomas, and other intellectuals who were
variously described as "sentimental choir boys," "sky pilots," and
"clerical gentry." The ACWA's sponsorship was also condemned, for
the IWW claimed that the clothing workers were only interested in
the textile workers because they wanted to absorb them in their own
"machine." [109]

These attacks damaged ATWA on a number of occasions. At the
time of the dyers' helpers' strike, the IWW refused to hand relief
funds over to ATWA because there was no guarantee that the money
would not be used to pay the ATWA staff members. [110] During a two-
month strike at a small broad-silk mill in December 1920, the IWW
opposed the ATWA leadership and a number of confrontations between the rival unions occurred on picket lines. In February 1920 the
IWW even charged that the ACWA/ATWA had supplied the Federal
Bureau of Investigation (FBI) with names of its supporters who were
picked up in an FBI raid on the remnants of the anarchist organizations in Paterson. [111]

While nothing could stem the IWW's own decline, these attacks
further weakened ATWA's own fragile base. By fall 1921 the ATWA
decided to give up its Paterson charter and encouraged its members
to enroll in the ASW. This meant that the ASW had clearly emerged
as Paterson's leading union by 1922 when it led a successful fourteen-

week strike against the Johnson-Cowdin Company's attempt to reimpose the forty-eight-hour week.[112] This strike did much to put the ASW on a permanent footing as the Johnson-Cowdin Company was one of the largest ribbon firms in Paterson. During the next few years, the ASW concentrated on preventing any further deterioration of working conditions in Paterson.[113] This steady determination to build an organization on sound footing meant that the ASW was in a position to lead the partially successful broad-silk strike against the three- and four-loom system that lasted from August to December 1924.[114] In this regard, it is significant that the 1924 strike, like that of 1913, was fought largely to oppose the stretch-out.[115] Only unions solidly grounded in the workplace could hope to lead the gritty battles in which Paterson silk workers engaged.

It is also hardly surprising that the ASW was not able to bridge Paterson's ideological divisions. By the time of the 1928 silk strike, a sharp division had developed between those who supported the Communist Party and its far-reaching concerns and those who continued to favor an exclusively local workplace orientation. Because of this conflict, the old-line leaders of the ASW even began to make approaches to their long-time enemies in the UTW.[116]

The 1928 dispute is also revealing in that it demonstrates that the different political orientations of ethnic and occupational groups continued to be an important factor in Paterson. Large numbers of ASW Jewish broad-silk weavers were also members of the Communist Party, while the ASW leaders were almost entirely ribbon weavers of German and English descent. It is particularly striking that not a single significant leader of the ASW was Jewish.[117] Building an industrial union in Paterson remained an enormous task both because ribbon weavers, broad-silk weavers, and dye-house workers preferred to act separately and because ethnic groups continued to uphold differing traditions. Though Paterson's silk workers showed a remarkable ability to bounce back from defeats, these sectoral and ethnic differences greatly hampered their ability to forge a union that could command the loyalty of all workers.

NOTES

[1]David Montgomery, *Workers' Control in America* (New York, 1979), 96–97.

[2]For the 1913 strike, see Melvyn Dubofsky, *We Shall Be All: A History of the Industrial Workers of the World* (Chicago, 1969), 263–85. For the 1914 strikes, see James D. Osborne, "The Paterson Strike of 1913: Immigrant Silk Workers and the IWW" (M.A. thesis, University of Warwick, 1973), 131–35.

[3]Exact data for 1916 is not available. These numbers are based upon the U.S. Department of Commerce, Bureau of the Census, *Fourteenth Census of the United States: 1920,* Volume 9: *Manufactures: Reports for States with Statistics for Principal Cities* (Washington, D.C., 1923), table 42, 952–55.

[4]These figures were compiled from N.J. Department of Labor, Bureau of Industrial Statistics, *The Industrial Directory of New Jersey* (Paterson, N.J., 1918), 466–79.

[5]*Fourteenth Census*, 10: table 130, 231.

[6]*Industrial Directory of New Jersey,* 466–79.

[7]Albert H. Heusser, ed., *The History of the Silk Dyeing Industry in the United States* (Paterson, N.J., 1927), 207–59.

[8]U.S. Commission on Industrial Relations, *Industrial Relations, Final Report,* Senate Executive Doc. no. 415, 64th Cong., 1st sess., 1916, 3:2413–15, 2424–25 (hereafter, *Report of CIR*).

[9]Nancy Fogelson, "They Paved the Streets with Silk: Paterson, New Jersey, 1913–1924," *New Jersey History* 97 (Autumn 1979): 136.

[10]For the Jewish weavers, see Detroit IWW (later, WIIU) *Industrial Union News,* March 1912.

[11]For a historical novel that contains a vivid description of these and other events in Lodz, see I. J. Singer, *The Brothers Askenazi* (New York, 1936; reprint, New York, 1980).

[12]Melech Epstein, *Jewish Labor in the U.S.A.* (New York, 1950), 1:xix.

[13]Nora Levin, *While Messiah Tarried: Jewish Socialist Movements, 1871–1917* (New York, 1977), 322–23.

[14]Epstein, *Jewish Labor in the U.S.A.* 1:xix; minutes of national executive meetings, Workmen's Circle, 112, YIVO Institute for Jewish Research, New York.

[15]The WIIU was originally named the Detroit IWW as it was founded when Daniel De Leon led a faction from the national IWW in 1908. It changed its name in 1916. The WIIU was closely connected to the Socialist Labor Party, which was meant to be its political arm. See Patrick Renshaw, *The Wobblies* (New York, 1968), 72.

[16]James D. Osborne, "Industrialization and the Politics of Disorder: Paterson Silk Workers, 1880–1913" (Ph.D. diss., University of Warwick, 1979), 215–30.

[17]For an excellent analysis of Italian emigration to Paterson, see ibid., 176–207.

[18]Mary Brown Sumner, "The Broad Silk Weavers of Paterson," *The Survey* 37 (March 16, 1912): 1932–35.

[19]Dubofsky, *We Shall Be All,* 277.

[20]Detroit *Industrial Union News,* April 1912, April 1913; *Report of CIR*, 3: 2478–83.

[21]Ibid., 2467.

[22]Detroit *Industrial Union News,* October 1918.

[23]Ibid., October 1912, August and December 1917, August 1918.

[24]For more information on this point, see David J. Goldberg, "Immigration, Intellectuals, and Industrial Unions: The 1919 Textile Strikes and the Experience of the Amalgamated Textile Workers of America in Passaic and Paterson, New Jersey, and Lawrence, Massachusetts" (Ph.D. diss., Columbia University, 1984).

[25]For the point of view of the "easterners," see Renshaw, *The Wobblies,* 119–47.

[26]*Report of CIR*, 3:2464. For a description of the IWW's strategy of struggle that is applicable to Paterson, see Mike Davis, "The Stop Watch and the Wooden Shoe: Scientific Management and the Industrial Workers of the World," *Radical America* 8 (January-February 1975): 89–91.

[27]For the IWW's membership, see "Report of E. T. Drew for May 12, 1918,"

Department of Justice, Bureau of Investigation, Record Group 65, 200813, National Archives, Washington D.C.

[28]During its brief existence, the BASW led no strikes and concentrated on attacking the left-wing unions. See Shichiro Matsui, *The History of the Silk Industry in the United States* (New York, 1928), 219; *Paterson Evening News*, September 11, 1915, and September 18, 1916.

[29]Ibid., February 5, 7, 1916.

[30]Ibid., March 17, 20–25, 1916; *Paterson Press-Guardian*, March 17, 22, 24, 27, 1916.

[31]Ibid., March 25, 1916. Following this triumph, practically all of Paterson's major firms, including the dye houses, granted the nine-hour day. See N.J. Bureau of Industrial Statistics, *Thirty-ninth Annual Report: 1917* (Trenton, N.J., 1917), 190–93.

[32]*Paterson Evening News*, April 3, 1916.

[33]Ibid., April 5, 12, 15, 1916; *Paterson Press-Guardian*, March 27–28, April 8, 1916.

[34]For Quinlan's change of affiliations, see Osborne, "Paterson Strike of 1913," 120.

[35]*Paterson Evening News*, September 13, 1917, September 13, 1918; New York *Daily News Record*, June 28, 1918.

[36]For this last point, see *New York Call*. March 30, 1916.

[37]New York *Daily News Record*, April 17, 1918.

[38]*Paterson Evening News*, April 17, 1918.

[39]A complete list of the groups that participated in the original meetings has not been located. For the list presented here, see *Paterson Press-Guardian*, January 3, 1919.

[40]Ibid., January 6, 1919; *Textile Worker* (December 1918):319. This latter source was a journal published in New York, not to be confused with Paterson *Textile Worker* (cited in note 109).

[41]The purpose of Golden's letter was to clarify the UTW's demands as there had been some confusion over whether the union sought forty-four or forty-eight hours. See *Paterson Press-Guardian*, January 23, 28, 1919; *Paterson Evening News*, January 31, 1919; *New York Call*, February 7, 1919.

[42]*Paterson Evening News*, February 3, 4, 1919.

[43]Paterson *Sunday Chronicle*, February 9, 1919; *Paterson Press-Guardian*, February 7,8, 1919; *New York Call*, February 3, 11, 1919.

[44]Valerie Conner, *The National War Labor Board* (Chapel Hill, N.C., 1983), 50–67.

[45]"Transcript of the Proceedings: The Silk Manufacturing Committee versus the United Textile Workers of America, February 13, 1919," National War Labor Board, Record Group 2, 1123, National Archives, Washington, D.C.

[46]"Silk Manufacturing Conference Committee versus the United Textile Workers of America," ibid.

[47]Paterson *Morning Call*, February 15, 1919.

[48]*New York Call*, February 15, 1919; Paterson *Sunday Chronicle*, February 16, 1919.

[49]Paterson *Morning Call*, February 18–20, 1919.

[50]The most objective account of this dispute is in *Paterson Evening News*, February 16, 1919.

[51]*Paterson Press-Guardian*, February 8, 1919.

[52]For the key role of the ACWA at this time, see Montgomery, *Workers' Control in America*, 106.

[53]*New York Call*, February 9, 1919; New York *Rebel Worker*, March 15, 1919; New York *New Textile Worker*, April 10, 1920

[54]Paterson *Sunday Chronicle*, February 9, 1919.

[55]"Silk Manufacturing Conference Committee versus the United Textile Workers of America."

[56]Most commentators assumed that the war technically was not over until a peace treaty had been signed. See *Paterson Press-Guardian*, April 10, 1919.

[57]Much of the UTW's reaction was feigned as there was no reason to expect anything other than a forty-eight-hour ruling. See ibid., April 10, 12, 15, 1919; *Paterson Evening News*, April 11, 14, 1919.

[58]For the ATWA's founding convention, see "Minutes of the First ATWA Convention," Department of Justice, Bureau of Investigation, Record Group 65, 361492, Nation Archives, Washington, D.C.

[59]For Thomas's activities after his release from prison, see *New York Call*, February 16, March 5, 14, 1919.

[60]For example, see Robert W. Dunn, "At Lawrence: Preparing the Workers for a New World," *Young Democracy* 1 (April 15, 1919).

[61]Detroit *Industrial Union News*, August 9, 1919; Chicago *New Solidarity*, January 3, 1920.

[62]See Henry Berger to William Ford, June 22, 1919, Lusk Papers, reel 4, Tamiment Library, New York University.

[63]Detroit *Industrial Union News*, August 9, 1919.

[64]For the prior activities of Hubschmidt and Derrick, see *Paterson Evening News*, October 23, 1915; *Paterson Press-Guardian*, November 20, 1918.

[65]Solon de Leon, *The American Labor Who's Who* (New York, 1925), 99; *Paterson Evening News*, September 13, 1917.

[66]"Fellow Members of the Amalgamated," Lusk Papers, reel 3, Tamiment Library.

[67]Ibid., reel 3.

[68]*Paterson Evening News*, July 1, 8, 15, 1919.

[69]New York *Rebel Worker*, August 15, 1919.

[70]Paterson *Sunday Chronicle*, July 13, 1919; "Report by Intelligence Officer, Camp Merritt, New Jersey, June 5, 1918," War Department, General Staff, Military Intelligence Division (1917–41), Record Group 165, 10110–406, National Archives, Washington, D.C.

[71]William Shriver, *The Silk Workers of Paterson: A Pioneering Study* (New York, 1929), 18, pamphlet in Paterson Public Library; Matsui, *History of the Silk Industry*, 43; *Paterson Press-Guardian*, June 27, 1919.

[72]*Paterson Evening News*, July 26, 1919.

[73]*Paterson Press-Guardian*, July 30, 1919.

[74]The reporters were unclear about how many workers walked out on the first day. See *Paterson Evening News*, August 2–4, 1919.

[75]Ibid., August 14–16, 1919.

[76]Ibid., August 9, 1919.

[77]Ibid., August 16–25, 1919; New York *New Textile Worker*, August 16, September 13, 1919.

[78]*Paterson Evening News*, October 10, 1919.

[79]See Osborne, "Industrialization and the Politics of Disorder," 215–30; James E. Wood, "History of Labor in the Broad-Silk Industry of Paterson, New Jersey, 1872–1940" (Ph.D. diss., University of California, 1941), 177–89.

[80]*Paterson Press-Guardian*, August 25, September 8, 1919; *Paterson Evening News*, August 25, 26, September 6, 8, 17, 1919.

[81]"Unions, Strikes and Violence," *The World Tomorrow* 2 (October 1919): 269.

[82]The concealed weapon was a broken broom handle with an iron roller attached. See *Paterson Press-Guardian*, August 12, 1919.

[83]Norman Thomas, "Organization or Violence," *The Nation* 109 (October 4, 1919): 461.

[84]Textile Workers' Union of America Records, Biographical File, reel 4, State Historical Society of Wisconsin, Madison, Wisconsin.

[85]*Paterson Evening News*, January 17, 20, 1919.

[86]These figures were compiled from *Davison's Silk Trade* (New York, 1915–20). See also Fogelson, "They Paved the Streets with Silk," 140–41.

[87]"Report from National Organizations Committee, September 10, 1924," minutes of national executive meeting, Workmen's Circle, YIVO Institute for Jewish Research, New York. This document does not give the exact year in which the chapter was dissolved, but it was probably 1919 or 1920.

[88]"Report from the National Organization Committee, October 5, 1924," ibid.

[89]New York *New Textile Worker*, January 3, 1920.

[90]Assistant Chief of Staff for Military Intelligence to Director of Military Intelligence, December 16, 1920, War Department, General Staff, Military Intelligence Division (1917–41), Record Group 165, 10110–00–6, National Archives, Washington, D.C.

[91]See the "Constitution and By Laws of the Associated Silk Workers, Organized in Paterson, August 5, 1919." (Copy in Paterson Public Library.) See also *New York Call*, August 5, 1919.

[92]For the ATWA's optimism in this regard, see New York *Daily News Record*, July 31, 1919; New York *New Textile Worker*, August 16, 1919.

[93]New York *Daily News Record*, August 7, 1919.

[94]*Paterson Press-Guardian*, October 13, 1919.

[95]*Paterson Evening News*, September 6, 1919.

[96]*Paterson Press-Guardian*, March 25, 1919; *Report of CIR*, 3: 2956; *New York Daily News Record*, April 24, 1917. Although a majority of its members were ribbon weavers, the ASW was an industrial rather than a craft union.

[97]Dubofsky, *We Shall Be All*, 281.

[98]The ATWA had established its own school which offered courses and lectures on a wide range of topics. See Tamiment Scrapbook Collection, scrapbook 20, Tamiment Library.

[99]"Constitution and By Laws of the Associated Silk Workers."

[100]For the rebellion against the Boot and Shoe Workers Union, see Thomas Norton, *Trade Union Policies in the Massachusetts Shoe Industry, 1919–1929* (New York, 1932).

[101]Fogelson, "They Paved the Streets with Silk, " 142.

[102]New York *New Textile Worker*, June 7, 1919.

[103]For the active recruitment of the UTW's ribbon weavers, see *Paterson Evening News*, August 3, 1920.

[104]Just before launching the open-shop campaign, the Paterson Employers' Association reorganized itself as the Associated Industries of Paterson. See New York *Daily News Record*, August 17, 1920; *Paterson Press-Guardian*, August 7, 1920.

[105]These proposals were made in a series of newspaper advertisements. See *Paterson Evening News*, September 24, 25, October 11, 18, 21, 25, 28, November 5, 8, 11, 15, 18, 26, 1920.

[106]*Paterson Press-Guardian*, September 17, 1920; *Paterson Evening News*, January 9, 1921.

[107] For Starr's earlier comments, see "Transcript of the Proceedings: United Textile Workers of America versus Silk Manufacturers' Conference Committee, March 19, 1919," National War Labor Board, Record Group 2, 1123, National Archives, Washington, D.C. For his later comments, see *Paterson Evening News*, January 11, April 27, 1921.

[108] *Paterson Evening News*, August 30, September 6, 21, October 7, 1920.

[109] See the only surviving copy of the Paterson IWW's newspaper, *Textile Worker*, November 1919, Tamiment Scrapbook Collection, scrapbook 20, Tamiment Library. See also New York *Rebel Worker*, September 1, 1919; Chicago *New Solidarity*, February 28, 1920, and March 27, 1920.

[110] Paterson *Textile Worker*, November 1919, in Tamiment Scrapbook Collection, scrapbook 20, Tamiment Library.

[111] New York *New Textile Worker*, December 6, 1919; Chicago *New Solidarity*, February 28, 1920, March 27, 1920.

[112] New York *New Textile Worker*, September 3, 1921.

[113] Federal Mediation and Conciliation Service Records, Record Group 280, 17/1682, National Archives, Washington, D.C.

[114] See in particular "Report of the Labor Group to the General Conference of the Silk Industry," January 18, 1923, ibid., 170/1727.

[115] There is no in-depth account of the 1924 strike. For an article that touches on some of the issues, see Fogelson, "They Paved the Streets with Silk," 142–47.

[116] Wood, "History of Labor in the Broad Silk Industry," 345; Louis Franis Bundez, "A Real United Front," *Labor Age* 20 (October 1931): 11–12, 29.

[117] This observation is based on the names of the ASW's leaders that appear in "Report of the Labor Group to the General Conference of the Silk Industry, January 18, 1923," Federal Mediation and Conciliation Service Records, Record Group 280, 170/1727, National Archives, Washington, D.C.

6

Labor Conflict and Technological Change: The Family Shop in Paterson, New Jersey

▪ PHILIP J. McLEWIN ▪

A PATERSON NEWSPAPER editorial noted with astonishment, "Paterson's first strike in which labor is interested mainly as an 'innocent bystander' is now in progress and marks a new epoch in the troubles of the silk industry. . . . We now have a strike of employers."[1] In the summer of 1936 a strike was conducted by 250 small-business proprietors in the Paterson broad-silk industry against other businessmen. Newspaper reporters understandably had difficulty comprehending this extraordinary event, in which suppliers of woven silk struck against buyers. The American Federation of Silk Workers was not involved; its leaders characterized the strike as a "civil war, not a class war."[2]

Like the strikes of 1913 and 1924, the economic changes leading up to 1936 are very significant in the history of the Paterson silk industry. Although historically unique to Paterson, these changes also serve as an illustration of the diverse means by which organizational innovation is a response to conflict within the workplace. The 1936 strike was the result of management practices adopted in the broad-silk industry over the previous quarter century. Specifically, the Paterson silk manufacturers adapted the putting-out system of seventeenth-century England to control labor in twentieth-century Paterson.[3] The action of the Paterson silk manufacturers was, according to the industry's trade association, a "strange reversal of economic evolution."[4] The putting-out system was revived, as it were, by the mill owners as a way to maximize labor productivity without inviting serious disruptions because of worker resistance.

From the 1860s, Paterson broad-silk workers had successfully resisted unilateral management control of shop-floor practice through their willingness and ability to conduct frequent and extended strikes. The 1913 silk strike continued this tradition of protracted conflict. In Paterson broad-silk manufacturing, as in other industries, there was a clear link between internal conflict over work assignments and external conflict in the form of strikes. What is unique to Paterson is the way this linkage was destroyed. After 1913 central mills were subdivided, and weavers were faced with a choice either of becoming proprietors of small family shops or of accepting unemployment. Work was put out to these shops on a commission basis by "converters," many of whom were former Paterson mill owners.

In these new circumstances the weavers (now also proprietors) were ensnarled in a complex set of relationships with creditors who held liens on their equipment, landlords who owned the buildings housing the family shops, and converters who, like the seventeenth-century merchant-capitalists, owned the raw materials and arranged for commission contracts. The result was subjugation of the family shop proprietors and, more generally, a fragmentation of the Paterson broad-silk weavers that effectively eliminated their ability to conduct general strikes.

CONFLICT IN THE BROAD-SILK INDUSTRY

The events of the 1913 strike have been told often and well.[5] The strike has generally been treated by historians as an important episode in American radical unionism, and particularly as part of the movement of the IWW from Lawrence, Massachusetts, through Paterson, and on to the free-speech struggles in the West. But it is equally significant if seen as a watershed in Paterson's history. The 1913 strike was both the culmination of forty years of industrial conflict in this city and the impetus for the establishment of the family-shop system, which dominated silk production for twenty-five years afterward.

The pattern of intense strike activity was the subject of comment as early as 1877, when the president of the Paterson Board of Trade wrote that "strikes in silk mills are more frequent than perhaps in any other industry."[6] During the last two decades of the nineteenth century, New Jersey silk workers struck far more often than those in other states.[7] This pattern continued into the early twentieth century; between 1905 and 1913 there were forty-eight strikes in Paterson. Clearly, the city remained the "storm center of the textile industry."[8] The treasurer of the Silk Association of America testified before an industrial commission in 1901 on the movement of silk mills from Paterson to Pennsylvania. He argued that wages were not the only consideration since Pennsylvania laborers "were less liable to labor troubles which are incident to Paterson." When asked if labor troubles had increased, he replied, "I doubt that . . . the same spirit of unrest exists in Paterson today as it ever did."[9]

The number of looms assigned to each weaver was the most important issue in the struggle for control of the labor process. As early as 1883 weavers struck against two separate mills that attempted to increase loom assignments.[10] Often called "stretch-out" or "speed-up," the introduction of this system also precipitated the 1913 strike.[11] Silk manufacturers like Henry Doherty, who first introduced the new four-loom system to Paterson, claimed they needed it to remain competitive. There had been less labor resistance to the system in other silk-producing regions, and the employers viewed the workers' protests in Paterson as attempts to impose "arbitrary restrictions."[12] The weavers thought it involved an intensification of work and they would not share in the gains. They also recognized that by doubling loom assignments unemployment would increase, further strengthening the mill owners' position. The lines were clearly drawn by (and in) 1913. The workers refused to accept the four-loom system; the silk manufacturers insisted it was their right to introduce it.

The silk manufacturers were confronted with a militant work force willing and able to conduct frequent, lengthy strikes. But the manufacturers themselves were also willing to take decisive action. The president of the Silk Manufacturers' Association of Paterson said during 1913, "no legitimate business can stand the method of attack of the IWW, but we'd rather go to the wall at once than yield everything we own to them by degrees."[13] In one of the most unusual twists in labor history, the silk manufacturers did eventually yield what they owned. Yet ultimately those who remained active in the industry gained greater control over the labor process by contracting out work on a commission basis.

DEVELOPMENT OF THE FAMILY SHOP

"The silk manufacturing business, in general, is in the merchant-capitalist stage" wrote Matsui in 1930 about the Paterson broad-silk industry of the 1920s.[14] The role of the seventeenth-century merchant-capitalists was carried out by twentieth-century silk converters. They provided the unfinished material to commission weavers and picked up the woven broad-silk cloth for further processing or sale. Actual production was conducted by families in rented mill space with looms purchased on credit. The cottagers of seventeenth-century England had their parallel with the commission weavers of twentieth-century Paterson.

For nearly three generations after its introduction in the 1840s, the stock-carrying broad-silk mill (the traditional mill that produced for inventory) was the dominant form of industrial organization in Paterson. Owners of these mills purchased thrown silk, hired workers to prepare the warps and operate the looms, and sold the woven broad cloth directly for finishing or to large retailers. These were independent businesses, producing goods in anticipation of orders to come. Some of them employed their own sales force.[15]

When the mill owners introduced commission weaving to Paterson, the result was a unique form of industrial organization: the family shop.[16] The shops were operated on a commission basis, but with two distinguishing characteristics; they were very small, with fewer than twenty looms per shop, and all or nearly all of the workers were family members.[17] Wages in the normal sense were not paid, rather family members shared in the net proceeds of the business.[18]

A few of these family shops were set up in homes or garages. There were even shops in a former synagogue, a stable, and a dance hall.[19] But the use of power looms made it necessary for most to be located in mill buildings constructed to withstand the vibration and sway of these machines.[20] When Lewis Hine visited Paterson in 1937 for the Works Progress Administration, he photographed the interior of a mill building that had been subdivided into multiple shops, separated by chicken wire. A survey of 150 shops conducted around the time of Hine's visit showed they were concentrated in sixteen mill buildings. The survey cited an example of six separate buildings that previously housed six different mills then contained sixty-one family shops, not to mention nine other miscellaneous commercial tenants.[21]

Experimentation with the family-shop form of industrial organization took place by 1913. A correspondent for the *Outlook* covering the 1913 strike was probably referring to the family shop when he reported that "there are many small firms in Paterson doing business in back lots."[22] Also in 1913 a system was described in which "boss weavers" and "warper foremen" had purchased five to ten looms and made arrangements with a selling agent to purchase their output.[23] Yet by 1915 only five shops in Paterson produced on a commission basis, less than 2 percent of the total.[24]

Commission weaving grew rapidly, increasing from roughly 25 percent of all mills in the early 1920s to nearly 60 percent by the mid-1930s (see table 1). But this gives only a general indication of the growth of family shops, since not all commission mills relied on family labor. Shops using family labor were very small. Based on a survey of 384 mills in 1936, an industrial consultant for the city of Paterson found that more than 90 percent of shops using all or part family labor had twenty or fewer looms. By contrast, nearly 85 percent of the mills (both commission and stock-carrying) with no family labor had twenty-one or more.[25] By the mid-1930s the Paterson broad-silk industry was divided three ways into independent or stock-carrying mills, commission mills, and family shops. Based on a survey of 147 mills, over 60 percent of them used family labor exclusively or partially and these accounted for about one-third of the output of the looms (see table 2).

An industrial organization based on the use of family labor in small commission weaving shops had no historical precedent in Paterson. Even after it developed, the family shop remained principally confined to this city.[26] According to the secretary of the Paterson Chamber of Commerce, "this condition does not exist in any other industry in the world to the degree it exists in Paterson."[27]

Market conditions during World War I are often used to explain their growth. There was, in fact, a threefold increase in the value of silk products sold between 1914 and 1919.[28] In an attempt to meet this unprecedented level of demand, the stock-carrying mills contracted with commission shops for some of their work.[29] In the process, the number of family shops increased from five in 1915 to nearly one-hundred and fifty in 1920.[30]

The unusual conditions of wartime demand and high profits are also used to explain how working people found an opportunity to realize their "big dreams" by becoming owners of small shops.[31] According to the vice president of a silk mill, "everybody has the crepe georgette fever" caused by "an unprecedented inflation during 1919 and 1920 [which] encouraged shoe-makers, policemen, barkeepers, grocers, hardwaremen, rabbis, anybody to plunge into this intricate business."[32] Others have stressed the importance of newly arrived immigrants who became proprietors.[33] Of one-hundred men who first entered into business in family shops between 1926 and 1936, however, ninety-six had been employed previously in the broad-silk industry. The largest group, eighty of the ninety-six, had been weavers; thirteen were from the skilled trades (warpers, twisters, and loom fixers); and three had been foremen. The median number of years of employment in the broad-silk industry for the ninety-six men was

Table 1
GROWTH OF COMMISSION WEAVING, PATERSON, 1904–36

Year	Commission Mills		Stock-carrying Mills		Mixed Mills[a]		Totals
	no.	%	no.	%	no.	%	
1904	—	—	—	—	—	—	190
1909	—	—	—	—	—	—	276
1914	—	—	—	—	—	—	291
1919	252	43.9	—	—	—	—	574
1921	—	—	—	—	—	—	593
1923	—	—	—	—	—	—	614
1924	121	23.4	359	69.3	38	7.3	518
1925	198	33.2	376	63.1	22	3.7	596
1926	209	30.4	405	59.0	73	10.6	687
1927	215	33.4	369	57.3	60	9.3	644
1928	203	36.4	318	57.1	36	6.5	557
1929	201	38.9	278	53.8	38	7.3	517
1930	247	47.9	158	30.6	111	21.5	516
1931	235	49.2	146	30.5	97	20.3	478
1932	243	51.0	126	26.4	108	22.6	477
1933	242	53.2	124	27.2	89	19.6	455
1934	260	54.7	144	30.3	71	15.0	475
1935	285	59.4	119	24.8	76	15.8	480
1936	224	57.4	99	25.4	67	17.2	390

Sources: *Monthly Labor Review* 29 (August 1929):281–82; James E. Wood, *Employment Experience of Paterson Broad-Silk Workers, 1926–1936: A Study of Intermittency of Employment in a Declining Industry,* U.S. Works Progress Administration, report L–3 (Philadelphia, 1939), 111. Percentages have been rounded.

[a]Mixed mills includes commission, stock-carrying, and those not specified in *Davison's Rayon and Silk Trade* (New York, 1904–36).

Table 2
DIVISION OF THE BROAD SILK INDUSTRY, PATERSON, 1935

Type of Mill	Mills		Looms	
	no.	*%*	*no.*	*%*
Family shop[a]	89	60.5	1,102	32.9
Commission weaving[b]	32	21.8	942	28.1
Stock-carrying mill	26	17.7	1,307	39.0
Total	147	100.0	3,351	100.0

Source: Adapted from Silk Textile Work Assignment Board, "Report upon Contract Weaving in the Rayon and Silk Industry," report no. 4387, Washington, D.C., April 27, 1935, mimeograph copy in Paterson Public Library, 4½. Percentages have been rounded.

[a]All or part family labor with fewer than twenty looms; 17 percent of these shops sold on their own account and were not commission weavers.

[b]No family labor either for commission weaving or stock-carrying mill.

Table 3
CONCENTRATION AMONG CONVERTERS, PATERSON, 1935

	Converters		Commission Weavers		
Size[a]		*no.*	*no. under con- tract*	*no. per con- verter*	*%*
Smallest 20%		16	16	1.0	3.1
Second 20%		16	32	2.0	6.2
Middle 20%		16	41	2.6	8.0
Fourth 20%		16	66	4.1	12.8
Largest 20%		15	359	23.9	69.8
Total		79	514	33.6	99.9

Source: Adapted from Silk Textile Work Assignment Board, "Report upon Contract Weaving in the Rayon and Silk Industry," report no. 4387, Washington, D.C., April 27, 1935, mimeographed copy in Paterson Public Library, 2½. Percentages have been rounded.

[a]Measured in quintiles.

16.2 years. The men with eleven to fifteen years of experience formed the largest segment, at 31.3 percent of the total. This was more than one-third larger than the second-highest group, men with six to ten years of experience, comprising 19.8 percent of the total.[34]

Why did the weavers become small-scale capitalists? According to an industrial consultant hired by the city of Paterson, "laborers operating under constant threat of strikes, have in many instances set up their own small shops, working on commission for the converter."[35] But this is inconsistent with the historical record of industrial conflict in Paterson. It is doubtful that workers who had struck so often and for so long would consider the strike a "constant threat." Rather, it was a weapon that, if they became small-scale capitalists, they would have to give up.

More generally, this analysis fails to explain why family shops did not develop on a significant scale in other silk regions. High wartime demand affected those areas as well. Given the presence of a less militant work force, there were probably proportionally more weavers willing to become proprietors in these regions. It also does not explain the continued expansion of the family shop in Paterson long after demand fell to normal levels. The national silk industry was changing. As early as the 1880s Paterson silk capitalists were moving all or parts of their operations to rural areas in eastern Pennsylvania. Labor there was cheaper and more docile. As transportation costs fell, making New York more accessible to outlying regions, Paterson lost some of its geographical advantages as well. There was a cost squeeze, which forced the Paterson mill owners to seek out new ways to accumulate and meet the new competition.

Within this context, struggle for control over the workplace was the key element: Paterson mill owners were confronted with militant workers when they attempted to reform the existing system of industrial organization. The four-loom system failed in Paterson because workers resisted its introduction.[36] Therefore, it is instructive to approach the issue from the opposite direction. It is not a question of why the weavers chose to become small-scale capitalists, but rather why the Paterson mill owners abandoned the stock-carrying format for the older putting-out system of commission weaving. Why was the broad-silk industry fragmented instead of integrated during the 1920s? Why did the local silk manufacturers avoid entering into even loose combinations, much less mergers, to control output and minimize financial risks?[37] This is especially curious because New Jersey led the nation in trusts, combinations, and mergers after 1889. This contradiction has been attributed to the individualism of Paterson entrepreneurs.[38] According to this view, their status and power derived from individual control over the mills. But this misses the point that mill owners did give up direct control over the manufacturing process when they sold their looms and rented space in their buildings to family shop weavers. To understand this is to move away from explanations involving the psychology of individualism and the economics of market demand. It means focusing instead on the antagonistic relationship between Paterson broad-silk weavers and mill owners.

The long history of industrial conflict in Paterson, culminating in the 1913 strike, led the mill owners to seek new ways to increase their control over the labor process and laborers. The loom assignment struggles concretely demonstrated that an intensification of work effort could not be achieved without the Paterson silk manufacturers strengthening their domination of the social relations of production. A significant shift in industrial organization was needed. By transforming workers into small-scale capitalists—broad-silk weavers into family-shop proprietors—this became possible.

A writer for the *New York Times* correctly reported the two great alternatives confronting the mill owners: leave Paterson or stay and change the organizational technology. According to the reporter, family shops were not very numerous when large mills "impatient under pressure from organized labor" began to move to other states, "where labor would trouble them less and where competitors were enjoying the advantages of child labor." The reporter outlined the alternative: "Other large operators who remained behind in Paterson, however, recognized in the 'family loom' an escape from organized labor and other irksome regulations. They sold their looms to workers on the installment plan, or they turned them over to machinery exchanges which did it. The larger operators became brokers or converters, with no more responsibility for labor conditions."[39]

Around the time of the 1913 strike some mill owners were subdividing their buildings and renting to commission shops. According to a study of commission weaving published in 1929: "twenty-odd years ago [in 1909] the original owners retired from business after the death of the senior member of the firm and following serious labor troubles. The mill represented a large investment in land and buildings and, in line with established custom in Paterson, it was offered for rent."[40] This operation became so successful that by 1929 the mill building was enlarged to twice the original size and it housed about forty family shops. Renting an entire mill or mill floors was an "established custom" in 1909; but subdividing it into cubicles was, in retrospect, an experiment with enormous implications. The reference to "serious labor troubles" is significant, since later many prominent mill owners became converters to avoid them.[41] "In other words, the manufacturer has turned converter and his employees commission manufacturers."[42] They continued to control the labor process and production, however, through contracting with the newly established family shop to weave on a commission basis.

Within this context of the mill owners abandoning the existing system of silk manufacturing and introducing commission weaving, many weavers were faced with a difficult choice. Given the prospect of closing a mill, employers were not hesitant to demand "concessions" from their workers. In Paterson, these involved the purchase of looms to preserve jobs. "There have been cases in recent years," wrote Wood in 1939, "in which operators have given their workers the alternative of buying the machines on which they work or quitting them. In agreeing to provide the former workers with orders, the operator has sometimes established himself as a converter."[43]

If the weaver refused the offer, the alternative was the prospect of imminent unemployment, uncertainty about its duration, and perhaps ultimately a change in vocation. This creates a coercive context which calls into question the voluntary nature of the choice, especially one based on the long range plans of weavers. Alexander Williams of the American Federation of Silk Workers observed bluntly that the family shop "became simply a process of leading men to 'buy their own jobs.'"[44] It is hard to argue with that conclusion. Mill owners, not weavers, initiated the process. Under the threat of a mill closing, the weavers were forced to make a very difficult and severely constrained choice.

LABOR'S RESPONSE

The first real test of the family-shop system as a means for tempering local labor militancy came in 1924. One of the principal issues was loom assignments. According to a statement prepared by the Associated Silk Workers Union, conditions in the mills had reached a "breaking point" because of the rapid growth of the three- and four-loom system during the early 1920s. The union accused the manufacturers of taking advantage of the economic slump to "force this evil system on the workers," hence the only solution was a general strike.[45]

On the first day of the strike Adolph Lessig, a local labor leader in 1913, claimed that "the mill owners cannot afford to keep their mills idle long."[46] Because it was the slack season, he may have overstated the pressure. But mill owners who wished to maintain production had a way out. By putting out their work to family shops on a commission basis they were able to meet their own production schedules. [47] The family shop became a unique resource for breaking the strikers' solidarity and the strike itself. According to some accounts, the only silk weaving taking place during the second week of the strike was in the family shops. [48]

These shops were difficult for the Associated Silk Workers to handle. Apparently the union attempted to close some of them down. [49] But with nearly 250 small shops with twenty looms or less, the sheer number of them made picketing difficult to organize and sustain. Since most of the shops used only family labor, on what basis could the weavers be organized to strike? They could not strike against themselves. The most compelling reason for the family shops to continue operating was, not surprisingly, financial. Because a substantial number of them were always near bankruptcy, the strike provided a chance for them to revive, even to thrive, for its duration. [50]

Under these circumstances it is surprising the strike lasted as long as it did. In an apparent union victory, as many as one-hundred mills reached settlements at the end of the second week of the strike agreeing to restrict loom assignments. [51] But there was never a definitive end to the strike, and during September and October the remaining weavers returned without gaining any concessions. By November 1924, the mills that had settled first were violating their agreements, but the union decided not to reopen the strike. [52] The way was clear for mill owners to increase loom assignments. [53]

The ultimately pathetic symbol of what happened in Paterson was a weaver who worked four looms—two for one family shop and two for another located just across the aisle. [54] If the 1913 strike demonstrated to mill owners that they had to find a solution to mitigate worker militancy and stabilize capitalist social relations of production, the 1924 strike proved that they had found one in the family shop. [55] Workers, too, realized that the old solidarity had been terribly and permanently fractured, for this was the last general strike in the Paterson silk industry. Weavers' resistance to "buying one's job" was surely weakened.

SOCIAL RELATIONS OF PRODUCTION

The inability of weavers to mount effective strikes was the most obvious impact of the family shop on the Paterson system of industrial relations. The whole industry was "revolutionized" and with it the social relations of production. Large silk manufacturers were able to make people work for them diligently and realize a profit from their labor through the family shop. In a formal sense, a contract to deliver finished goods replaced the employment contract; familial relationships within the shops replaced worker-employer relationships within the mills.

In 1921 A. K. Baker, a mill owner, wrote an article describing the growth of commission weaving. A notice appeared about his firm, Baker and Company, in the same issue: "The company is supervising the manufacture of silk piece goods for manufacturers and wholesalers who place their orders for consignments or commission weaving with Paterson mills. They procure reliable mills to manufacture goods. Their services include a dependable personal supervision of manufacturing at the mill, a reliable audit of silk records, and safeguarding against the delivery of goods not strictly up to contract."[56] By 1921 the number of family shops had become significant enough to attract attention in the industry's trade journal. But the shops were also a new and untested means for ensuring diligent application of labor. A. K. Baker obviously thought there was a need for direct personal supervision of commission weavers, but he was wrong.

The family shop proved to be a harsh system increasing the control of the mill owners over production and the labor process, even though they divorced themselves from direct ownership of the instruments of production.[57] A new group of converters, including former Paterson mill owners, were the primary beneficiaries of this system.[58] The older, established converters purchased previously manufactured greige (gray) goods from independent, stock-carrying mills for further processing or resale. The converting function itself was expanded and transformed when commission contracts were made with family shops. The converters now owned the raw silk as well, but more significantly, they initiated production and controlled the producers.[59] Multiple sourcing and debt were the two general means that allowed the converters to dominate the family shops. Multiple sourcing refers to a practice gaining popularity today whereby a single company purchases identical inputs from more than one supplier. In the terminology of neoclassical economic theory, this is an oligopsony, where relatively few buyers purchase from many sellers.

Estimates of the number of converters with substantial operations making contracts in Paterson in the mid-1930s range from four or five to about two dozen.[60] The concentration characteristic of oligopsony can be observed in a study of seventy-nine converters operating in Paterson; the largest 20 percent of them (only sixteen in absolute numbers) had 70 percent of the commission weavers under contract (see table 3).[61] Each one of the largest had agreements with an average of twenty-four family shops. Since the typical shop contained twelve looms, the largest sixteen converters had direct access to nearly three-hundred looms each. Compared to the stock-carrying mills that averaged less than fifty looms each, this was a substantial number.[62] The largest single converter controlled seventy-three family shops, with about 875 looms combined, compared to the largest single standard mill with 730 looms.[63]

Converters maintained complete flexibility as to where they purchased broad-silk goods. Within the city of Paterson they could buy from literally hundreds of family shops or even switch back and forth between commission contracting and purchasing from stock-carrying mills. They could also purchase from other silk regions, including the Allentown area of eastern Pennsylvania.[64]

The most important basis for multiple sourcing was the existence of serious excess capacity in the Paterson commission-weaving industry.[65] Each shop was essentially interchangeable from the converters' point of view. Their ability to substitute shops under conditions of excess (even expanding) capacity resulted in intense competition among the family shops. Compared with other silk textile regions, competition was much keener in Paterson.[66] Multiple sourcing and competition define the general conditions enabling converters to control commission weavers. The specific instrument of control was the contract. It called for the production of specified quantities of cloth at a certain commission rate per yard. Two important features of the contract reflect the domination of the converter over the commission weaver. They were verbal and exclusive: Because they were verbal, the contracts were flexible at the discretion of the converter; because they were exclusive, an individual commission weaver had a contractual relationship with only one converter at any given time.[67]

Converters maintained they needed the exclusive contract to ensure there would be no intermingling of different batches of raw materials or finished cloth by the commission weavers.[68] In practice, this meant that commission weavers had no security beyond the current contract. Even this was illusory. Inevitably disagreements arose between a converter and a commission weaver over the quality of goods, production schedules, the measurement of yardage manufactured, and who would assume the loss associated with falling market prices for woven cloth during the contract period. There were no grievance or arbitration procedures. Unless these disputes were settled to the satisfaction of the converter, the latter could effectively stop the contract by withholding delivery of raw materials. This forced the commission weaver back into the market seeking a new contract under conditions of excess capacity in the industry. [69]

In addition to their ability to withhold materials, converters could stop money payments for work in progress. The usual practice was for converters to pay commission weavers weekly or biweekly during the contract period. [70] This represented a quasi-wage that the weavers used to cover the costs of operating the shop. Obviously, withholding these payments put serious financial pressure on the commission weaver who had to meet rent, equipment mortgage, and utility expenses. [71] This practice brings us to a further reason why the commission weavers were in a subordinated position. Steve Marglin has put it forcefully by observing that "debt was not a business arrangement, but subjugation." [72]

Easy entry of business firms describes a market condition associated with intense competition. But it was not simple for individual weavers to become proprietors. They had to have investment funds. During the period of most rapid growth up to the mid-1920s, the typical family shop proprietor purchased eight looms requiring a median expenditure of $808.00. [73] This is roughly equivalent to eleven months of income for industrial workers during the same period. [74] Remarkably, of one-hundred family-shop proprietors surveyed in the mid-1930s, thirty-two of them paid cash for their machinery. The others typically made a 50 percent down payment and assumed a mortgage for the remainder. [75] In the context of the Paterson broadsilk industry described here, it is difficult to believe these relatively large sums of cash were accumulated to purchase a business. It seems more plausible, following the lifetime earnings and spending pattern of workers, that this was money set aside for medical needs and retirement. [76]

As might be expected, savings from wages was the most common source of these funds. This was the case in nearly 90 percent of the shop. [77] Since wages have historically been low in textiles—silk is no exception—it must have been very difficult to accumulate savings in such amounts. In fact, few weavers could do this out of their own individual incomes. Family savings had to be pooled. [78] Family members who appeared to be joining the capitalist class by purchasing the instruments of production were, in actuality, becoming illiquid workers (by putting their cash reserves and savings into fixed assets). When faced with the dilemma of losing a job versus buying looms, those who chose the latter risked a lifetime of family savings. [79] During a period when there was no social security, unemployment insurance, medical insurance, pension plans, or food stamps to help bridge a period of financial crisis, the absorption of family savings substantially increased the vulnerability of weavers and their families to unemployment. Now, instead of modest accumulated savings to call upon, they had a debt. Fixed business expenses replaced a family nest egg.

But the loss of savings and, for the majority, the assumption of mortgages for looms was just the beginning of debt accumulation. Floor space had to be rented in mill buildings. In the early 1930s the monthly rent for a shop with twelve looms was about $45.00 per month, or roughly equivalent to the monthly wages of an employed weaver. This included power and light for a one-shift operation. Family shops were often in arrears. The records of one landlord showed rent owing for several shops ranging from $300.00 to nearly $700.00. [80] The debt instruments were held by a combination of converters, landlords, and machinery dealers, including some former stock-carrying mill owners. In many cases converters actually held the bill of sale and mortgage and insurance policies on the looms and other machinery in a family shop. [81] They were in a position of forcing foreclosure on a family shop just by withholding contracts and demanding that the bills be paid. Then, because converters held the machinery lien, they could choose either to set the same weavers up in business again, or to sell the machinery to other families. [82]

Of the shops 90 percent operated on a month-to-month tenancy. [83] Turnover was very high. It was not uncommon in Paterson to have fifteen or twenty failures and new starts a week. [84] During 1925, for example, 111 shops closed but 189 opened. In combination, nearly 60 percent of the total shops during this one year were either closed or newly opened. [85] This was at a time when the value of silk products sold in Paterson was reaching the peak level after World War I. [86]

This data does not suggest how an individual family-shop owner fared. A study of one-hundred family-shop owners in business in 1936 showed that exactly half of them went through a dissolution of proprietorship at some time. [87] Some liquidations can be explained by such factors as disputes among the family members or closing a successful shop to reopen two new ones. But most were due to poor business. [88] Since converters directed business to commission weavers of their choosing, they controlled who survived. According to a report issued by the National Recovery Administration, "the turnover among these small firms is very high, a condition which, it is asserted, has been due in most instances to unscrupulous converters upon whom this group is very dependent." [89]

Debt had an additional and significant impact on the operation of the family shop. Traditional enterprises are managed to maximize profits. This is achieved by adjusting the rate of production to capture the most favorable trade-off between additional revenues from sales and rising additional costs of production. The family shop was operated differently. Production was maximized. [90]

The family shop had a cost structure similar to a public utility with high fixed costs relative to variable costs. In fact, for most family shops there were practically no explicit variable costs of production. Since only family members were employed in a majority of these shops, no wages were paid in the usual sense. Family members shared in the net proceeds after all other expenses were met. There were also no variable costs for raw materials since the converters provided the silk, and power and light were part of the monthly rent. [91] On the other hand, there were fixed payments for mortgages and rents, regardless of the level of output. With virtually no variable expenses, the additional cost of producing additional yardage was effectively zero. Thus, the higher the output the lower the unit or average cost of production, and the greater the net proceeds with a given commission-weaving rate.

Maximizing output involved working long hours intensively. "Generally," reported the *Monthly Labor Review*, "the hours are limited only by the physical endurance of the members of the families working in their own contract shops."[92] Another study found that fifty to seventy hours per week were worked in violation of labor standards, and concluded that "such excessive hours can easily be worked in a situation where members of a family are the only workers, where no labor organization exists and where the workers, being also owners, are more interested in total plant production than in the rate paid or the hours worked."[93]

As a result, commission-weaving costs have been estimated to be from one-third to one-half below those of regular stock-carrying mills. [94] It also provided the opportunity for converters to increase the degree of exploitation by lowering the commission-weaving rates so that the family shops cover only their fixed expenses with little or nothing left over for their labor. The prevailing commission rate in the mid-1930s was around the level of estimates for overhead in commission shops, suggesting this kind of squeeze had taken place. [95]

A financial study of two family shops in 1935 by the Silk Textile Work Assignment Board illustrates these forces. One twenty-loom shop produced 2,500 yards of cloth at $.05 per yard. Three family members (father, son, and daughter) received a net income of only $2.54 each for a forty-hour week. If amortization of machinery owned by them were included, there would have been a net loss. This shop also employed three nonfamily weavers and paid them $14.00 each for the week ($6.00 less than the standard wage for Paterson weavers in stock-carrying mills). Three brothers and a sister fared better in a second shop with twelve looms. In a forty-hour week they produced 1,300 yards of cloth at just under $.06 per yard and realized a net income of just over $11.00 each. They employed no outside labor.[96]

According to a former weaver, the family-shop proprietor "had to work like a jack-ass and at the end of the week got peanuts."[97] Maximizing production must have placed a great strain on family relationships as they were transformed into a vehicle for self-exploitation for the ultimate benefit of the converter. Nothing is recorded about how Paterson families managed to function both at home and in the shop under the conditions described here. A major sociological study using diaries and oral histories remains to be done.[98] Nonetheless, it is abundantly clear that family members had no choice but to work at their maximum capacity, probably under the strict supervision of the male proprietor in his family role as husband and father.

The long hours of intense work were spent in extraordinarily bad physical surroundings. Each shop occupied a minimum of space in the subdivided mill buildings. The shops were extremely crowded, the looms poorly spaced, sometimes as little as a foot separating them. Looms were not always bolted to the floor and thus moved about. The constant pounding and vibrations found in a mill with well-arranged looms was intensified with overcrowding. In nearly all the shops the looms were driven by overhead belts, exposing workers to safety hazards. In many instances the ceilings were low and the belts scarcely head high. Lighting was poor. None of the 150 shops in a survey had ventilation systems, and only thirteen had washstands.[99] It is no wonder they were called the "cockroaches of Paterson."[100] Labor standards had broken down; they were sweatshops.

In a sense, the commission weavers of the twentieth century were worse off than their counterparts three centuries earlier. At least the domestic workers in England had the ability to survive off the land when work was not put out to them.[101] The only economic resource the entire family in Paterson had was its shop.[102] Capital's requirement for a "free" labor force was painfully evident in Paterson, even if disguised. Entire families were free to enter into contracts with converters through their commission shops; but they were also free of any other means of survival and hence forced to make contracts under unfavorable circumstances. A report written for the National Recovery Administration concluded that "possibly the most widespread unfair practice has been the exploitation of commission weavers by converters."[103] The Paterson Industrial Commission report stated even more bluntly, "the converter constitutes a sort of Frankenstein to the silk industry."[104]

THE 1936 COMMISSION-WEAVERS STRIKE

On July 30, 1936, about 175 family-shop proprietors agreed to stop taking work from the half-dozen converters who provided them with silk for weaving. Thus began one of the most unusual strikes in Paterson's history, and probably in the history of industrial conflict. It was difficult for some outsiders to understand how small businesses could strike against other businesses. [105] Yet a staff writer for *Business Week* caught its essence as "a strike by workers who are at the same time small businessmen, after a fashion." [106] For those familiar with the family shop, and Paterson's history of industrial conflict, it was a logical outcome of the prevailing economic power relationships between the proprietors and converters.

The family-shop weavers formed the Silk Manufacturers Association as a means to act in a concerted fashion. When the association called the strike it was conducted in a manner vastly different from the picketing and mass rallies of traditional labor struggles. They established committees to contact family owners to elicit their cooperation. "It is not our intention to picket if there is no response," according to a statement issued by the Policy and Negotiating Committee, "in the latter event the textile machinery dealers and landlords will enter the situation," to demand overdue rents or payments. [107] The bill collector replaced the picket line. The family weavers were able to turn debt and differences between converters and landlords/machinery dealers to their own advantage—at least for a brief time. [108] They ultimately gained the cooperation of about 250 family shops, representing 70 percent of the family looms. [109]

Their demands were strictly economic. They proposed an increase in the commission-weaving rate from $.04 to $.05 per yard. [110] Thus, the typical twelve-loom family shop operating forty hours would add $12.00 per week to gross revenues. [111] The new rates were to be enforced by requiring converters to place work only with family shops belonging to the association, whose members agreed in advance to conform to the established price scale. [112] Price competition was to be eliminated.

Responding in an entirely predictable manner, one converter said "it is an easy matter for us to have our raw silk finished at our southern mills . . . , so you see, we will just send all our stuff down south where we have no labor troubles." [113] Despite these challenging claims, the converters agreed to the increase, and the major issue was how to maintain the new rates after the six-day strike was settled. According to Abe Brenman, a lawyer hired by the association to represent them, "the speed of success which attended this involvement has convinced many that only in collective action within an organization developed upon the needs of the industry can success be achieved."[114] These are hardly the words of the great labor leaders of the 1913 strike, but they are part of a common thread in Paterson's industrial and labor history. Paterson broad-silk workers, no matter what their condition, always struggled collectively to foster their interests. The family shop was an organizational innovation that simply made it much more difficult for them to carry on that struggle.

NOTES

[1]*Paterson Evening News,* July 30, 1936, 18.

[2]*New York Times,* July 29, 1936, sec. 1, 1.

[3]The putting-out system existed in the later Middle Ages, side by side with craft production. But the system was established "decisively" in the seventeenth century, according to E. J. Hobsbawm, "The Crisis of the Seventeenth Century," in *Crisis in Europe, 1560–1660,* ed., Trevor Aston (Garden City, N.Y., 1967). For a detailed description of the putting-out system, see Paul Mantoux, *The Industrial Revolution in the Eighteenth Century* (New York, 1961).

[4]*American Silk Journal* 51 (February 1932): 48.

[5]The best brief description and analysis is Philip S. Foner, *History of the Labor Movement in the United States* (New York, 1965), vol. 4, *The Industrial Workers of the World, 1905–1917,* chap. 4. In decreasing order of usefulness, see also Elizabeth Gurley Flynn, *The Rebel Girl: An Autobiography* (New York, 1973), chap. 4; Joyce L. Kornbluh, ed., *Rebel Voices: An IWW Anthology* (Ann Arbor, Mich., 1968), chap. 7; Melvyn Dubofsky, *We Shall Be All: A History of the Industrial Workers of the World* (Chicago, 1969), chap. 2; N.J. Bureau of Statistics of Labor and Industry, *Thirty-sixth Annual Report* (Trenton, N.J., 1913), 175–242; Graham Adams, Jr., *Age of Industrial Violence, 1910–1915* (New York, 1966), chap. 4; Morris Schonback, *Radicals and Visionaries: A History of Dissent in New Jersey.* The New Jersey Historical Series, vol. 12 (Princeton, N.J., 1964), chap. 4.

[6]James E. Wood, "History of Labor in the Broad-Silk Industry of Paterson, New Jersey, 1872–1940" (Ph.D. diss., University of California, 1941), 138. The quotation is cited from the Paterson Board of Trade, *Fourth Annual Report* (Paterson, N.J., 1877), 13.

[7]Between 1881 and 1900 there were 137 strikes in New Jersey, averaging seven per year. Each strike lasted over thirty days on average. By comparison, New York silk workers, with the second-highest number in the United States, struck ninety-seven times during this period. Each of these strikes averaged less than ten days each in duration. Wood, "History of Labor," 160. Of the 27,157 workers in the New Jersey silk industry in 1899, 15,943 were in Paterson. B. M. Selekman, H. R. Walter, and W. J. Couper, *Regional Survey of New York and Its Environs* (New York, 1928), vol. 1–B, *The Clothing and Textile Industries,* 93.

[8]Wood, "History of Labor," 265. Harold Z. Brown, "Cockroach Silk Bosses Breed Twelve-Hour Day," *Federated Press Eastern Bureau,* sheet 2, no. 3409, October 23, 1928, Tamiment Library, New York University.

[9]Morris W. Garber, "The Silk Industry of Paterson, New Jersey, 1840–1913: Technology and the Origins, Development, and Changes in an Industry" (Ph.D.

diss., Rutgers University, 1968), 228. Wood concluded, "a vigorous labor movement has existed in Paterson, but in most other silk-manufacturing areas the workers have fought less persistently for improvements in working conditions." Wood, "History of Labor," 511. The following sources all stress that the propensity of Paterson silk workers to strike caused serious difficulties for mill owners: James E. Wood, *Employment Experience of Paterson Broad-Silk Workers, 1926–1936: A Study of Intermittency of Employment in a Declining Industry,* U.S. Works Progress Administration, report L–3 (Philadelphia, 1939), 9; Shichiro Matsui, *The History of the Silk Industry in the United States* (New York, 1928), 1; U.S. Tariff Commission, *Broad-Silk Manufacture and the Tariff* (Washington, D.C., 1926), 93; Herbert Swan, *The Plain Goods Silk Industry: A Survey of Existing Conditions in Paterson, New Jersey* (Paterson, N.J., 1937), 39; Nancy Fogelson, "They Paved the Streets with Silk: Paterson, New Jersey, Silk Workers, 1913–1924," *New Jersey History* 97 (Autumn 1979): 139; "Contract Work in the Paterson, N.J., Silk Industry," *Monthly Labor Review* 29 (August 1929): 283; Paul W. Fuller, "Conference on Industrial Relations in Paterson," *The American Federationist* 35 (August 1928): 992; Ruth Tierney, "The Decline of the Silk Industry in Paterson, New Jersey" (M.A. thesis, Cornell University, 1938), 69; *Labor Age* 20 (December 1931): 17, copy in Tamiment Library; *American Silk Journal* 40 (November 1921): 55–56.

[10]Garber, "The Silk Industry," 239.

[11]Labor Research Associates, "Why Paterson Workers Strike," news release, n.d., Paterson Silk Strike, 1931 General File, mimeograph copy in Tamiment Library. Elizabeth Gurley Flynn, one of the principal organizers for the IWW in Paterson, wrote "the strike was caused by the speed-up system." Flynn, *The Rebel Girl,* 156.

[12]Dubofsky, *We Shall Be All,* 267.

[13]Adams, *Age of Industrial Violence,* 78–79.

[14]Matsui, *Silk Industry,* 177.

[15]Melvin T. Copeland and Homer W. Turner, *Production and Distribution of Silk and Rayon Broad Goods* (New York, 1935), 18; W. C. Henderson, "Evidence Study No. 37 of the Silk Textile Industry," National Recovery Administration, Washington, D.C., September 1935, mimeograph copy in Paterson Public Library, 3–4; *Broad Silk Manufacturer,* 105.

[16]Outwork in Paterson existed in the hand-loom era, but was largely extinct by the late 1880s. On the other hand, commission weaving had existed for a long time in some European centers of silk manufacturing. See William M. Poz, "Commission Weaving," *American Silk Journal* 38 (December 1919): 55. Instead of selling goods, the commission mills sold only their weaving services. Under contract, they agreed to supply a stock-carrying mill or converter with a specified amount of cloth. These mills seldom, if ever, purchased raw materials or finished the broadcloth. This was the function of the converter. Copeland and Turner, *Production and Distribution,* 11; Henderson, "Evidence Study," 18. There were small commission dye works using family labor and some hired help in Philadelphia around 1910, as well as roughly two dozen commission spinning or weaving shops in worsted woolen goods. *Official American Textile Directory: 1913* (Boston, 1913).

[17]Copeland and Turner, *Production and Distribution,* 18.

[18]Tierney, "Decline of the Silk Industry," 22.

[19]*American Silk Journal* 39 (March 1920): 79.

[20]*Monthly Labor Review* 29 (August 1929): 278.

[21]Silk Textile Work Assignment Board, "Report upon Contract Weaving in the Rayon and Silk Industry," report no. 4387, Washington, D.C., April 27, 1935, mimeograph copy in Paterson Public Library, 5.

[22]Gregory Mason, "Industrial War in Paterson," *The Outlook* (June 7, 1913): 286.

[23]James Chittick, *Silk Manufacturing and Its Problems* (New York 1913), 247–48. See Poz, "Commission Weaving," 55, who claimed that commission weaving was introduced in 1913. According to Wood, however, of one hundred family shops surveyed in 1936, two had started before 1911. Of the others in the sample, fifty-three had been established between 1911 and 1925, sixteen between 1926 and 1932, and twenty-nine between 1933 and 1936. Wood, *Employment Experience*, 34.

[24]Ibid., 20.

[25]Swan, *Plain Goods Silk Industry*, 8.

[26]Copeland and Turner, *Production and Distribution*, 18, 43; *Broad-Silk Manufacturer*, 103.

[27]*American Silk Journal* 41 (January 1922): 78.

[28]*Monthly Labor Review* 29 (August 1929): 282.

[29]Wood, *Employment Experience*, 20; Francis Markley Roberts, "Textiles," *The Story of New Jersey*, ed., William Starr Myers, vol. III (New York, 1945), 124; Fogelson, "They Paved the Streets," 140.

[30]Wood, *Employment Experience*, 20.

[31]Fogelson, "They Paved the Streets," 140. See also *American Silk Journal* 43 (January 1924): 93.

[32]E. Buhler, "Too Easy to Enter Silk Business," *American Silk Journal* 43 (May 1924): 88. In the same journal, Rabbi Harry Richmond of Paterson criticized cobblers, butchers, and "whatnot" for leaving their trades to become owners of family shops. Ibid. 39 (July 1920): 50.

[33]"Too Many Weavers Spoil Silk Industry," *Journal of Industry and Finance* 3 (November 1928): 11; Martin C. Mooney, "The Industrial Workers of the World and the Immigrants of Paterson and Passaic, New Jersey, 1907–1913" (M.A. thesis, Seton Hall University, 1969), 27; William Nelson and Charles A. Shriner, *History of Paterson and Its Environs: The Silk City* (New York 1920), 1:348.

[34]These numbers are from Wood, *Employment Experience*, 34, They are based on a National Research Project Field Survey of shops having twenty or fewer looms. See also the *New York Times*, April 12, 1936, sec. 2, 1; A. K. Baker, "The Growth of Commission Weaving," *American Silk Journal* 40 (July 1921): 73; Max Rosenstock, "The Broadsilk Situation in Paterson," *Silk* 19 (December 1926): 37.

[35]Swan, *Plain Goods Silk Industry*, 4.

[36]Wood found that in 1924 the four-loom system was not yet in general use in Paterson. Wood, *Employment Experience*, 103.

[37]There were, of course, large mills in other places. Five or six large companies, each with two thousand to five thousand looms, produced 20 to 25 percent of U.S. broad silk, according to *Broad-Silk Manufacturer*, 6. In Pennsylvania the "chain-of-mill" system was used as a device to mitigate labor problems. It consisted of a company operating several mills in geographically separate locations. Ibid., 98.

[38]Garber, "The Silk Industry," 225; Fogelson, "They Paved the Streets," 139.

[39]*New York Times*, April 12, 1936, sec. 2, 1.

[40]*Monthly Labor Review* 29 (August 1929): 278.

[41]Tierney, "Decline of the Silk Industry," 23; *New York Times*, April 12, 1936, sec. 2, 1.

[42]Swan, *Plain Goods Silk Industry*, 5.

[43]Wood, *Employment Experience*, 40.

[44]*New York Times*, April 12, 1936, sec. 2, 1.

[45]*Paterson Evening News*, August 8, 1924, 1.

[46]New York *Daily Worker*, August 15, 1924, 1.

[47]Matsui, *Silk Industry*, 224.

[48]New York *Daily Worker,* August 22, 1924, 2.

[49]Outside a mill building housing several family shops, 107 strikers were arrested, the largest number at any one time during the strike. *New York Times,* September 5, 1924, sec.1, 1.

[50]New York *Daily Worker,* August 27, 1924, 3.

[51]*Paterson Evening News,* August 21, 1924, 1.

[52]Wood, "History of Labor," 341–42.

[53]For the 1926–36 period, Wood concluded that "by far the most significant change affecting labor requirements in the local industry was the raising of the loom assignment . . . [resulting] . . . by and large, from an increase in the work load." Wood, *Employment Experience,* 49. He found that six looms per weaver was the most common assignment in 1938. Ibid., 47. For other estimates of increased loom assignments, see Swan, *Plain Goods Silk Industry,* 13.

[54]Brown, "Cockroach Silk Bosses."

[55]The proportion of commission mills increased from 23 to 33 percent of all mills between 1924 and 1925. This proportion rose gradually to nearly 60 percent by 1936; in no other single year was there such a dramatic change. Wood, *Employment Experience,* 111.

[56]Baker, "Growth of Commission Weaving," 76.

[57]Henderson, "Evidence Study," 4.

[58]Wood, *Employment Experience,* 40.

[59]About 40 percent of the converters fell into the new category. They were based principally in New York and many had offices in Paterson, which was the center of commission weaving in the United States. Silk Textile Work Assignment Board, "Report," 1–2; Swan, *Plain Goods Silk Industry,* 32.

[60]The lower estimate is from the *New York Times,* April 12, 1936, sec. 2, 1; the estimate of twenty-four converters in Paterson is from Wood, "History of Labor," 29. Swan estimated there were six or seven. Swan, *Plain Goods Silk Industry,* 30.

[61]Silk Textile Work Assignment Board, "Report," 2½.

[62]Swan, *Plain Goods Silk Industry,* 8.

[63]Ibid.; Silk Textile Work Assignment Board, "Report," 2½.

[64]Copeland and Turner, *Production and Distribution,* 50; Swan, *Plain Goods Silk Industry,* 30.

[65]Copeland and Turner, *Production and Distribution,* 3; Henderson, "Evidence Study," 3–4.

[66]Swan, *Plain Goods Silk Industry,* 22.

[67]Swan (ibid., 30) stressed their exclusive nature and Wood (*Employment Experience,* 19) their verbal nature. It was suggested in Silk Textile Work Assignment Board, "Report," 2, that the exclusive contract was the norm but not universal. There was even an informal market in the streets bordering Paterson's City Hall (called "The Curb"), where some silk goods were sold outside the converter system. Wood, *Employment Experience,* 16.

[68]Swan, *Plain Goods Silk Industry,* 30.

[69]Wood, *Employment Experience,* 19.

[70]Swan, *Plain Goods Silk Industry,* 31.

[71]The industrial consultant for the city of Paterson concluded that "the silk mills which do only a commission business are in a very unenviable position." Ibid., 30.

[72]Steve Marglin, "What Do Bosses Do? The Origins and Functions of Hierarchy in Capitalist Production," *Review of Radical Political Economics* 6, no.2 (Summer 1974): 80.

[73]Wood, *Employment Experience,* 36.

[74]The average annual earnings in all industries, excluding farm labor, was $889.00

per year for the 1904–25 period. U.S. Bureau of the Census, *Historical Statistics of the United States, Colonial Times to 1957* (Washington, D.C., 1960), 91.

[75] Wood, *Employment Experience*, 37.

[76] A conceptual point emphasized by the "life cycle hypothesis" in macroeconomic theory is that the propensity of people to save out of income is greater in the middle years of their lives than in the early and late years. See A. Ando and Franco Modigliani, "The Life Cycle Hypothesis of Savings: Aggregate Implications and Tests," *American Economic Review* 53 (March 1963), 55–84.

[77] Wood, *Employment Experience*, 37.

[78] Ibid.

[79] A Rabbi Richmond wrote of "the savings of a lifetime" lost by many family shops during the post–World War I depression. See *American Silk Journal* 39 (July 1920): 50.

[80] According to Swan, 75 percent of Paterson weavers earned less than $15.00 per week, and over 50 percent earned less than $12.00 per week. Swan, *Plain Goods Silk Industry*, 9. Swan also reported cases of back rent ranging from $600.00 to $700.00, and equipment mortgages from $2,000.00 to $3,000.00. Ibid., 20. The rent information given in the text is based on a survey of 118 shops in the Silk Textile Work Assignment Board, "Report," 7½–8.

[81] Wood, "History of Labor," 31; Swan, *Plain Goods Silk Industry*, 31; Silk Textile Work Assignment Board, "Report," 2. William M. Poz advised converters (whom he called operators) to write contracts containing these provisions. William M. Poz, "Broadsilk Commission Weaving," *Silk* 20 (February 1927):31–32.

[82] Henderson, "Evidence Study," 31.

[83] Silk Textile Work Assignment Board, "Report," 7.

[84] Copeland and Turner, *Production and Distribution*, 1.

[85] Wood, *Employment Experience*, 28.

[86] *Monthly Labor Review* 29 (August 1929): 281–82.

[87] Wood, *Employment Experience*, 38. See note 23 above for the length of operation of the family shops in this sample. In the sample, of the fifty shops that closed, thirty-two had closed only once, twelve closed twice, five closed three times, and one shop closed five times.

[88] Ibid.

[89] Henderson, "Evidence Study," 4.

[90] Silk Textile Work Assignment Board, "Report," 7.

[91] Rents included forty hours per week for power. A surcharge was imposed for additional usage, but this was a very small variable cost of production. Ibid.

[92] *Monthly Labor Review* 29 (August 1929): 279.

[93] Silk Textile Work Assignment Board, "Report," 7.

[94] Ibid. However, estimates from the National Federation of Textiles, an industry research group, indicated there was little difference between the weaving costs of regular mills and the commission shops. Their analysis did not explicitly identify Paterson. But since this was the center of commission weaving, it is safe to assume Paterson was one of the regions included. Copeland and Turner, *Production and Distribution*, 24.

[95] *Business Week* (August 8, 1936): 13, reported the current commission rate was around $.04 per yard, depending on the type of cloth woven.

[96] Silk Textile Work Assignment Board, "Report," 9–10.

[97] Hyman Gurinsky, interview, Paterson, N.J., May 5, 1980.

[98] Fogelson interviewed family-shop owners for her study of the 1924 strike, "They Paved the Streets." More generally, Eli Zaretsky, *Capitalism, The Family and Personal Life* (New York, 1976), briefly analyzed some features of the family under the

putting-out system.

[99] For a detailed decription of these conditions, see Silk Textile Work Assignment Board, "Report," 5–7, and Swan, *Plain Goods Silk Industry*, 20–21.

[100] Grace Hutchins, *Labor and Silk* (New York, 1929), 24.

[101] Zaretsky, *Capitalism, The Family and Personal Life*, 46.

[102] In a survey of ninety-one shops, the family members included primarily spouses, sons, and daughters of the proprietor, but it also extended to fathers, mothers, uncles, nieces, cousins, and even in-laws (sisters, fathers, mothers, daughters) and grandmothers. Silk Textile Work Assignment Board, "Report," 4.

[103] Henderson, "Evidence Study," 31.

[104] Swan, *Plain Goods Silk Industry*, 33.

[105] *New York Times*, July 26, 1936, sec. 1, 1.

[106] *Business Week* (August 8, 1936): 13.

[107] *Paterson Evening News*, City-Suburban Edition, July 7, 1936, 1. See also the *New York Times*, July 29, 1936, sec. 1, 1, and *Business Week* (August 8, 1936): 12.

[108] In fact, a machinery dealer was one of the "spearheads" of the strike. *Paterson Evening News*, August 7, 1936, 24.

[109] *New York Times*, July 31, 1936, sec. 1, 21.

[110] *New York Times*, July 30, 1936, sec. 1, 20. As already suggested, the increased commission rate could also have made the difference between just breaking even and having some positive income for the family shop.

[111] This assumes 2.5 yards per loom per hour, based on estimates from Henderson, "Evidence Study," 9.

[112] *New York Times*, August 1, 1936, sec. 1, 25.

[113] *Paterson Evening News*, Final Edition, July 30, 1936, 6, statement by Nat Kluger of H. Kluger and Sons.

[114] Ibid., City-Suburban Edition, September 4, 1936, 4.

Bibliographical Note

T HE PURPOSE OF THIS BIB-
liographical note is to present a survey of basic sources concerning
the silk industry in Paterson, New Jersey, upon which the foregoing
essays have drawn and future research may rely. These references
have been organized in the customary divisions: primary sources,
both published and archival; and secondary sources, including books,
dissertations, and articles.

PRIMARY SOURCES

Most studies on the history of Paterson have relied to some extent
on daily and weekly local newspapers, considerable runs of which are
extant. For the nineteenth century these include the *City Herald,
Paterson Daily Guardian, Paterson Daily Press, Paterson Labor Standard, Paterson Pencillings, Paterson Weekly Call, Paterson Weekly
Press,* and *Silk Herald.* Their twentieth-century successors were the
Morning Call, Paterson Evening News, Paterson Press-Guardian,
and *Sunday Chronicle.* New York's labor press also reported frequently on events in Paterson, especially periodicals such as the
socialist *New Textile Worker, New York Call,* and *Textile Worker,* as
well as the IWW journals *New Solidarity* and *Solidarity* (Chicago), and
Industrial Union News (Detroit), later published by the Workers'
International Industrial Union. The textile-trade *Daily News Record*
(New York) is still being published. For the manufacturers' views as
well as reports on markets and technology, researchers should use
two trade journals published monthly from the 1870s and 1880s: *Silk*
and *American Silk Journal.* Other industry journals concerned specific aspects of the silk industry. For dyeing, *Textile Colorist*

(Philadelphia) is particularly helpful, and in general, *Textile American* (Manchester, N.H.), *Textile Record* (Philadelphia), and *Textile World* (Boston) offer useful information occasionally, as well as details on labor conflicts and market trends.

Government publications federal and state, are more detailed and plentiful after 1900 than before. Printed volumes of the federal censuses provide useful statistics after 1850, both for population and manufacturing. Special volumes of the census series for each decade contain surprises, like the comprehensive age and ethnic breakdowns for Paterson women workers in a supplement to the 1900 population set, *Statistics of Women at Work* (Washington, D.C., 1907), tables 9–12, 23, 26–29. Manuscript schedules of the population and manufacturing censuses for Passaic County are found in the National Archives, Washington, D.C. At present, both series are open to researchers on microfilm for 1850–80; the population series is also open for 1900 and 1910.

Important published federal reports include: U.S. Industrial Commission, *Report of U.S. Industrial Commission: Report on the Relations and Conditions of Capital and Labor . . .* (Washington, D.C., 1900–1902), vol. 14, with valuable Paterson material; U.S. Immigration Commission, *Immigrants in Industries: Silk Goods Manufacturing and Dyeing* (Washington, D.C., 1907–10), of this vast study, part 5 concerned Paterson; and U.S. Commission on Industrial Relations, *Industrial Relations, Final Report*, Senate Executive Doc. no. 415, 64th Cong., 1st sess., 1916, the third volume of which treated extensively the 1913 strike in Paterson. Debates over the tariff on foreign-made silks yielded at least two volumes of trade statistics, price series, and recommendations: U.S. Tariff Commission, *Silk and Manufacture of Silk* (Washington, D.C., 1918) and U.S. Tariff Commission, *Broad Silk Manufacturer and the Tariff* (Washington, D.C., 1926). The latter reproduced weaving price-lists current in Paterson from 1909 through the 1920s. The *Federal Report on Woman and Child Wage Earners* (Washington, D.C., 1911), vol. 4, *Silk*, concerned both labor exploitation and unions. The U.S. Department of Labor's *Monthly Labor Review* had occasional feature articles on Paterson in the 1920s and 1930s. The U.S. Works Progress Administration, National Research Project, based in Philadelphia, commissioned James E. Wood's study, *Employment Experience of Paterson Broad-Silk Workers, 1926–1936: A Study of Intermittency of Employment in a Declining Industry*, U.S. Works Progress Administration, report L–3 (Philadelphia, 1939), as well as Lewis Hine's photographs of mill interiors and "cockroach shops" (Record Group 69, Still Pictures Section, Audiovisual Division, National Archives). The National

Archives also include files on efforts to resolve twentieth-century Paterson factory disputes (Records of the Federal Mediation and Conciliation Service, Record Group 280, and the papers of the National War Labor Board, Record Group 2).

Annual reports from the New Jersey Bureau of Statistics of Labor and Industries commenced in 1878 but grew progressively less detailed after the 1890s. They continued after 1914 as the reports of the state Bureau of Industrial Statistics. Similarly, the early annual reports of the state inspector of factories and workshops offered firm-by-firm employment figures from the mid-1880s until shortly after the turn of the century. *The Industrial Directory of New Jersey,* released triennially after 1900 by the New Jersey Bureau of Statistics, is much less satisfactory, as it was in part a promotional piece that omitted many small firms. Beginning in 1874, the Paterson Board of Trade published annual reports, and in the 1930s the Paterson Industrial Commission published occasional studies, most notably Herbert Swan's *The Plain Goods Silk Industry: A Survey of Existing Conditions in Paterson, New Jersey* (Paterson, N.J., 1937).

Private-sector industrial directories can be of considerable value for research, as they were printed annually for commercial users and identify firms by names, address, and products, and often add information on machinery, officers, and buyers' needs. Two main series of these directories cover the 1890–1940 period: the *Official American Textile Directory,* published in Boston by *Textile World;* and *Davison's Textile Blue Book,* or its more specialized *Davison's Silk Trade* (after 1895), which became *Davison's Silk and Rayon Trade* in 1929.

The Tamiment Library, New York University, has a vast collection of documents and pamphlets in labor history. Of particular importance is the Tamiment Scrapbook Collection, which includes papers of the Amalgamated Textile Workers of America and the only surviving copy of the Paterson IWW's newpaper, *Textile Worker,* from November 1919. The State Historical Society of Wisconsin, Madison, Wisconsin, is the repository for the papers of the Textile Workers Union of America, portions of which bear on the silk industry. In the local Paterson area, three historical museums have collected artifacts and materials of considerable importance. The American Labor Museum, Haledon, New Jersey, together with the Paterson Museum and the Passaic County Historical Society, both in Paterson, jointly sponsored a 1984 exhibition, "Life and Times in Silk City," and published a catalog that displays some of their holdings. In addition, the Passaic County Historical Society holds the important Pelgram and Meyer Collection, consisting of eight pattern books of silk samples. The Paterson Public Library holds a copy of George W.

Carey, "The Vessel, the Deed and the Idea: Anarchists in Paterson, 1895–1908" (manuscript, 1978–79), as well as valuable printed materials, maps, and directories of Paterson. The Ryle Family Papers are in a private collection.

SECONDARY SOURCES

Published works are arranged below in three categories: the history of Paterson; the silk industry; and workers and their experience. In the first class are a cluster of late nineteenth-century compendiums, the publication of which was sparked by the interest in local history following the centennial celebrations of the United States in 1876 and Paterson in 1892. In chronological order, the most important of these are: L. R. Trumbull, *A History of Industrial Paterson* (Paterson, N.J., 1882); W. Woodford Clayton and William Nelson, *The History of Bergen and Passaic Counties* (Philadelphia, 1882); Richard Edwards, ed., *Industries of New Jersey* (New York, 1883); Charles A. Shriner, *Paterson, New Jersey* (Paterson, N.J., 1890); Edward B. Haines, comp., *Paterson, New Jersey, 1792–1892: Centennial Edition of the Paterson Evening News* (Paterson, N.J., 1892); William Nelson, *Biographical Cyclopedia of New Jersey* (New York, 1913); William Nelson and Charles A. Shriner, *History of Paterson and Its Environs*, 3 vols. (New York, 1920); and Charles A. Shriner, *Random Recollections* (Paterson, N.J., 1941).

The first important survey of the post-Civil War silk industry was L. P. Brockett, *The Silk Industry of America* (New York, 1876), copyrighted by the recently founded Silk Association of America, followed shortly by W. C. Wyckoff, *The Silk Goods of America* (New York, 1879). The standard work on subsequent development is Shichiro Matsui, *The History of the Silk Industry in the United States* (New York, 1928). For biographies of firms in the dyeing sector, see Albert H. Heusser, ed., *History of the Silk Dyeing Industry in the United States* (Paterson, N.J., 1927). Melvin T. Copeland and Homer W. Turner, *Production and Distribution of Silk and Rayon Broad Goods* (New York, 1935), and E. B. Alderfer and H. E. Michl, *Economics of American Industry* (New York, 1950), chap. 25, sketch the outlines of crisis and decline in the industry through the mid-twentieth century. International trade relations are treated in Frank Mason, *The American Silk Industry and the Tariff,* American Economic Association Publications, ser. 3, vol. 11 (n.p., 1910).

The best single volume on industrial practice in the silk industry is James Chittick, *Silk Manufacturing and Its Problems* (New York,

1913). For a more technically precise discussion of production techniques, see the two works of E. A. Posselt, *Silk Throwing* (Philadelphia, 1915) and *Wool, Cotton, Silk: From Fibre to Finished Fabric* (Philadelphia, 1911). Either is read more profitably in conjunction with Louis Harmuth, *Dictionary of Textiles* (New York, 1924), the most thorough contemporary review of terminology for the industry. For labor, documents relating to the 1913 strike are reproduced in Joyce L. Kornbluh, ed., *Rebel Voices: An IWW Anthology* (Ann Arbor, Mich., 1964), chap. 7. Full studies include the National Industrial Conference Board, *Hours of Work as Related to Output and Health of Workers: Silk Manufacturing* (Boston, 1919); William Shriver, *The Silk Workers of Paterson: A Pioneering Study* (New York, 1929); Grace Hutchins, *Labor and Silk* (New York, 1929); and Robert W. Dunn and Jack Hardy, *Labor and Textiles* (New York, 1931). See also Philip C. Newman, "The First I.W.W. Invasion of New Jersey," *Proceedings of the New Jersey Historical Society* 58 (1940): 268–83.

Scholarly interest in Paterson has been revived in the last decade, as the contents of this volume indicate. Yet a few earlier theses and dissertations are worthy of note: Carlo Altarelli, "History and Present Conditions of the Italian Colony of Paterson, New Jersey" (M.A. thesis, Columbia University, 1911); Robert R. R. Brooks, "The United Textile Workers of America" (Ph.D. diss., Yale University, 1935); Ruth Tierney, "The Decline of the Silk Industry in Paterson, New Jersey" (M.A. thesis, Cornell University, 1938); Philip C. Newman, "The IWW in New Jersey, 1912–1913" (M.A. thesis, Columbia University, 1940); James E. Wood, "History of Labor in the Broad-Silk Industry, Paterson, New Jersey, 1872–1940" (Ph.D. diss., University of California, 1941); Morris W. Garber, "The Silk Industry of Paterson, New Jersey, 1840–1913: Technology and the Origins, Development, and Changes in an Industry" (Ph.D. diss., Rutgers University, 1968); and Martin C. Mooney, "The Industrial Workers of the World and the Immigrants of Paterson and Passaic, New Jersey, 1907–1913" (M.A. thesis, Seton Hall University, 1969). Recent dissertations and theses include: Delight W. Dodyk, "Winders, Warpers, and Girls on the Loom: A Study of Women in the Paterson Silk Industry and their Participation in the General Strike of 1913" (M.A. thesis, Sarah Lawrence College, 1979); James D. Osborne, "Industrialization and the Politics of Disorder: Paterson Silk Workers, 1880–1913" (Ph.D. diss., University of Warwick, 1980); Robert P. Volyn, "The Broad Silk Industry in Paterson, New Jersey: A Troubled Industry in Microcosm, 1920 through 1935" (Ph.D. diss., New York University, 1980); Richard D. Margrave, "The Emigration of Silk Workers from England to the United States of America in the Nineteenth Century" (Ph.D. diss., University of London, 1981); Helena Flam, "Beyond Democracy: Work, Credit, and Politics in Paterson, New Jersey, 1890–1930" (Ph.D. diss., Columbia University, 1983); David J. Goldberg, "Immigration, Intellectuals and Industrial Unions: The 1919 Textile Strikes and the Experience of the Amalgamated Textile Workers of America in Paterson and Passaic, New Jersey, and Lawrence, Massachusetts" (Ph.D. diss., Columbia University, 1984); and Howard Harris, "The Transformation of Ideology in the Early Industrial Revolution: Paterson, New Jersey, 1820–40" (Ph.D. diss., City University of New York, 1985).

Other than Christopher Norwood's *About Paterson: The Making and Unmaking of an American City* (New York, 1974), no book-length studies of Paterson have been published in the last generation. The 1913 strike has been featured in accounts of the IWW: Philip S. Foner, *History of the Labor Movement in the United States* (New York, 1965), vol. 4, *The Industrial Workers of the World, 1905–1917* and Melvyn Dubovsky, *We Shall Be All: A History of the Industrial Workers of the World* (Chicago, 1969). Material on Paterson also appears in related studies: Joseph R. Conlin, *Big Bill Haywood and the Radical Union Movement* (Syracuse, N.Y., 1969); Robert Rosenstone, *Romantic Revolutionary: A Biography of John Reed* (New York, 1975); and Fred Thompson, *The IWW: Its First Fifty Years* (Chicago, 1955). The autobiographies of two radical leaders are also relevant to the general strike: William D. Haywood, *Bill Haywood's Book: The Autobiography of William D. Haywood* (New York, 1929) and Elizabeth Gurley Flynn, *The Rebel Girl: An Autobiography* (New York, 1974). The autobiography of a Paterson "mill girl" has also been published: Lini DeVries, *Up from the Cellar* (Minneapolis, Minn., 1979). Steve Golin, who is preparing a book-length analysis of the 1913 strike, has published three articles based on his research: "Defeat Becomes Disaster: The Paterson Strike of 1913 and the Decline of the IWW," *Labor History* 24 (Spring 1983): 223–49; "Bimson's Mistake: Or How the Paterson Police Helped to Spread the 1913 Strike," *New Jersey History* 100 (Spring-Summer 1982): 57–86; and "The Paterson Pageant: Success or Failure," *Socialist Review*, no. 69 (May-June 1983): 45–80. Two papers drawn from James D. Osborne's dissertation have also been published: "Paterson: Immigrant Strikers and the War of 1913," in Joseph R. Conlin, ed., *At the Point of Production: The Local History of the IWW* (Westport, Conn., 1981), and "Italian Immigrants and the Working Class in Paterson: The Strike of 1913 in Ethnic Perspective," in Paul A. Stellhorn, ed., *New Jersey's Ethnic Heritage* (Trenton, N.J., 1978). Caroline Golab's "Comments" in the latter volume enrich the context of Osborne's studies. A recent contribution to the literature is George W. Carey, *"La Questione Sociale* and Anarchist Working-Class Newspapers, Paterson, New Jersey," in Lydio Tomasi, ed., *Italian Americans: New Perspectives in Italian Immigration and Ethnicity,* forthcoming, Center for Migration Studies, New York.

Beyond the 1913 strike, the two most important scholarly evaluations of Paterson's history are credited to Herbert G. Gutman and are available in his collection, *Work, Culture, and Society in Industrializing America* (New York, 1976). First published in the late 1960s, they are titled "The Reality of the Rags-to-Riches 'Myth': The Case of the Paterson, New Jersey, Locomotive, Iron, and Machinery Manufacturers, 1830–1880," and "Class, Status, and Community Power in Nineteenth-Century American Industrial Cities: Paterson, New Jersey: A Case Study." Other work includes "Northeast Historical Archaeology: 1974 Symposium on Industrial Archaeology, Paterson, New Jersey," a special issue of the *Journal of the Council for Northeast Historical Archaeology* 4 (Spring 1975); Michael Ebner, "Mrs. Miller and 'The Paterson Show': a 1911 Defeat for Racial Discrimination," *New Jersey History* 86 (Summer 1968): 88–91; Nancy Fogelson, "They Paved the Streets with Silk: Paterson, New Jersey, Silk Workers, 1913–1924," *New Jersey History* 97 (Autumn 1979): 133–48; Robert Snyder, "The Paterson Jewish Folk Chorus: Politics, Ethnicity, and Musical Culture," *American Jewish History* 74 (1984): 27–44; Sidney Edelstein, "Politics, Phoenix, and Paterson: Textile Processing in New Jersey," *American Dyestuff Reporter* 50 (February 20, 1961): 21–26; Helena Flam, "Democracy in Debt: Credit and Politics in Paterson, New Jersey, 1890–1930," *Labor History* 18 (Spring 1985): 439–62; and Delight W. Dodyk, "Women's Work in the Paterson Silk Mills: A Study in Women's Industrial Experience in the Early Twentieth Century," in *Women in New Jersey History,* ed. Mary R. Murrin (Trenton, N.J., 1985), 11–30.

Index

Contributors

PHILIP B. SCRANTON is associate professor of history at Rutgers University in Camden, New Jersey. He holds a Ph.D. in history from the University of Pennsylvania. Scranton is the author of *Proprietary Capitalism: The Textile Manufacture at Philadelphia, 1800–1885* (New York: Cambridge University Press, 1983) and articles in *American Quarterly, Technology and Culture, Journal of Urban History,* and *Pennsylvania Magazine of History and Biography.* He is working on a study of the decline of the Philadelphia-area textile industry in the twentieth century.

RICHARD D. MARGRAVE holds a Ph.D. in history from the University of London, with a dissertation entitled "The Emigration of Silk Workers from England to the United States of America in the Nineteenth Century."

STEVE GOLIN is professor of history at Bloomfield College in Bloomfield, New Jersey. He holds a Ph.D. in history from Brandeis University. Golin is completing a monograph on the 1913 Paterson silk strike and has published articles in *Labor History, Socialist Review,* and *New Jersey History.*

PATRICIA C. O'DONNELL is the former director of the Goldie Paley Design Center of the Philadelphia College of Textiles and Science. She has a M.A. from the University of Pennsylvania and a M.A. from the University of Delaware.

DAVID J. GOLDBERG is an assistant professor of history at Cleveland State University in Cleveland, Ohio. He holds a Ph.D. in history from Columbia University, with a doctoral dissertation entitled "Immigration, Intellectuals, and Industrial Unions: The 1919 Textile Strikes and the Experience of the Amalgamated Textile Workers of America in Passaic and Paterson, New Jersey, and Lawrence, Massachusetts."

PHILIP J. MCLEWIN is associate professor of economics at Ramapo College in Mahwah, New Jersey. He holds a Ph.D. in economics from Cornell University and prepared *The Paterson Silk Strike of 1913: With an Industrial and Labor History,* 1978, distributed by Icarus Films, New York.

DELIGHT W. DODYK is a lecturer in women's history at Drew University in Madison, New Jersey. She holds a M.A. in history from Sarah Lawrence College, with a thesis entitled "Winders, Warpers, and Girls on the Loom: A Study of Women in the Paterson Silk Industry and Their Participation in the General Strike of 1913."

JOHN A. HERBST is executive director of the American Labor Museum in Haledon, New Jersey. He holds a M.A. in museum education from the Bank Street College of Education and is the co-author of *Life and Times in Silk City: A Photographic Essay of Paterson, New Jersey* (Haledon, N.J.: American Labor Museum, 1984).